"Ashley D. Ross has done those of us who think resilience has meaning in disaster recovery a great favor. This book establishes the definition of resilience in a nuance and important way. No longer are we left with a rudimentary discussion of resilience. Ross has attached methodological heft to the meaning of resilience. Going forward, we can discern just what can be termed a resilient response to disaster and what is not."

—Roland V. Anglin, *Rutgers University*

"Ashley D. Ross is a rising star among the next generation of scholars who study natural hazards and disasters. Her book represents an important contribution to the field, effectively filling a niche in how emergency managers and elected officials perceive their own community's disaster resilience relative to an empirical assessment of local resilience in these same jurisdictions. Her findings are particularly relevant to our emerging understanding of this often misunderstood concept, while providing key insights into how we can improve our national policy in order to better assist local communities achieve this still elusive aim."

—Gavin Smith, *University of North Carolina*
at Chapel Hill & Executive Director,
Department of Homeland Security Coastal
Hazards Center of Excellence

Local Disaster Resilience

In the past decade, the Gulf Coast states—Texas, Louisiana, Mississippi, Alabama, and Florida—have experienced a series of natural and manmade disasters, including the unprecedented events of Hurricane Katrina and the BP *Deepwater Horizon* oil spill, that not only devastated the region but also called into question our national emergency management system. In response to the missteps and failures in management surrounding these focusing events, government agencies and policy practitioners have looked to recast emergency management. Community resilience has emerged as a framework to facilitate improvements in preventing, managing, and recovering from disasters. Despite the promotion of resilience, a shared understanding of the concept and how it is applied on the local level where it is purported to develop remains limited. *How is disaster resilience perceived by local government officials and translated into disaster management practices?*

Ashley D. Ross systematically explores disaster resilience through secondary data sources and original surveys of county emergency managers and elected municipal officials. She creates and analyzes a measure of capacity for disaster resilience that spans 75 Gulf Coast counties. Additionally, she assesses perceptions and experiences of local officials across 56 counties and 122 municipalities in the Gulf Coast region. The findings of these analyses shed light on how resilience is understood by local officials and on the attributes and circumstances that facilitate the development of resilience on the local level.

Local Disaster Resilience fills a critical gap in the literature by applying existing theories and models to a region that has experienced the worst disasters the United States has faced in the past decade. It also provides tools to advance our knowledge of disasters in an interdisciplinary manner by offering county-level data and teaching guides on Gulf Coast disaster resilience.

Ashley D. Ross is an Assistant Professor of Political Science at Sam Houston State University. Her research focuses on comparative public policy with an emphasis on local governments. In addition to this work on local disaster resilience, her research has examined decentralization in Latin America, education policy in Texas, and environmental policy among municipalities in Costa Rica.

Routledge Research in Public Administration and Public Policy

Local Disaster Resilience

Administrative and Political Perspectives

Ashley D. Ross

Routledge
Taylor & Francis Group

LONDON AND NEW YORK

First published 2014
by Routledge
711 Third Avenue, New York, NY 10017

and by Routledge
2 Park Square, Milton Park, Abingdon, Oxfordshire OX14 4RN

*Routledge is an imprint of the Taylor and Francis Group,
an informa business*

First issued in paperback 2015

Library of Congress Cataloging-in-Publication Data

Ross, Ashley D.
Local disaster resilience : administrative and political perspectives /
  Ashley D. Ross.
      pages cm — (Routledge research in public administration and public
policy)
  1. Environmental disasters—Government policy—Gulf Coast (U.S.)
2. Natural disasters—Government policy—Gulf Coast (U.S.)
3. Emergency management—Gulf Coast (U.S.)   4. Disaster relief—
Gulf Coast (U.S.)   5. Crisis management in government—Gulf Coast
(U.S.)   6. Gulf Coast (U.S.)—Environmental conditions.   I. Title.
  GE146.R67 2013
    363.34'5610976—dc23
    2013027662

ISBN 978-0-415-82333-3 (hbk)
ISBN 978-1-138-19444-1 (pbk)
ISBN 978-0-203-55191-2 (ebk)

Typeset in Sabon
by Apex CoVantage, LLC

This book is dedicated to my grandmother, Tanalita Palm, who taught me at an early age to explore the world through reading and writing. I know she would have been pleased to read this.

Contents

Tables

Figures

Acknowledgments

The research reported in this book was funded by the Department of Homeland Security (DHS) Summer Research Program for Minority Serving Institutions. Support for fieldwork was also given by Texas A&M University—Corpus Christi through faculty research enhancement grants.

Thank you to Gavin Smith, Thomas Richardson, and Robert Whalin, DHS Coastal Hazards Center of Excellence (CHC), for their belief in the project and thoughtful guidance along the way; to Luis Cifuentes and Ron George, Texas A&M University—Corpus Christi (TAMUCC) Research Office, for generously extending institutional backing of this research; and to Joseph Jozwiak, TAMUCC Department of Social Sciences, for contributing departmental resources to free up my time to devote to this work.

I also thank the following individuals for their administrative support of the project: Patti Obenour, Oak Ridge Institute for Science and Education; Anna Schwab, DHS CHC at the University of North Carolina at Chapel Hill; LaShon Lowe, DHS CHC at Jackson State University; and Maricela Alexander, TAMUCC College of Liberal Arts.

I am also obliged to those who gave their time in providing feedback on this research. Thank you to David Yoskowitz, TAMUCC Harte Research Institute, and Mike Wetz, TAMUCC Department of Marine Biology, as well as Walter Peacock and John Cooper, Texas A&M University Hazard Reduction and Recovery Center, for their input and encouragement. I also offer my gratitude to Wendy Strain for her patience and expertise in editing the manuscript.

A huge thanks to the student research assistants that contributed to this project: Debbie Abraham, Melissa Beeler, Michael Bueno, Jesse Clifton, Patrick Doty, Nicole Dritz, Samantha Duffy, Logan Harrell, Sandra Joslyn, Marcus Pierre, Gina Wilson, Roshae Wilson, and Charden Virgil. I extend a special thank you to Melissa Beeler who worked on this project from its inception until the very end. Her dedication and GIS skills were invaluable. I credit her with the creation of all the maps in the book.

I am also indebted to the following faculty for their assistance and time in recruiting research assistants: Sam Brody, Texas A&M University at Galveston Department of Marine Sciences; Jim Garand, Louisiana State University

Department of Political Science; Meherun Laiju, Tougaloo College Division of Social Sciences; and Ann-Margaret Esnard, Florida Atlantic University School of Urban and Regional Planning. Thank you also to Melissa Stewart, University of West Florida, for connecting me to research participants.

A heartfelt thanks is extended to the research participants involved in this project. (A list of names is not provided to preserve their anonymity.) The insight and time given by these individuals made this work possible.

Finally, I extend a personal thank you to Gabe for his unwavering encouragement as I worked on this project. I am also indebted to my parents and Chad and Chrissie for their considerable support. Thank you to *all* my family for cheering me on!

1 Introduction
Local Disaster Resilience

Community resilience to disasters is fundamentally local. Commonly referred to as "bouncing back," disaster resilience involves the strengths a community develops to prepare for, respond to, and recover from disasters. These strengths are reflective of the community population—their economic resources, health, mobility, and activity in local groups. They are also comprised of the institutions and infrastructure the community has developed to prepare for disasters as well as the measures taken to protect the environment. But what makes resilience inherently a local phenomenon is the collective action these strengths empower. The most important aspect of community disaster resilience is the way it enables change through the design of local solutions to local problems. It, therefore, is a way to frame capacity-building needed to be ready for a disaster and an approach to inclusive, collaborative decision-making following a disaster event. In this regard, resilience is an incredibly important resource. Unfortunately, this resource has not been fully tapped. The concept of resilience is fuzzy, and the conditions that facilitate its development are not entirely clear. It is the aim of this book to deepen our understanding of resilience by applying the concept to localities across the Gulf Coast in an effort to answer the big question: *How is community disaster resilience understood and practiced on the local level?*

Why the Gulf Coast? The localities along the Gulf of Mexico coast in the states of Alabama, Florida, Louisiana, Mississippi, and Texas have experienced the worst natural and environmental disasters in our nation's history with Hurricane Katrina in 2005 and the BP *Deepwater Horizon* oil spill in 2010. Remarkably, they have largely recovered from these events and have lessons to share from this. These disaster events as well as others throughout the collective history of the Gulf Coast region have also shaped our federal emergency management framework. To appreciate how resilience fits into this bigger picture, we need an understanding of the Gulf Coast. Even more so, we need perspectives from the local level.

LOCAL PERSPECTIVES

This study examines resilience from the perspective of local administrative and political elites, specifically county emergency managers and municipal elected officials. It is the job of county emergency managers to mitigate their community's risk to disasters and prepare citizens for emergencies. This task is considerable in today's interconnected but bureaucracy-laden disaster management field. It is often constrained by limited fiscal and human resources, unengaged citizens, and conflicting local government priorities. Some of this conflict originates with municipal elected officials, namely mayors and city council members, who tend to prioritize economic development and other issues popular with voters over disaster planning and mitigation. Local political elites' priorities and activities, however, do not always conflict with emergency management goals. Policies and programs spearheaded by mayors and city council members can foster community resilience. Taken together, the two perspectives of county emergency managers and municipal elected officials provide valuable insight on local governance of the development of resilience.

To capture the perspectives of local administrative and political elites, interviews and surveys were conducted with county emergency managers and municipal elected officials to assess their understanding of resilience and the way they manage disasters. Responses to the survey create a sample of 56 counties and 122 municipalities across the Gulf States of Alabama, Florida, Louisiana, Mississippi, and Texas. These surveys are complemented by a dataset that measures capabilities for resilience using secondary sources across a broader sample of 75 counties in the Gulf Coast region.

CONTRIBUTIONS OF THIS STUDY

The county and municipal surveys capturing resilience perceptions as well as the county-level secondary dataset on resilience capacities is used to address gaps in our knowledge of community disaster resilience. The first relates to the inconsistent use of the term "resilience" in emergency management arenas. Some have criticized scholars and federal agencies alike for referring to resilience in multiple and often contradicting ways. This issue is addressed by examining the meanings county emergency managers assign to the concept of community resilience. Examination of shared meanings of resilience gives us an idea of how resilience is understood on the local level.

Another gap in our understanding of resilience is specific to the Gulf Coast. There is also a need for updated assessments of capacities for resilience that are comparable across the region. This study presents a county-level index comprised of the most recent information available and analyzes this data to identify trends linked to variation in capacities. The findings of these analyses can meaningfully inform policy choices to build local capacity for resilience.

Finally, this study addresses the lack of knowledge we have about the conditions that facilitate resilience, particularly collaboration and coordination, during the response and recovery stages of disasters. This is explored through local administrative and political elites' perceptions of disaster response and recovery. Additionally these perceptions are paired with county capacities to delineate the factors that encourage and impede resilient action. The results of these analyses expand our understanding of the local government attributes that develop disaster resilience.

OVERVIEW OF CHAPTERS

Chapter 2 outlines the concept and study of community resilience as both a set of adaptive capacities and an adaptive process. Adaptive capacities refer to the strengths a community has for disaster response and recovery such as a diversified economy, mitigation policies and programs, sound support systems, and protected natural barriers. Community adaptive capacities also involve citizens' social capital and willingness to work together to solve local problems. The adaptive process is characterized by impromptu action, coordination of resources and collective action, engagement of the community, and institutionalizing policy solutions developed during disaster recovery. A conceptual framework is presented specifying how adaptive capacities are translated into the adaptive process when a disaster strikes. Adaptive capacities developed prior to a disaster should enable collective action to respond and recover from the event.

Chapter 3 details the research design of the study. It traces disaster events across the Gulf Coast and ties them to the development of our federal emergency management framework. It also describes the counties and municipalities in the study sample, elaborating on the criteria for the sample as well as the economic and population characteristics of these cases. An overview of the county and municipal surveys is also given specifying the questionnaire themes, the administration of the survey, and the response rate of each.

Chapter 4 answers the question: *How is community resilience understood by county emergency managers?* This chapter outlines how resilience has been treated by federal and state emergency management directives and then compares this to the perceptions of resilience held by local officials. Meanings assigned to resilience by county emergency managers are grouped, and a regression analysis is presented that identifies the county-level factors related to perceptions of resilience.

Chapter 5 answers the question: *What factors explain county-level adaptive capacities for resilience?* This chapter presents an adaptive capacity index for 75 counties across the Gulf Coast that builds on two important models of capacity—the Disaster Resilience of Place designed by Susan Cutter and her colleagues as well as the Community Disaster

Resilience Index designed by researchers at Texas A&M University's Hazard Reduction and Recovery Center. The construction of the adaptive capacity index is detailed including a discussion of its components. Spatial trends in the data are examined, and several propositions regarding which factors influence county adaptive capacity are empirically tested.

Chapter 6 analyzes the adaptive process to determine: *How have the attributes of the adaptive process been evident in recovery to recent disasters?* A case study of response to the BP *Deepwater Horizon* oil spill is offered to illustrate the characteristics of the adaptive process at work. Additionally, coordination during the adaptive process is examined in more detail by looking at the role, activities, and perceptions of emergency managers and local elected officials. Regression analyses are presented that identify the factors associated with good ratings of coordination in past disasters.

Chapter 7 answers: *What factors facilitate local disaster resilience?* Using data explored in the previous chapters, county adaptive capacity is overlapped with perceptions of the adaptive process to create profiles for high, moderate, and low resilience. Additionally, county adaptive capacities are compared to emergency manager perceptions of their jurisdiction's resilience in the event of a (hypothetical) severe disaster to identify the factors related to overestimations of resilience. Chapter 8 concludes the study by connecting the key findings of the chapter analyses to research questions that may be explored by future studies.

This book has features to enable teaching and research on the topic of community disaster resilience. Each chapter poses a series of discussion questions at the end that can be used by instructors in public administration and emergency management courses to further explore the concept of resilience. For researchers, the raw data and method used to construct the adaptive capacity dataset for 75 counties across the Gulf Coast are provided in the appendix. Additional data are also offered in the appendix reporting the various resilience ratings analyzed throughout the book. Sharing this data is motivated by the goal to expand our collective knowledge through the use of comparative benchmarks of disaster resilience. For more teaching and research materials related to this project as well as table and figures related to analyses in this book, visit the website: localdisresilience.com.

2   The Concept of Disaster Resilience

The word *resilience* has become part of our everyday vernacular. News headlines buzz with the term: "Euro Resilience Hints at Shift in Currency's Role,"[1] "New York Giants Prove Resilient Again in Super Bowl XLVI,"[2] "Haiti's Earthquake Tests Resilience of Capital's Hair Stylists, Now Working in Streets."[3] The word has appeared in the title of memoirs such as the late Elizabeth Edwards' *Resilience: Reflections on the Burdens and Gifts of Facing Life's Adversities* and has been the topic of numerous self-help books, including *Building Resilience in Children and Teens: Giving Kids Roots and Wings* and *The Resilience Factor: 7 Keys to Finding Your Inner Strength and Overcoming Life's Hurdles*. Musicians have featured resilience in their band names and album titles,[4] and on any given day you can even find hundreds of references to the word on Twitter, with tweets ranging from the poetic— "Dreamers can't be tamed **#resilience**"[5]—to the more serious—"65% of Nairobi's population live in densely populated slums. Thoughts on building **#resilience.**"[6]

Often we use the term resilience to stir emotion, inspire, and motivate. It was cited by Martha L. Loudder as "the most important characteristic that you can have to succeed" at a recent Texas A&M University's commencement ceremony.[7] In a speech given May 2012, United States President Barack Obama reflected on our nation's recent economic challenges, saying Americans "have the skills to claim their dreams" for America is a county of "grit and resilience."[8] Queen Elizabeth evoked similar sentiments in her address to the British Parliament during her 2012 Diamond Jubilee, stating: "We are reminded here of our past, of the continuity of our national story and the virtues of resilience, ingenuity and tolerance which created it."[9] While resilience is a commonly used word—and an emotionally powerful one—it is difficult to nail down one definition because its meaning changes as a result of the context in which it is used.

As the examples above demonstrate, we use the word resilience in reference to individuals, sports teams, businesses, economies, and nations and in the context of psychological crises and triumphs, economic downtowns, and disasters. For each of these, the term resilience has different meanings. Psychological resilience, for example, is typically understood as emotional coping in times of stress.[10] While economic resilience indicates the ability of an economic system to withstand shocks,[11] disaster resilience is often referred to as "bouncing back" to normal after a hazardous event.[12] These broad meanings, however, mask the complexity of defining resilience that exists within these contexts. The definition and use of the term resilience is not always agreed upon in specific fields of study, and this is particularly true for the study of resilience in hazards and disaster research.

In disaster policy and research communities, resilience emerged as a priority issue in the National Science and Technology Council's Subcommittee on Disaster Reduction's (SDR) 2005 Grand Challenges Report.[13] While resilience was introduced as a focal point of hazard scholar Dennis Mileti's 1999 seminal assessment of hazard research,[14] it was not until SDR's 2005 report that there was a call for the systematic assessment of resilience.[15] A focus on resilience spread among federal agencies and was officially introduced into the Department of Homeland Security's lexicon with the Homeland Security Advisory Council's 2006 Critical Infrastructure Task Force Report.[16] This report asserted that resilience should be "the overarching strategic objective" for national policy and planning. Since then resilience has framed federal homeland security and emergency management policy, trickling down from the federal to subnational levels of government and among agencies such as the Gulf of Mexico Alliance, as the guiding principle for responding to and recovering from disasters. "The policy goal is clear and pragmatic—if communities can increase their resilience then they are in a much better position to withstand adversity and to recover more quickly than would be the case if there were few or no investments in building resilience."[17]

The timing of its adoption as a guiding principle for emergency management followed Hurricane Katrina in 2005. Resilience became a way to recast a system that failed on all levels, shifting "disaster management from a focus on protecting critical infrastructures toward the creation of 'resilient communities.'"[18] Policy-makers have embraced resilience as a more proactive way to engage the community in preparing for emergencies and reducing disaster impacts.[19] Consequently, resilience studies have also increased among academics. This chapter explores how scholars conceptualize and study disaster resilience with the aim of identifying common threads that can be woven together to constitute a working framework to use in exploring Gulf Coast disaster resilience.

THE CONCEPTUAL ORIGINS OF RESILIENCE

The term resilience originated in the fields of physics and mathematics where it refers to the quality or ability of a material or system to return to its original state after stress rather than breaking. *Merriam Webster's* definition is: "the capability of a strained body to recover its size and shape after deformation caused especially by compressive stress."[20] Picture, for example, a metal spring that is put under a large, heavy object. Once this pressure has been removed, the ability and rate to which the spring bounces back to its original shape is its resilience.

C.S. Holling, an ecologist, was the first to use resilience as a metaphor. He adapted the term in the 1970s to describe ecological systems, asserting that a resilient system has the "ability to absorb change and disturbance."[21] Because resilience is an element in stability analysis,[22] Holling clearly distinguished between the two, noting that stability is "the ability of a system to return to an equilibrium state" and "the more rapidly it returns, and with the least fluctuation, the more stable it is."[23] In contrast, resilience is the ability "to absorb changes . . . and still persist."[24] Stability, then, is marked by a rapid return to normal while resilience is characterized by absorbing the impact of change and still existing. Resilient systems, unlike stable systems, may considerably fluctuate from the original equilibrium.

Following Holling's work, political scientist Aaron Wildavsky was the first to apply resilience to social sciences. In *Searching for Safety*, Wildavsky, sets up resilience and anticipation as alternative strategies for decision-making in the context of risk and uncertainty. Anticipation is "a mode of control by a central mind; efforts are made to predict and prevent potential dangers before damage is done" while resilience is "the capacity to cope with unanticipated dangers after they have become manifest, learning to bounce back."[25] Anticipation as a decision-making strategy is best for risks that are predicted and well understood, and policies made by this method invest resources into specific defenses to counter specific threats.[26] On the other hand, resilience is flexible and adaptable requiring improvisation in the use of available resources to create what is needed in the moment.[27] But it is also a bit more. To be truly resilient, organizations learn from threats and build greater capacity to prevent and manage future events.[28]

Like Wildavsky, scholars from a variety of disciplines including psychology, public health, economics, national security, and hazard mitigation have adopted resilience as a frame, exploring the way entire societies, communities within these societies, and individuals within these groups respond to disasters.[29] This widespread use of the term resilience has produced a myriad of definitions within hazards research.[30] Rather than reach a consensus that could be translated into applicable tools, critics say that this scholarship has treated resilience as "an umbrella concept for a range of system attributes that are deemed desirable."[31]

Most definitions within hazards and disaster management research highlight capacities, describing resilience as the general ability to "bounce back"; the ability of communities to survive external stress and disturbance;[32] or the ability to prevent, withstand, and recover from loss.[33] But others reject the notion of "bouncing back" because it implies returning to a previous state, which in Holling's terms would exhibit stability and not resilience. Further, in the context of disasters, returning to the ways things were, as hazards scholar Douglas Paton points out, "captures neither the reality of disaster experience nor its full implications."[34] Therefore, some scholars conceptualize resilience as a process of adaptation, deliberate action, and policy learning. They, like Wildavsky, consider resilience to occur if communities have learned by making meaningful choices to solve post-event issues and capitalize on the new opportunities offered.[35]

Dual Conceptualization

While the definition of resilience offers a variety of ways to bound the term, there are two underlying components, both of which are linked to adaption. One, resilience is a set of capacities that enable adaption. These capacities refer to the strengths and weaknesses of a system (i.e., an ecological system, a society, a community, a household) that affect how it is able to adjust to a disruption. Two, resilience is also a process of adaptation. This process requires behavior to modify the way of doing things in response to a disruption; this means that a resilient response to a disaster may entail changes that produce a "new normal" rather than a return to exact pre-disaster conditions. Sociologist and disaster scholar Kathleen Tierney describes the components of resilience within the disaster management process, stating:

> The term implies both the ability to adjust to "normal" or anticipated stresses and strains and to adapt to sudden shocks and extraordinary demands. In the context of hazards, the concept spans both pre-event measures that seek to prevent disaster-related damage and post-event strategies designed to cope with and minimize disaster impacts.[36]

In addition to being both a set of capacities and an adaptive process, resilience should be understood as a dynamic phenomenon—changing with time and different sets of actors. Therefore it is not an outcome or end point;[37] rather resilience describes the qualities of a system, specifically its capacity for responding to and recovering from a disaster, and the process of adapting to the impacts of a disaster event and taking action to prevent future crises. When we speak of resilient outcomes, however, we can understand this as referring to the degree to which policies, programs, or results have contributed to the development of adaptive capacities or facilitated the adaptive process.

DISASTER RESILIENCE AS ADAPTIVE CAPACITIES

Adaptive capacities are the resources that enable resilient responses to hazard events. They can exist on an individual (e.g., one person or household) or collective (e.g., neighborhood or city) level. They prepare individuals and communities for emergency and disaster events.

Emergencies happen when a community interacts with a hazard. *Hazards* are naturally occurring (e.g., hurricanes) or environmental (e.g., oil spills).

When hazards intersect with a community then an emergency is triggered and a disaster possible.[38] A *disaster* occurs "when hazard activity results in significant loss or disruption to established social processes, functions, activities and interactions."[39] Defining disaster in this manner supports that disasters are socially-bound—they occur within communities where damages are felt—while hazards exist independently.[40] Emergency management[41] seeks to prepare communities for possible emergencies and disaster events.

There are four stages of emergency management: mitigation, preparedness, response, and recovery. *Mitigation* involves "actions taken before a disaster to decrease vulnerability, primarily through measures that reduce causalities and exposure to damage and disruption or that provide passive protection during disaster impact."[42] These measures often focus on the development of structures such as dams and levees but also entail building and land-use regulations to reduce vulnerability and risk to hazards.[43] *Preparedness* refers to actions taken to bolster emergency response capabilities including warning systems, evacuation routes, supplies, and communication procedures established prior to disaster and emergency events.[44] Preparedness can also entail "developing a response plan and training first responders to save lives and reduce disaster damage, identifying critical resources, and developing necessary agreements among responding agencies, both within the jurisdiction and with other jurisdictions."[45] *Response* is the action taken immediately before, during, and after a disaster to save lives, clear debris, and minimize damage. In general, response activities are preparedness plans in action.[46] *Recovery* refers to the short-term activities to restore vital support systems (e.g., roads) as well as the long-term activities to rebuild properties and social and economic functioning.[47] During the recovery stage, a community may engage in developing plans and policies that reduce an area's vulnerability to future disaster losses; this feeds back into the mitigation phase of disaster, making the process cyclical. The mitigation and preparedness stages of emergency management allow for the establishment and improvement of adaptive capacities that are drawn upon in the response and recovery stages.

Adaptive capacities refer to characteristics that either enable resilience and/or detract from vulnerability. *Vulnerabilities* are "inherent characteristics or qualities of systems that create the potential for harm or differential ability to recover following an event."[48] While "resilience is often viewed as an antidote to vulnerability,"[49] Disaster scholar David King contends that vulnerability and resilience are independent of one another, stating:

> Vulnerability is not the opposite of resilience. These characteristics of an individual or a community are best seen as separate scales that may intersect on specific characteristics, but it is quite possible for a community to be both vulnerable and resilient simultaneously, i.e., a low income or indigenous closely-knit community that has endured many floods or cyclones and has learned to minimize loss.[50]

Often vulnerabilities are "immutable"; for example, being very old makes one more vulnerable to disaster events but age cannot be changed. Vulnerabilities are also created. Coastal communities all over the United States have chosen to develop homes and businesses along the water, increasing their risk to disasters by placing themselves dangerously close to hazard events while at the same time degrading natural systems such as sand dunes and wetlands that provide barriers to hazards.[51] As sea levels rise due to climate change, these development choices will only make coastal populations more vulnerable.[52] Our vulnerabilities—both individual characteristics and collective circumstances—necessitate that we work diligently as communities to enhance our adaptive capacities so that our responses to disasters may be more resilient.

Individual Adaptive Capacities

In general, individuals are more likely to be resilient if they have: access to information—especially preparedness information and knowledge of services available post-disaster; ample resources—both financial and tangible goods that sustain them post-disaster; time and opportunity to manage activities that engender resilience; and linkages to others in society that provide personal and communal support.[53] Numerous sectors of society are comprised of individuals that may not have these resources. Typically, these include the poor, unemployed, nondominant language speakers, older and younger populations, the ill or medically dependent, and the physically disabled or mentally challenged. Particular attention to enabling and protecting these populations is needed for capacity building.

Personal Income and Employment
Many poor individuals lack the assets needed to prepare for recovery from a disaster. The poor are also the least likely to have the time and opportunity to take part in activities that develop resilience such as attending emergency preparedness meetings. For many communities poverty overlaps with minority group populations; socioeconomic status is inherently tied to racial and ethnic social structures that exist in society.[54] For other communities it involves households that may not be considered poor in conventional terms but whose property value represents a larger proportion of their total assets.[55] In these scenarios damaged property is proportionally more costly to repair or replace, especially in the absence of homeowner's or renter's insurance.[56] In addition to the poor, unemployed individuals are also likely to have low resilience because they lack not only financial resources but also employer health insurance to help cover costs of injury or illness, which may occur as a result of a disaster event.[57]

Information Access
Access to local information is critical for disaster preparedness. Individual access to information about emergencies and disasters depends to some

degree on level of education and primary language. Those with higher education are more likely to have access to disaster information in varied forms; moreover they are more likely to act upon this information.[58] On the other hand, nondominant language speakers (i.e. those individuals who do not speak or speak to a limited degree English) are less likely to have access to mainstream information that enables sound preparation for disasters and guides individuals to available services post-event.[59] As a result they tend to rely on information from friends and family that could be inaccurate.[60]

Social Support and Engagement
Individuals that have and are engaged in a wide network of friends and acquaintances should have a good base of support to assist them in the event of a disaster.[61] Moreover, engagement in social networks may reinforce other factors tied to individual capacity for disaster resilience including place attachment[62] and collectivism.[63] However, Buckle asserts that individuals must also engage in formal community networks to strengthen their individual capacity for resilience; in particular he points to participation in community outreach programs and playing an active role in collective decision-making related to disaster management.[64] Beyond these modes of participation, modern technology is being used in disaster management programs to facilitate individual participation virtually through social media.[65]

Special Needs and Dependent Individuals
Older, senior populations as well as the very young rely more on others in society for daily needs and functioning.[66] The physically disabled and mentally challenged also require the help of caregivers, especially during disruptions and emergencies. Therefore, these individuals are dependent on others for information, resources, mobility, and general activities that are involved in preparation for and recovery from disasters. They are also the most likely to be medically dependent which makes loss of electricity or technology even more perilous during a disaster event.

Studies of Individual Resilience
Studies of individual resilience have underscored the importance of individual and family income, information access, and social support for the development of adaptive capacities. In a study of New Orleans, Louisiana, hazards scholar Timothy Beatley finds that much of the city's population did not return after Hurricane Katrina due to lack of employment and affordable housing.[67] Not having the financial means to wait for new opportunities or rebuild, many of the poorest relocated. In an analysis of single-family homeowners in Florida, Anthony Peguero found that nondominant English language speakers were less likely to use government publications as a source of information; instead they relied on family and friends for information, which could increase their vulnerability due to inaccuracies.[68] Regarding social support, research on the Vietnamese-American community in east

New Orleans has shown that the close community ties among this group, founded on a shared history, facilitated the rebuilding of this neighborhood post–Hurricane Katrina.[69]

While these studies highlight that individual characteristics are linked to resilience, it is critical to recognize that these traits do not directly equate to lower or higher resilience. Rather, these characteristics are connected to circumstances that may limit resilience. It may be that a poor individual can improve their individual and household capacities for resilience beyond their economic means, for example, by being more connected to their neighbors, taking an active role in disaster preparations and community meetings. Studies of disaster resilience have demonstrated that while economic, health, and other factors affect individual resilience, those circumstances can be mitigated by a proactive approach on part of the individual and community.

One example of such research is a study conducted by hazards scholar Alison Cottrell that found women in Northern Australia relied heavily on social networks in case of emergency events.[70] In this region flooding and cyclone events are common, particularly during the wet season. The nature of local labor markets means that many women are often left alone to care for families because their husbands' employment takes them away from home. Additionally, some women in the area provide for their families on very limited incomes. To navigate these challenges, women purposively set up support networks utilizing family and friends to prepare for various natural hazards scenarios ranging from arrangements to pick up friends' children if separated from their mother during an emergency event to checking in on a friend's home during a flood. They also managed risk through these informal networks; for instance, women shared information on which homes would flood to others looking for rentals. Moreover, they took advantage of formal networks by utilizing local day care and community centers for help with not only child care but also with learning strategies for managing finances and preparing for emergencies. This action strengthened these women's capacities for disaster resilience beyond their individual means; it also contributed to the collective capacity of the community by cultivating social networks.

Collective Adaptive Capacities

On one level collective adaptive capacities are simply an aggregation of individual adaptive capacities. For example, a community with a population of wealthy individuals can be considered to collectively have greater resilience; they presumably have the economic resources to protect themselves and homes from disaster damages with insurance and the means to rebuild and recovery easily. The collective demographic characteristics of a community represent the social aspect of adaptive capacities, and they are largely indicative of a community's vulnerabilities to hazards. While this is one part of collective adaptive capacities, there are other components to be considered.

Collective adaptive capacities occur on multiple dimensions including a community's economy, institutions, infrastructure, environment, and community capital. Economic adaptive capacity refers to the economic robustness of a community and its ability to recover from economic disruption post-disaster. Institutional adaptive capacity is built around a community's disaster mitigation policies, for example its response and recovery plans. Infrastructure capacity refers to the way a community's roads, highways, and public services affect resilience. Similarly, ecological capacity refers to the way a community has managed its natural resources that serve as barriers to disaster impacts. And finally, community capital refers to the networks among individuals and the collective action that emerges among community members. Together these represent the potential a community has of effectively responding to and recovering from a disaster; a resilient community maintains and develops these capacities in ways elaborated below.

Economic Capacities

Economic resilience is the ability of communities to withstand financial disruption and cushion themselves against damage and loss.[71] At best, disasters disrupt local commerce, but severe disasters destroy places of business, displace populations, and suspend local economies for indefinite periods of time. Communities that have more equal distributions of wealth, high human capital, a stable and growing workforce, and a diverse economy can withstand the shock of disasters better than those that lack in these attributes.

Wealthy communities have more robust economic resources at their disposal therefore have greater recovery capacity. But Mileti cautions that high income inequalities even among wealthy communities may intensify disaster damages as poorer populations strain local programs in terms of assistance with jobs, housing, and basic services.[72] This was the reality in St. Bernard Parish, Louisiana after Hurricane Katrina; many of those that could afford to leave moved to nearby communities that were not as vulnerable to flooding.[73] The shifting demographics of the community have affected parish government revenue because it is largely based on property taxes. This in turn has influenced the availability of services that are now in high demand as the community as a whole is much needier.

Beyond wealth, a sustainable economy requires diversity.[74] Economies that rely on a few key industries for economic well-being lack the capacity to recover quickly from disasters if these sectors are affected.[75] This is particularly relevant in coastal communities where the majority of economic activity is generated by a few industries including fishing, oil development, and tourism.

The vulnerability of coastal economies was exposed by the BP *Deepwater Horizon* oil spill. The spill occurred April 2010 off the coast of Louisiana and dumped over 200 million gallons of oil into the Gulf of Mexico resulting in bans on commercial fishing and effectively shutting down tourism in states that experienced oil on their beaches. This included Baldwin County, Alabama whose tourist industry contributes to approximately 25 percent of the state's travel-related revenue.[76] When its pristine beaches were polluted with oil and tar balls as a result of the oil spill, the county experienced a 9 percent drop in tourist/travel related employment in 2010 compared to 2009—the equivalent of 2,532 jobs. Three years after the spill, the Louisiana Department of Wildlife and Fisheries reported that the oyster catch was down 27 percent from the average haul between 2002 and 2009.[77] Similar challenges continue for fishing and crabbing that is severely damaging in a state where the seafood industry accounts for one of every 70 jobs and generates $2.4 billion in revenue.[78]

Institutional Capacities

Institutional adaptive capacities refer to a way a community has mitigated against hazard risk or implemented plans and policies to reduce vulnerability to hazards.[79] Mitigation involves the improvement of built structures such as levees to protect communities from hazards as well as the implementation of land-use policies and building codes to reduce risk to hazards.[80] Planning is an important aspect of mitigation as plans for disaster response and recovery establish procedures and goals that guide collective action during disaster events.

There are two types of mitigation—project and process, also referred to as structural and nonstructural or hard and soft.[81] Public administration scholar, Thomas Birkland borrows the terms "project" and "process" mitigation from Philip Ganderton to refer to the construction of structures to resist hazards and the development of policy tools to alter behavior to reduce risk, respectively.[82] Project mitigation includes the building of levees, floodwalls, and beach groins to protect communities from natural forces. Process mitigation involves planning, zoning, and building codes that set up regulations to reduce vulnerable development.

While both types of mitigation have the potential to strengthen capacity for resilience, Birkland cautions that "promoting mitigation is not the same thing as promoting resilience." Not all mitigation is inherently resilient. For example, project mitigation programs to re-nourish beaches may encourage continued development along coastlines that are high-risk to flooding and storm surges. Process mitigation such as zoning and land-use policies potentially create controversy as they can threaten economic development.[83] Consequently, local elected officials are often reluctant to engage in the politics of it, focusing their efforts on more immediate actions that have a consensus of public support behind them (e.g., unemployment, crime). Mitigation through planning for hazards is also not popular among local government officials,[84] but emergency planning is required of localities.

In accordance with the Disaster Mitigation Act of 2010, state and local governments are required to develop disaster plans for federal funding pre- and post-disaster.[85] States also have specific rules for counties and municipalities regarding emergency plans; however, these vary. For example, Florida is the only state in the Gulf Coast region that requires local governments to have comprehensive plans and stipulates that they must address hazards.[86] Despite these mandated plan requirements that encourage the development of plans prior to a disaster event, most are developed in the aftermath of a disaster due to the way federal funding incentivizes assistance.[87]

Infrastructure Capacities

Infrastructure capability refers to the robustness of community support systems or "lifelines" that include electricity, gas, transportation, telephones, water systems, and sewerage systems.[88] These systems support community activities on a daily basis. In the event of an emergency or disaster, they are critical for response and recovery. For example, roadways and highways affect disaster evacuation pre-event and provide routes for assistance post-disaster. Water and sewerage systems fundamentally affect the health of community; if inoperable, the public is at high risk. Infrastructure quality and integrity, therefore, is imperative for the development of capacities. Also important to consider is the way a community's lifelines are connected. Interdependencies between support systems can impede restoration of service in the aftermath of a disaster. Therefore, it is imperative that communities assess the vulnerabilities of their infrastructure and make contingency plans to ensure that the most basic needs (e.g., water and medical transport) are met.[89]

Ecological Capacities

Ecological capacities refer to a community's natural barriers to hazards. The natural environment includes features such as sand dunes, forests, and vegetated areas that protect communities against disaster damages by absorbing and reducing hazard impacts.[90] Wetlands, for example, significantly reduce storm surge. A community that preserves these natural barriers strengthens its adaptive capacity. Preservation includes restricting and directing urban development away from these areas through land-use planning and zoning regulations.[91] Moreover, it can involve the reinstatement of natural barriers. In the aftermath of Hurricane Katrina, multiple initiatives for the restoration of wetlands emerged across the Gulf Coast and in Louisiana in particular.[92] This idea has even been transplanted to urbanized areas in different forms. For example, innovative plans emerged in response to Hurricane Sandy to ring Lower Manhattan with grassy networks of land-based parks alongside patches of wetlands and salt marshes to buffer against storm surge.[93]

Community Capital

Community capacity for resilience refers to the supportive connections that exist among individuals that make them capable of collaboration. Paton refers to this as "soft resilience,"[94] and political scientists call this "social capital."[95] Community capacity is fostered, for example, by citizens who are actively engaged in community organizations, parent-teacher associations, and church and volunteer groups. Investing in farmer's markets, supporting block parties and festivals, promoting community clubs and organizations, and establishing new community spaces are ways Beatley proposes local governments can develop community capacity.[96] Research has shown that socially resilient communities are able to work together to confront local issues,[97] share social values,[98] are networked to one another through organizations such as churches,[99] and offer personal and community support to one another post-disaster.[100] Resilience "can be forged and sustained through community engagement in activities concerned with identifying and dealing with local issues even if they have little or nothing to do with hazard readiness per se."[101]

Some scholars have pointed to community competence as an important aspect of community capital.[102] Community competence refers to the degree of involvement of citizens in solving collective issues. A community that has a high degree of competence capitalizes on the social capital that exists within their locality, taking advantage of supportive networks to facilitate the identification and resolution of collective problems. In this sense, we could say that social capital is a prerequisite for community competence.[103] It is, however, not a guarantee of competence. It is possible for a community to have a high degree of social capital or networks among its citizens but low competence if those citizens did not value involvement or were not given the opportunity to participate in decision-making as related to disasters.

Studies of Collective Adaptive Capacities

Many studies focus on one aspect of adaptive capacity. For example, a recent analysis of social capacity in Galveston, Texas, after Hurricane Ike found that lower neighborhood social capacity (or in the authors' terms greater "social vulnerability") was related to lower rates of evacuation prior to the storm.[104] Additionally, low social capacity was connected to low rates of applying for and receiving assistance post-disaster. Similarly, a study of flood events in Texas found that institutional capacity, measured as the number of flood mitigation measures implemented and the number of dams constructed, was associated with lower odds of flood causality deaths.[105]

Other studies of adaptive capacity have moved to analyzing the aggregation of community abilities for resilience. Hazards scholar Susan Cutter and her colleagues have created a model called the Disaster Resilience of Place (DROP) for assessing adaptive capacities on the county level. The model focuses on five components: 1) *Social resilience*—measured as the county population's education, age, proportion of citizens with disabilities, English language use, vehicle access, and health insurance recipients; 2) *Economic resilience*—measured as housing capital, average business size, and employment; 3) *Institutional resilience*—measured as mitigation efforts, plans, and prior disaster experience; 4) *Infrastructure resilience*—measured as vulnerable properties in county, building codes, and health care facilities; and 5) *Community capital*—measured as the number of religious adherents and the number of civic organizations. Using census data as well as other secondary sources, Cutter and her colleagues measured resilience across these five components to produce a resilience score for 736 counties in FEMA's Region IV, including the states of Kentucky, Tennessee, North Carolina, South Carolina, Mississippi, Alabama, Georgia, and Florida. They found several patterns among the resilience scores across this region, including: rural counties had low levels of overall resilience while urban counties ranked the highest in terms of social resilience; and inland counties and those counties encompassing capital cities and major industrial hubs demonstrated higher levels of economic resilience. These capacities are important as they imbue communities with strengths needed to engage in the adaptive process if a disaster were to occur.

DISASTER RESILIENCE AS AN ADAPTIVE PROCESS

Resilience is not only a set of capacities but also a process by which individuals and communities respond to, recover from, and act to reduce vulnerabilities to disasters. Adaptive capacities are often overwhelmed by large, destructive disasters. Even communities with robust economies, connected and trusting citizens, formalized disaster plans, sound infrastructure, and progressive zoning and land-use policies can be derailed by a disaster event. In the face of severe disruption it is the community's response that holds the most promise for resilience. Echoing this, editors of the book *Designing Resilience*, Arjen Boin, Louise Comfort, and Chris Demchak elaborate:

> [C]risis and disaster researchers have consistently shown that there is very little political leaders and public administrators can do during the immediate aftermath of a catastrophe (especially when they lack accurate knowledge of the unfolding event). It turns out that disaster plans do not work, communication fails, and command-and-control doctrines backfire—only after some time can skilled or talented crisis managers impose some kind of order. Ultimately the quality of the response critically depends on the capacity to enhance improvisation, coordination, flexibility, and endurance—qualities that we typically associate with resilience.[106]

A resilient response to a disaster engages the community in the adaptive process which can be characterized by four attributes:

- *Improvisation:* The adaptive process of resilience begins when local solutions are initiated to meet local needs post-disaster. Impromptu action to restore functioning and rebuild the community tends to be more flexible and needs-driven.[107] However, to be truly resilient—to create outcomes that improve the community in a sustainable way— improvisation should be balanced with planning, ideally recovery planning devised pre-disaster.[108] By implementing those plans, communities can proceed in a flexible manner to connect available resources with needs that have emerged as most important in the specific context created by the disaster event.

- *Coordination:* Connecting resources to meet response and recovery needs post-disaster is an imperative part of the adaptive process. Coordination is needed to restore critical infrastructure and meet basic needs following a disaster event, and collaboration among stakeholders is critical in the recovery process for positive, sustainable solutions to be implemented.[109] Much of the job of local administrative and political elites is to lead this coordination.[110]

- *Engagement of the community:* Involvement of the community and key stakeholder groups in decision-making related to recovery projects is needed to create outcomes that are sustainable and that adapt to—ideally, improve upon—the post-disaster environment.[111] Engagement of broad community groups should help produce better solutions as a diverse set of interests is represented and local knowledge is aggregated.[112] Additionally, community engagement in recovery initiatives can create a sense of unity amidst devastation, which in itself is resilient by enhancing community ties, and can also generate a "buy-in" of various groups as they feel invested in decision-making.

- *Endurance:* Recovery solutions that emerge in the post-disaster context are often put together piecemeal over a long period of time. To ensure that the outcomes created continue beyond the disaster event, the lessons learned must take on some quality of endurance.[113] Formalizing programs and plans into policy is one way that endurance can be achieved. In other circumstances, lessons learned may be so profound that it becomes part of the community's collective memory, and thus part of social norms and behavior in the post-disaster environment.

These four characteristics can be identified in theoretical models that trace the adaptive process through the disaster event stages. They are also evident in documented cases of community response and recovery to disaster events. While theory provides a precise framework of the adaptive process of resilience, the case studies demonstrate that the development of resilience in reality is messy. The characteristics of the adaptive process may manifest to varying degrees in different contexts. But central to the adaptive process in theory and practice is the coordination of collective action that capitalizes on local knowledge to experiment and flexibly deal with local circumstances.[114]

Theoretical Models of the Adaptive Process

Scholars have developed theoretical models of resilience to trace the adaptive process in response to disasters over time. These models set up a linear process that begins with a community's adaptive capacities, flows through the disaster event, and progresses through disaster response and recovery. A community's adaptive capacities are matched against the disaster event characteristics, setting it on a trajectory within this process. If adaptive capacities are not overwhelmed by the disaster, the process ends with a state of stability and a high level of recovery. On the other hand, if a community's capacities are exceeded, the process either opens the door for adaptive resilience, ending in an altered environment with a high degree of recovery, or continues to perpetuate existing dysfunction, furthering vulnerabilities and resulting in a low degree of recovery. Two models of this process are discussed below; each presents a nuanced version of how resilience develops, highlighting in different ways the four characteristics of the adaptive process— improvisation, coordination, community engagement, and endurance.

Cutter et al.: The Disaster Resilience of Place Model

The Disaster Resilience of Place (DROP) model, devised by Susan Cutter and her colleagues is one foundational framework of resilience.[115] In this model resilience is defined as "the ability of a social system to respond and recover from disasters and includes those inherent conditions that allow the system to absorb impacts and cope with an event, as well as post-event, adaptive processes that facilitate the ability of the social system to re-organize, change, and learn in response to a threat."[116] A community's inherent resilience refers to its collective strengths to withstand disasters based on qualities of its institutions, infrastructure, economy, demographics, and community capital. These capacities are termed "antecedent conditions" because they exist prior to a disaster and position the community's response to the event. Sometimes, however, these capacities are not enough and may be overwhelmed by a severe disaster.

The balance of a community's adaptive capacities, coupled with predetermined coping mechanisms, and the disaster characteristics (i.e. duration, rate of onset, intensity, magnitude) is referred to as "absorptive capacity." In the event that a community's absorptive capacity is not exceeded, meaning that the community's adaptive capacities and coping strategies successfully mitigate the disaster, the model predicts a high level of recovery. On the other hand, if a community's absorptive capacity is exceeded, it has the opportunity to engage in the adaptive process. Absorptive capacity may be overwhelmed in two scenarios: 1) The disaster is so large that community capacities cannot cope with it; 2) The disaster is less severe but the community's existing capacities are insufficient to handle its impact.[117] If either of these scenarios presents itself, then the community may exercise adaptive resilience.

The process of adaptive resilience plays out for different communities under varying circumstances, but it should entail some form of improvisation and social learning. Improvisation involves "impromptu actions which may aid in the recovery process," and social learning is considered to be "the diversity of adaptations and the promotion of strong local social cohesion and mechanisms for collective action."[118] Social learning takes place "when beneficial impromptu actions are formalized into institutional policy for handling future disaster events and is particularly important because individual memory is subject to decay over time."[119] Social learning may take the form of new or modified disaster plans. In all, "both the degree of recovery and the potential knowledge gained from the adaptive resilience process influence the state of the social, natural, and built environment systems and the resultant antecedent conditions for the next event."[120]

Norris et al.: Model of Stress Resistance and Resilience Over Time

Another important model of resilience is offered by psychiatry professor and disaster scholar Fran Norris and her colleagues. This model is termed the Model of Stress Resistance and Resilience over Time. Resilience here is considered to be "a process linking a set of adaptive capacities to a positive trajectory of functioning and adaptation after a disturbance."[121] Resilience is distinguished from resistance, which, similar to Holling's concept of stability, as a state where a community's resources have effectively blocked the stressor (or disaster) without resulting in a state of dysfunction. Resistance is the ideal outcome of disturbances, particularly for dangers that occur with some frequency and can be planned for. But, resistance (or stability) may not be a preferable or a resilient outcome in all circumstances if additional precautions are needed to accommodate the altered environment brought on by the disturbance or disaster event. "The resilience of systems . . . depends upon one component of the system being able to change or adapt in response to changes in other components; and thus the system would fail to function if that component remained stable."[122]

The balance between adaptive capacities and the stressor (or disaster) determines if resistance or transient dysfunction occurs. Adaptive capacities refer to a community's resources networked across the areas of economic development, social capital, information and communication, and community competence.[123] Additionally, to be a set of capacities that sufficiently promote resilience, these resources should exhibit the qualities of robustness, redundancy, and rapidity. Robustness indicates the "ability to withstand stress without suffering degradation."[124] Redundancy refers to the substitutable quality of resources; on a social level, redundancy is built into resources when there is more than one way to solve a problem.[125] Rapid resources are those that can be quickly accessed and used.[126]

When a community's resources are sufficiently robust, redundant, or rapid to buffer or neutralize the immediate impact of the stressor (disaster), resistance is the outcome.[127] Total resistance, however, is expected to be rare, particularly with severe or highly surprising events. Transient situational dysfunction, a state where the stressor temporarily overwhelms community resources, is more likely. In this state of dysfunction, the resilience process occurs when resources are mobilized in such a manner that permits "a return to functioning, adapted to the altered environment."[128]

While plans may prove to guide action during the recovery process, "communities must exercise flexibility"[129] and pursue problem-solving approaches that "allow for innovation and localized variations in response."[130] This process may produce adaptations that are not the "qualitative equivalent of pre-event functioning," but the post-disaster altered environment is "not necessarily superior in level or character or effectiveness to pre-event functioning; it is simply different."[131] The alternative to resilience is vulnerability which occurs when resources were not sufficient to engage in the resilient process. The outcome of vulnerability is persistent dysfunction. Resilience, on the other hand, should produce a "new normal" and also support the building of collective community capacities.

Common Components of Theoretical Models
The DROP model by Cutter and colleagues and the Model of Resistance and Resilience over Time by Norris and colleagues conceptualize the development of the adaptive process somewhat differently, but underlying both are the attributes of the adaptive process. The following summarizes how the models incorporate the four characteristics of adaptive resilience:

- *Improvisation* is a key marker of the adaptive resilience process in the DROP Model. The model by Norris et al. also emphasizes flexibility in decision-making to create innovative and localized solutions.
- *Coordination* is inherent to resilient response and recovery efforts as both models encourage the mobilization of resources to restore community functioning as well as create improvements to the post-disaster environment. Norris et al. put particular focus on the coordination of community groups, noting that "pre-existing organizational networks and relationships are the key to rapidly mobilizing emergency and ongoing support services for disaster survivors."[132]
- *Community engagement* is also evident in both models. Norris et al. note that involving the community in the recovery process allows community members to "assess and address their own vulnerabilities to hazards, identify and invest in their own networks of assistance and information, and enhance their own capacities to solve problems."[133] For Cutter et al. community engagement is important for creating meaningful impromptu action and formalizing solutions through policy learning.
- *Endurance* is treated differently by the models. For Cutter et al. it is achieved when social learning has occurred, particularly when recovery initiatives are written into policy and the community takes action to enhance pre-event preparedness. For Norris et al. the endurance of resilient action is broader and manifested in general social change or a shift to recognizing that disaster experiences and prevention is community-based.

Beyond underscoring the four attributes of the adaptive process, a comparison of the two theoretical models reveals a set of commonalities important to the concept and study of disaster resilience. The first is: *Disaster severity is critical.* In both models reviewed, a community's capacities were balanced against the severity of the disaster—its intensity, duration, rate of onset, and magnitude. Very severe disasters almost always exceed a community's resources and abilities to manage the event impacts. Given that disaster trends point to increasing frequency and intensity, understanding how disaster severity affects community resilience is ever more important. Facing a severe disaster, we would expect a community that can survive the immediate, short-term dysfunction and effectively regroup to utilize its resources in a creative and adaptable way is best positioned to recover in a resilient way. This recovery, however, should not look like the pre-event environment, which is highlighted by the next point.

Resilience produces a "new normal." The process of resilience is defined in both models as occurring when adaptation takes place. This new normal is structured to meet the challenges the disaster has presented, remedying issues that may have caused the community to be vulnerable to the hazard in the first place. As such, disasters present opportunities to improve social conditions, building codes, and mitigation plans. If these are institutionalized into policy and social norms, then they are more enduring and will have a better chance of enhancing the community's response to the next disaster event. This cyclical nature of resilience is highlighted in the final take-away point.

Resilience develops over time. Both models depict resilience as unfolding over time. The adaptive capacities of resilience are critical in the short-term, determining whether a community is overwhelmed or not by a disaster event. In the long-term, the adaptive process of resilience draws upon the capacities not destroyed by the event and creatively pieces together solutions for recovery. These decisions directly affect a community's capacities, ideally by enhancing them and avoiding the perpetuation of existing vulnerabilities. Therefore, in the long-term, resilience feeds back into the base conditions that can equip a community to withstand a disaster. Identifying that resilience develops over time recognizes that it is a lengthy, complicated, often messy process. It also underscores that resilience does not happen by chance. Rather, it "requires a conscious effort on the part of people, communities and societal institutions to develop and maintain the resources and processes required to ensure this can happen and that it can be maintained over time."[134] This point is highlighted by case studies of disaster response and recovery, two of which are discussed in the following section.

Case Studies of the Adaptive Process

Central to the adaptive process of resilience is the coordination of and collaboration among community groups in ways that capitalize on local knowledge to experiment and flexibly deal with local circumstances.[135] Therefore, the adaptive process is highly localized, relying heavily on the ability of the community to act collectively to improve post-disaster conditions. In many ways post-disaster adaptation is unique to the community context, but to generate resilient results it should demonstrate four characteristics: improvisation to solve local problems and meet needs, coordination among groups, engagement of the broad community, and learning that is formalized in some way to last beyond the disaster event. The following two case studies are representative of how the four characteristics of the adaptive process manifest in different contexts—Miami post–Hurricane Andrew and New Orleans post–Hurricane Katrina.

Women Will Rebuild Miami after Hurricane Andrew, Case Study by Elaine Enarson and Betty Morrow[136]

Hurricane Andrew hit South Florida on August 24, 1992, leaving a path of destruction that was 18 miles wide.[137] Infrastructure supporting a population of 375,000 was wiped out; nearly 100 health facilities and schools as well as most fire and police stations were severely damaged or destroyed. Entire communities were devastated. More than 180,000 people were left homeless,[138] and property damages exceeded $25 billion.[139] In response, the federal government provided more than $10 billion in grants and loans[140] and private donations poured in.[141]

To raise relief funding and coordinate the distribution of both public and private aid, community leader, Alvah Chapman, was personally asked by President George H. Bush to establish the nonprofit organization We Will Rebuild. Chapman drew upon his extensive personal and political network to appoint the founding board members including political, business, and civic leaders in Miami-Dade County.[142] The board initially included very few women and minorities; "the widespread impression was that [the] job of rebuilding destroyed communities was now firmly in the hands of Miami's elite male-dominate, mostly Anglo, downtown business community."[143] Further exacerbating this impression was the organization's direction of funds for primarily business and economic recovery.[144] In response, sociologists Elaine Enarson and Betty Morrow in their edited volume *The Gendered Terrain of Disaster,* detail how Women Will Rebuild, a coalition of over 50 existing women's groups from civic service clubs to immigrant groups to female business owners, emerged to call attention to the inequalities in disaster recovery and lobby for change.

Women Will Rebuild was a grassroots effort that purposively took on a decentralized structure. The group committed to an informal consensus decision-making process[145] and established from the outset short-term goals which focused on applying political pressure to the We Will Rebuild campaign. Their goals were to include 15 more women on the We Will Rebuild Board of Directors and allocate at least $2.5 million for women's health, housing, employment, education, and day care.[146] To organize their efforts, Women Will Rebuild formed working committees and established bimonthly meetings as well as a system of hotline communication among activists.[147] Their lobbying effectively compelled the organization to include new women members, including the director of Women Will Rebuild, as well as establish two new committees—Families and Children and Domestic Violence.[148] Furthermore, the pressure exerted by the organization influenced the funding of teen pregnancy programs and childcare services by We Will Rebuild—areas previously passed over by the committee in favor of business and economic initiatives.

While some hoped that Women Will Rebuild would develop into a permanent multicultural women's coalition, it formally disbanded in 1993 when its goals were largely met. Even though this organization did not endure institutionally, Enarson and Morrow assert that the group has another legacy:

> We found wide consensus that when Miami is struck again by a hurricane, as it will certainly be, women will be far more engaged as active and empowered responders. If only to co-opt their opposition, mainstream disaster response organizations and groups are now unlikely to exclude women. A broader base of acknowledged female leadership is evident in the metropolitan area. Personal and professional networks have been created or strengthened among Miami's diverse women's groups, ensuring that future responses to crisis or disaster are also less likely to be racially or culturally exclusive. These are important dimensions of nonstructural mitigation, leading toward more disaster-resilient communities.[149]

The Emergence of Innovative Health Care in New Orleans after Hurricane Katrina, Case Study by Karen DeSalvo[150]

The quality of care for the Medicare population in the state of Louisiana a decade ago ranked the lowest in the nation but the highest in terms of cost of care.[151] In the city of New Orleans, the issue of quality of care was largely rooted in the low density of primary care physicians per capita and the failure to support primary care programs in community health centers. This resulted in limited access to primary care by the city's low-income, uninsured, and predominantly minority groups. This lack of care contributed to the high rates of chronic illness experienced by New Orleanians, including obesity, diabetes, heart disease, and asthma.[152] An opportunity emerged to improve the New Orleans region health care system amidst the devastation of Hurricane Katrina, which struck Louisiana on August 29, 2005. New Orleans Health Commissioner Karen DeSalvo, in the book *Resilience and Opportunity: Lessons from the U.S. Gulf Coast after Katrina and Rita*, documents how the community came together following Katrina, began planning early for a new health infrastructure, and effectively implemented an improved system that is now a model of community health care.

The state-run public hospital known as Charity Hospital was the heart of the greater New Orleans area health system for 275 years until Hurricane Katrina struck the Gulf Coast. The storm flooded the city and caused the hospital to close its doors for 14 months leaving hundreds of thousands of individuals without access to their principle source of care.[153] Ambulatory facilities were also severely damaged, and only three of 16 hospital facilities, all of which were in the suburbs of the city, were able to operate, albeit limitedly, following Katrina.[154] The issue of primary care for the city's vulnerable population became critical and the community responded.

In the early days of emergency response activity, volunteers established makeshift care sites across the New Orleans area to meet the urgent care needs of first responders, those left behind, and those quickly returning to the city.[155] Not only were immediate urgent care needs met early on, only two months following Katrina, local health care providers and organizations also came together to plan and make recommendations for a new system to meet the long-term primary care needs of the city's population.[156] At this critical juncture, those involved seized the opportunity to not only respond to the disaster and adapt to post-disaster realities but to also improve conditions. On this, DeSalvo notes:

> . . . [T]he community began to consider a policy framework that would support the vision of a more patient-centered and effective health sector than the one decimated by Katrina. Broad reform was discussed, but inevitably attention was focused on the needs of the safety net to serve the low-income population, given that more than half of the population's health care was supported through some sort of public program. The efforts at rebuilding and redesign began early and in earnest, with stakeholders working simultaneously to restore services and to develop a policy framework that would guide and support the new vision and infrastructure.[157]

The consensus emerged among stakeholders that the New Orleans' health care system needed to move from a hospital-centered safety-net model to a distributed primary care system as primary care was recognized as the key to better health outcomes, better efficiency, and reduced costs.[158] This new system focused on the creation of "medical homes" or community-based health care sites.[159] Many of these sites were those that emerged in the grassroots efforts that began in the early days of response. Some of these sites were federally qualified as health centers and free clinics while others were independently operated by academic, government, or faith-based groups.[160]

Developing a sustainable finance structure for the new health care system became the biggest challenge, and the solution required extensive collaboration of community health care providers and multiple government agencies over the span of three years. In 2007, New Orleans area health care providers came together to secure interim support by requesting federal government aid during a hearing of the House Oversight and Investigations Subcommittee of the Energy and Commerce Committee.[161] Congress met this request through the establishment of a special grant provided by Health and Human Services which awarded $100 million to the state of Louisiana to support and expand a community-based health care network. While significant, this funding only served as a bridge to more permanent financing. Initially, there were efforts to enact insurance coverage expansion in Louisiana, but these efforts failed. To protect the new health care system, federal and state governments worked together with considerable input from local leaders to redirect traditional hospital financing to support the community health care sites.[162] The resulting organization, the Greater New Orleans Health Service Corps, was awarded additional grants to recruit and retain health care professionals to the area. These recruitment efforts have been successful and, DeSalvo notes, have been critical to the overall success of the community health network.[163] This funding ensured that the innovation that emerged in response to the disaster endured to improve the post-disaster community. In all, the New Orleans community worked to be resilient—not to return to "normal" but to adapt and improve their primary health care system for the uninsured population.

Lessons Learned from Case Studies

Both of the case studies highlighted the adaptive process in action, particularly how improvisation, coordination among groups, engagement of the community, and learning contributes to resilient outcomes. First, the coalition Women Will Rebuild in Miami, Florida post-Hurricane Andrew and the community health care centers in New Orleans, Louisiana post-Hurricane Katrina emerged as impromptu responses to post-disaster needs. Neither were mandated groups, controlled from the top while both demonstrated decentralized structures and flexibility in their operations. Second, both efforts engaged various community stakeholders in the pursuit of recovery goals. Women Will Rebuild was a coalition of more than 50 women's groups with diverse interests and the Louisiana community health center initiative was promoted by various health care providers and concerned members of the broader New Orleans area community. Third, collaboration was critical to the success each group achieved. Women Will Rebuild worked with the nonprofit We Will Rebuild to encourage more inclusion of women and minority groups in the recovery process, and the New Orleans community health center initiative involved the collaboration of health care providers with state and federal agencies to secure funding for the centers. Fourth, each case demonstrated learning that endures past the disaster event. Even though Women Will Rebuild did not last as an organization, it impacted the community's approach to disaster recovery by learning that successful recovery efforts must be inclusive of all groups. The New Orleans community health care center efforts were successful in institutionalizing the program and securing funding for its operation. Both created outcomes that improved the community's conditions in the post-disaster environment.

In addition to demonstrating how improvisation, coordination, engagement of the community, and endurance is part of the adaptive process, comparison of these two case studies illustrates other features of resilience that are worth noting. The first is: *The way the adaptive process develops is unique to community context.* Communities have legacies and collective histories that are not destroyed by disaster events. Often these legacies promote inequalities or inefficiencies that, if not addressed post-disaster, may perpetuate. The cases above illustrated that the elite-controlled board of We Will Rebuild was a manifestation of Miami's elite male-dominated, mostly Anglo, downtown business community; the centralized health care system that existed pre-Katrina was a 275-year-old institution. While disasters opened a window of opportunity to alter these dynamics, the focal point of the resilience process for each community was unique to its historical legacy.

The second take-away point from these illustrative case studies is: *Resilience may require a mix of top-down and bottom-up action.* While resilience is fundamentally a strategy to meet local needs with local solutions, designing and implementing these solutions often requires collaboration with state and federal officials particularly for securing funding of recovery projects. Both case studies detailed above involved top-down influences. In the case of Miami, We Will Rebuild was a group organized from above—recall that President Bush requested Chapman's leadership and was charged with the responsibility for directing private and public funding. In the case of New Orleans, funding for the operation of the community health centers involved negotiations between state and federal government agencies along with the input of local leaders. Both demonstrate that resilient outcomes may require that grassroots efforts coordinate with stipulations and action from the top of the disaster management framework, namely state and federal government agencies.

The final lesson learned from these case studies is: *Varying degrees of improvisation, coordination, community engagement, and learning exist within the adaptive process.* While the adaptive process is characterized by these attributes, they are not a "formula" for resilience. Rather, these characteristics mark attributes of post-disaster action that typically produce resilient outcomes. For example, improved land-use plans that affect a specific area might be achieved without widespread engagement of the community. Moreover, these characteristics may exist to varying degrees and still contribute to community resilience. For example, a higher degree of improvisation may create an action that is less likely to be formalized into policy. This does not, however, necessarily mean that resilient outcomes were not achieved. It is simply a matter of degree—a more resilient outcome may have been to institutionalize the action for the next disaster event. In all, the adaptive process is complex, and the characteristics that mark the adaptive process of resilience are dynamic, existing to varying degrees depending upon circumstance and context.

A GENERAL FRAMEWORK OF COMMUNITY DISASTER RESILIENCE

The literature, models, and case studies detailed in this chapter can be woven together to create a general framework of community disaster resilience. While resilience exists on both the individual and collective levels, the focus of this book is communities in the context of disaster events. Therefore, capacities are conceptualized to be aggregated to the municipal or county level, representing the collective ability of these units to respond and recover from natural and environmental disasters.

Broadly, disaster resilience can be defined as *a set of capacities that imbue a community with the strengths needed to respond, cope, and recover from a disaster event as well as a process of collective action enabled by these capacities to adapt to the post-disaster environment.* As shown in Figure 2.1 adaptive capacities are collectively comprised of a community's ties and social structure, economy, disaster institutions, basic infrastructure, and ecological attributes. A disaster resilient community is one that has a high degree of human capital (education, language skills, and health) as well as social capital and competence for collective action. It also has a diverse economy with a robust labor pool, disaster mitigation plans in place, sound infrastructure, and protected natural barriers to buffer against disaster impacts. These capacities exist and are developed on an ongoing basis. However, many of them are inherently tied to the disaster mitigation and preparedness stages, indicated by the solid arrows in the figure running to and from these stages in the process.

In the mitigation stage, communities act to prevent and reduce the severity of impacts through the development of building codes, land-use planning, and wetland preservation—among other activities.[164] The stakeholders

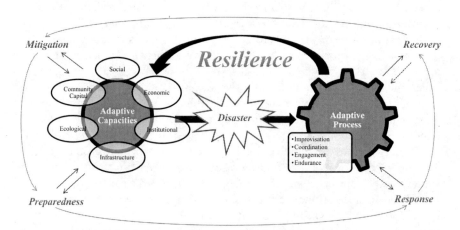

Figure 2.1   Conceptual Model of Local Disaster Resilience

involved are the local population, home and business owners, emergency managers, planners, public officials, and environmental experts. This stage is most closely tied to a community's institutional and ecological attributes of adaptive capacities.

The preparedness stage involves planning to protect human life and property from threats that cannot be controlled through mitigation.[165] Actions are taken during this stage to develop plans for coordinating emergency response, train emergency response personnel, devise evacuation plans and procedures, and stockpile equipment and medical supplies. The stakeholders involved in this stage include emergency managers, first responders, transportation employees, hospitals, and public officials. This stage is most closely related to a community's institutional and infrastructure capacities.

When a disaster strikes, a community's adaptive capacity is put to the test. Severe disasters generally overwhelm local abilities in the short-term, but many of these can rebound to be put to use in the adaptive process creating impromptu and coordinated solutions for disaster response and recovery. Response efforts focus on search and rescue, containing disaster damages, and securing needed supplies for those in the disaster impacted area.[166] Some of the stakeholders involved in response are the local population, first responders, nonprofits, faith-based groups, and the media. Recovery involves actions to rebuild damaged properties and restore economic and social disruptions.[167] It is a long process that involves multiple stakeholders including the local population as well as local, state, and federal government agencies and officials. Economic and business groups, insurance agencies, and local civic organizations are also involved.

Sometimes disasters are so severe that community capacities are temporarily degraded; in this case, immediate response efforts may be directed from entities outside the community. This possibility is represented by a dashed line running from the adaptive process to the disaster response stage. Disaster response, however, certainly influences the adaptive process. A sound response quickly restores basic community functioning, helping collective adaptive capacities to bounce back and become available resources for long-term response and recovery. This dynamic is represented in the figure by a solid arrow running from response to the adaptive process.

Recovery, on the other hand, is directly affected by the adaptive resilience process. The manner in which a community is able to collectively act to pursue recovery projects is not only dependent on the adaptive capacities that are at their disposal post-disaster event but also on the way groups work together. Highly resilient recovery outcomes are produced from impromptu, flexible actions that engage the community in coordinated collective action. Moreover, recovery efforts that take on these attributes should encourage additional action that is also resilient. A community that pursues recovery in a manner that is controlled from the top, excludes parts of the community, or neglects institutionalizing solutions may not see the same cascading benefits of the recovery process. This is represented in the figure by the solid arrow running from the adaptive process to recovery and by the dashed arrow running from recovery to the adaptive process.

Finally, as the figure illustrates, the adaptive process should produce outcomes that in turn affect the community's adaptive capacities. Resilient actions will contribute positively to adaptive capacities as they have adapted to the post-disaster environment and in some cases improved upon pre-disaster conditions. Specifically, social and economic inequalities may be reduced and mitigation and land-use planning may be improved. The adaptive process affecting the recovery stage then spills into the mitigation and preparedness stages for the next disaster event. In all, resilience should beget more resilience.

SUMMARY

Disaster resilience is both a set of adaptive capacities and an adaptive process. Adaptive capacities refer to the strengths a community has for disaster response and recovery. There are multiple types of capacity including: social, economic, institutional, infrastructure, ecological, and community capital. A community with a high degree of adaptive capacity has a population with low social vulnerability, a robust and diverse economy, reduced vulnerability to hazards as a result of mitigation policies and programs, sound support systems, and protected natural barriers to hazards. Additionally, a community with considerable adaptive capacities has a citizenry with high levels of social capital and community competence, willing and able to participate in collective decision-making. These adaptive capacities are translated into the adaptive process when a disaster strikes. Very severe disasters may temporarily degrade the community's abilities, but once restored the adaptive capacities developed prior to the event will imbue the community with strengths to engage in the adaptive process. The adaptive process is characterized by improvisation, coordination, engagement of the community, and endurance.

DISCUSSION QUESTIONS

1. Do you think resilience is a term that is over-used or misused in our society?
2. Can you come up with examples (possibly from your community) of how resilience is distinct from vulnerabilities? Can you think of an example where vulnerability has been created?
3. Which adaptive capacities do you deem critical for the resilience of your community? Why are these important?
4. Considering the four attributes of the adaptive process, are there specific community groups, leaders, or actors that may significantly influence the adaptive process in one regard?

5. How might communities ensure that the collective action they engage in during the adaptive process (after a disaster event) translates into strengthening their adaptive capacity for the next event?

NOTES

1. "Euro Resilience Hints at Shift in Currency's Role," last accessed August 2, 2012, *http://online.wsj.com/article/SB10001424052702303343404577511636 0529967418.html.*
2. "New York Giants prove resilient again in Super Bowl XLVI," last accessed August 2, 2012, *http://sportsillustrated.cnn.com/2012/writers/don_banks/02/05/ super.bowl.xlvi.snaps/index.html.*
3. "Haiti's earthquake tests resilience of capital's hair stylists, now working in streets," last accessed August 1, 2012, *http://rapadoo.com/2012/07/10/haitis -earthquake-tests-resilience-of-capitals-hair-stylists-now-working-in-streets -the-washington-post/.*
4. For example: *Resilience* by The Rentals, *Sound of Strength* by Resilience, and *Resilience* by Annabelle Chvostek.
5. Paulo Coelho, Twitter post, March 5, 2013, accessed March 8, 2013, https:// twitter.com/paulocoelho.
6. The Rockefeller Foundation, Twitter post January 27, 2013, accessed March 8, 2013, https://twitter.com/RockefellerFdn.
7. Martha L. Loudder, "Commencement Speech Transcript," (TAMU Faculty Senate Speaker, May 14, 2004), last accessed August 1, 2012, *http:// graduation.tamu.edu/04A_MarthaLoudder.html.*
8. "Text of Obama's Speech in Afghanistan," May 1, 2012, last accessed August 1, 2012, *http://www.nytimes.com/2012/05/02/world/asia/text-obamas-speech-in -afghanistan.html?pagewanted=1&_r=2.*
9. "Queen's Jubilee speech hails U.K.'s 'resilience'," March 20, 2012, last accessed August 1, 2012, *http://www.cbc.ca/news/world/story/2012/03/20/queen -jubilee-address.html.*
10. George A. Bonanno, "Loss, trauma, and human resilience: have we underestimated the human capacity to thrive after extremely aversive events?," *American Psychology* 4 (2004): 20–8.
11. Lino Briguglio et al., "Economic Vulnerability and Resilience," (Research Paper No. 2008/55), United Nations University, 2008.
12. Douglas Paton, "Disaster Resilience: Building Capacity to Co-Exist with Natural Hazards and Their Consequences," in *Disaster Resilience: An Integrated Approach*, ed. Douglas Paton and David Johnston (Springfield, IL: Charles C Thomas Publisher, Ltd., 2006), 3–10.
13. Susan L. Cutter, Christopher G. Burton, and Christopher T. Emrich, "Disaster Resilience Indicators for Benchmarking Baseline Conditions," *Journal of Homeland Security and Emergency Management,* 7(2010): 1.
14. Dennis S. Mileti, *Disasters by Design: A Reassessment of Natural Hazards in the United States,* (Washington, DC: Joseph Henry Press, 1999).
15. National Science and Technology Council, Subcommittee on Disaster Reduction, *Grand Challenges for Disaster Reduction,* (Washington, DC: National Science and Technology Council, 2005). Accessed June 30, 2013, *http://www .sdr.gov/docs/SDRGrandChallengesforDisasterReduction.pdf.*
16. U.S. Department of Homeland Security, Homeland Security Advisory Council, *Report of the Critical Infrastructure Task Force* (Washington, DC: DHS,

2006). Accessed June 30, 2013, *http://www.dhs.gov/xlibrary/assets/HSAC _CITF_Report_v2.pdf* .

17. Cutter, Burton, and Emrich, "Disaster Resilience Indicators," 1.
18. Mark de Bruijne, Arjen Boin, and Michel van Eeten, "Resilience: Exploring the Concept and Its Meanings," in *Designing Resilience: Preparing for Extreme Events*, ed. Louise K. Comfort et al. (Pittsburg: University of Pittsburg Press, 2010), 28.
19. Susan L. Cutter et al., "A Place-Based Model for Understanding Community Resilience to Natural Disasters," *Global Environmental Change*, 18 (2008): 598.
20. "Resilience," last accessed August 1, 2012, *http://www.merriam-webster.com/ dictionary/RESILIENCE*.
21. C.S. Holling, "Resilience and Stability of Ecological Systems," *Annual Review of Ecology and Systematics*, 4 (1973): 1–23.
22. Per Bodin and Bo L.B. Wiman, "Resilience and other stability concepts in ecology: Notes on their origin, validity, and usefulness," *ESS Bulletin*, 2 (2004): 33–43.
23. Holling, "Resilience," 17.
24. Ibid.
25. Aaron Wildavsky, *Search for Safety* (New Brunswick: Transaction, 1988), 22. Quoted in de Bruijne, Boin, and van Eeten, "Resilience: Exploring the Concept," 21.
26. de Bruijne, Boin, and van Eeten, "Resilience: Exploring the Concept," 21.
27. Ibid, 22–3.
28. Ibid, 23.
29. Fran H. Norris et al., "Community Resilience as a Metaphor, Theory, Set of Capacities, and Strategy for Disaster Readiness," *American Journal of Community Psychology*, 41(2008): 127–50.
30. See: Norris et al., "Community Resilience"; Community and Regional Resilience Initiative, *Community and Regional Resilience: Perspectives from Hazards, Disasters, and Emergency Management*, Susan L. Cutter, Lindsey Barnes, Melissa Berry, Christopher Burton, Elijah Evans, Eric Tate, and Jennifer Webb, CARRI Research Report 1 (Columbia: Hazards and Vulnerability Research Institute, University of South Carolina, 2008), accessed June 5, 2011, *http:// www.resilientus.org/library/FINAL_CUTTER_9–25–08_1223482309.pdf*; Timothy Beatley, *Planning for Coastal Resilience: Best Practices for Calamitous Times*, (Washington, DC: Island Press 2009).
31. de Bruijne, Boin, and van Eeten, "Resilience: Exploring the Concept," 28.
32. W. Neil Adger, "Social and Ecological Resilience: Are They Related?," *Progress in Human Geography*, 24 (2000): 347–64.
33. Philip R. Berke and Thomas J. Campanella, "Planning for Postdisaster Resiliency," *Annals of the American Academy of Political and Social Science*, 604 (2006): 192–207; Adam Rose, "Economic Resilience to Disasters: Towards a Consistent and Comprehensive Formulation," in *Disaster Resilience: An Integrated Approach*, ed. Douglas Paton and David Johnston (Springfield, IL: Charles C Thomas Publisher, Ltd., 2006), 226–45.
34. Paton, "Disaster Resilience: Building Capacity," 7.
35. Paton, "Disaster Resilience: Building Capacity"; Cutter et al., "A Place Based Model."
36. Kathleen Tierney, "Conceptualizing and Measuring Organizational and Community Resilience: Lessons from the Emergency Response Following the September 11, 2001 Attack on the World Trade Center," accessed June 30, 2013, *http://udspace.udel.edu/bitstream/handle/19716/735/PP329.pdf?sequence=1*
37. Norris et al., "Community Resilience."

38. Daniel Henstra, "Evaluating Local Government Emergency Management Programs: What Framework Should Public Managers Adopt?" *Public Administration Review,* 70 (2010): 236–46.
39. Paton, "Disaster Resilience: Building Capacity," 6.
40. David R. Godschalk et al., *Natural Hazard Mitigation: Recasting Disaster Policy and Planning* (Washington, DC: Island Press, 1999); Anthony Oliver-Smith and Susanna M. Hoffmann, ed.. *The Angry Earth: Disasters in an Anthropological Perspective* (New York: Routledge, 1999).
41. Throughout this book the terms "emergency management" and "disaster management" are used interchangeably. Emergency management certainly addresses more than disaster events; however, given that natural and environmental disasters are the focus of this book, the author takes the liberty to substitute the terms.
42. Kathleen Tierney, Michael K. Lindell, and Ronald W. Perry, *Facing the Unexpected: Disaster Preparedness and Response in the United States* (Washington, DC: Joseph Henry Press, 2001), 5.
43. Richard Sylves, *Disaster Policy & Politics: Emergency Management and Homeland Security* (Washington, DC: CQ Press, 2008), 22–3.
44. Mileti, *Disasters by Design,* 22–3.
45. Sylves, *Disaster Policy,* 23.
46. Walter G. Peacock et al., *Advancing the Resilience of Coastal Localities: Developing, Implementing and Sustaining the Use of Coastal Resilience Indicators: A Final Report,* (College Station: Hazard Reduction and Recovery Center, Texas A&M University, 2010), 23.
47. Mileti, *Disasters by Design,* 23.
48. *Community and Regional Resilience,* 2.
49. Beatley, *Planning,* 4.
50. David King, "Planning for Hazard Resilient Communities," in *Disaster Resilience: An Integrated Approach,* ed. Douglas Paton and David Johnston (Springfield, IL: Charles C Thomas Publisher, Ltd., 2006), 293.
51. Beatley, *Planning.*
52. Bruce Glavovic and Gavin Smith, *Adapting to Climate Change: Lessons from Natural Hazards* (London: Springer, forthcoming).
53. Philip Buckle, "Assessing Social Resilience," in *Disaster Resilience: An Integrated Approach,* ed. Douglas Paton and David Johnston (Springfield, IL: Charles C Thomas Publisher Ltd., 2006), 88–103.
54. Fernando I. Riveria and Marc R. Settembrino, "Sociological Insights on the Role of Social Capital in Disaster Resilience," in *Disaster Resiliency: Interdisciplinary Perspectives,* ed. Naim Kapucu, Christopher V. Hawkins, and Fernando I. Rivera (New York: Routledge, 2013), 48–60.
55. Barry Flanagan et al., "A Social Vulnerability Index for Disaster Management," *Journal of Homeland Security and Emergency Management,* 8 (2011): 1–22.
56. Kathleen Tierney, "Social Inequality: Humans and Disasters," in *On Risk and Disaster: Lessons from Hurricane Katrina,* ed. Ronald J. Daniels, Donald F. Keitl, and Howard Kunreuther (Philadelphia: University of Pennsylvania Press, 2006), 109–29.
57. M. E. Brodie et al., "Experiences of Hurricane Katrina Evacuees in Houston Shelters: Implications for Future Planning," *American Journal of Public Health,* 96 (2006): 1402–8.
58. Tierney, "Social Inequality."
59. Flanagan et al., "A Social Vulnerability Index."
60. Anthony A. Peguero, "Latino Disaster Vulnerability: The Dissemination of Hurricane Mitigation Information Among Florida's Homeowners," *Hispanic Journal of Behavioral Sciences,* 28 (2006): 5–22.

61. Buckle, "Assessing," 96.
62. Thomas J. Campanella "Urban Resilience and the Recovery of New Orleans," *Journal of the American Planning Association*, 72 (2006): 141–6.
63. Julia Perilla, Fran H. Norris, and Evelyn A. Lavizzo, "Ethnicity, Culture, and Disaster Response: Identifying and Explaining Ethnic Differences in PTSD Six Months After Hurricane Andrew," *Journal of Social and Clinical Psychology*, 21 (2002): 20–45.
64. Buckle, "Assessing," 96.
65. "Disaster Relief is the Tip of the Iceberg for Social Media," last accessed June 30, 2013, *http://www.psfk.com/2013/04/melissa-waggener-zorkin-psfk-2013.html*.
66. Buckle, "Assessing," 96.
67. Beatley, *Planning*.
68. Peguro, "Latino Disaster Vulnerability."
69. Karen Leong et al.,"Resilient History and the Rebuilding of a Community: The Vietnamese American Community of New Orleans East," *The Journal of American History*, 94 (2007): 770–79; Emily Chamlee-Wright and Virgil H. Storr, "Community Resilience in New Orleans East: Deploying the Cultural Toolkit within a Vietnamese American Community," in *Community Disaster Recovery and Resiliency: Exploring Global Opportunities and Challenges,* ed. DeMond S. Miller and Jason D. Rivera (Boca Raton, FL: Auerback Publications, 2011), 102–24.
70. Alison Cottrell, "Weathering the Storm: Women's Preparedness as a Form of Resilience to Weather-Related Hazards in Northern Australia," in *Disaster Resilience: An Integrated Approach,* ed. Douglas Paton and David Johnston (Springfield, IL: Charles C Thomas Publisher Ltd., 2006), 128–41.
71. Rose, "Economic Resilience."
72. Miletti, *Disasters*.
73. Subject #41, personal interview by Ashley Ross, Chalmette, Louisiana, June 7, 2012.
74. Buckle, "Assessing."
75. Beatley, *Planning*.
76. Alabama Travel Industry Economic Impact Report, last accessed August 1, 2012, *http://images.alabama-staging.luckie.com/publications/main-content/2010TourismReport.pdf*.
77. "Empty Nets in Louisiana Three Years After the Spill," last accessed June 30, 2013, *http://www.cnn.com/2013/04/27/us/gulf-disaster-fishing-industry*.
78. "Economic Impact," last accessed June 30, 2013, *http://louisianaseafood.com/why-buy-louisiana/economic-impact*.
79. C.E. Gregg and B.F. Houghton, "Natural Hazards," in *Disaster Resilience: An Integrated Approach,* ed. Douglas Paton and David Johnston (Springfield, IL: Charles C Thomas Publisher, Ltd. 2006), 19–37.
80. Godschalk et al., *Natural Hazard,* 5.
81. Robert O. Schneider, "Hazard Mitigation: A Priority for Sustainable Communities," in *Disaster Resilience: An Integrated Approach,* ed. Douglas Paton and David Johnston (Springfield, IL: Charles C Thomas Publisher Ltd., 2006), 66–86.
82. Thomas A. Birkland, "Federal Disaster Policy: Learning, Priorities, and Prospects for Resilience," in *Designing Resilience: Preparing for Extreme Events,* ed. Louise K. Comfort, Arjen Boin, and Chris C. Demchak (Pittsburgh: University of Pittsburgh Press, 2010), 109.
83. Sylves, *Disaster Policy,* 69.

84. Robert P. Wolensky and Kenneth C. Wolensky, "Local Government's Problem with Disaster Management: A Literature Review and Structural Analysis," *Review of Public Research,* 9 (1990): 703–25.
85. "FEMA Disaster Mitigation Act 2000," last accessed August 1, 2012, *http:// www.fema.gov/library/viewRecord.do?id=1935.*
86. *"Survey of State Land-Use and Natural Hazards Planning Laws,* 2009," accessed June 30, 2013, http://ofb.ibhs.org/page;jsessionid=549644DA1BD114 7F56D5BD822A8AE566?execution=e1s1&pageId=state_land_use.
87. Godschalk et al., *Natural Hazard,* 13.
88. David Johnston, Julia Becker, and Jim Cousins, "Lifestyles and Urban Resilience," in *Disaster Resilience: An Integrated Approach,* ed. Douglas Paton and David Johnston (Springfield, IL: Charles C Thomas Publisher Ltd., 2006), 40.
89. Johnston, Becker and Cousins, "Lifestyles."
90. Schneider, "Hazard Mitigation."
91. Beatley, *Planning.*
92. For example see: "Louisiana's Coastal Area—Ecosystem Restoration," last accessed June 30, 2013, *http://www.lca.gov/learn.aspx#;* "Wetlands Restoration," last accessed June 30, 2013, *http://www.commongroundrelief.org/ wetlands;* and "Natural Lines of Defense," last accessed June 30, 2013, *https:// healthygulf.org/our-work/natural-defenses/natural-defenses-overview.*
93. "Protecting the City, Before Next Time," last accessed June 30, 2013, *http:// www.nytimes.com/2012/11/04/nyregion/protecting-new-york-city-before -next-time.html?pagewanted=all&_r=0.*
94. Jerome Kahan, Andrew C. Allen, and Justin K. George, "An Operational Framework for Resilience," *Journal of Homeland Security and Emergency Management,* 6 (2009): 1–48.
95. Robert Putnam, "Bowling Alone: America's Declining Social Capital," *Journal of Democracy,* 6 (1995): 65–78.
96. Beatley, *Planning,* 36.
97. Douglas Paton and Li-ju Jang, "Disaster Resilience: Exploring All Hazards and Cross-Cultural Perspectives," in *Community Disaster Recovery and Resiliency: Exploring Global Opportunities and Challenges,* ed. DeMond S. Miller and Jason D. Rivera (Boca Raton, FL: Auerback Publications, 2011), 81–99.
98. Buckle, "Assessing."
99. Kahan, Allen, and George, "An Operational Framework."
100. Buckle, "Assessing."
101. Douglas Paton, "Disaster Resilience: Integrating Individual, Community, Institutional, and Environmental Perspectives," in *Disaster Resilience: An Integrated Approach,* ed. Douglas Paton and David Johnston (Springfield, IL: Charles C Thomas Publisher, Ltd. 2006), 313.
102. Buckle, "Assessing"; Norris et al., "Community Resilience"; Douglas Paton, "Community Resilience: Integrating Individual, Community and Societal Perspectives," in *Phoenix of Natural Disasters: Community Resilience,* ed. Kathryn Gow and Douglas Paton (New York: Nova Science Publishers, 2008), 13–31; and Julie Ann Pooley, Lynne Cohen, and Moria O'Connor, "Links Between Community Resilience: Evidence from Cyclone Affected Communities in North West Australia," in *Disaster Resilience: An Integrated Approach,* ed. Douglas Paton and David Johnston (Springfield, IL: Charles C Thomas Publisher, Ltd. 2006), 161–70.
103. Norris et al., "Community Resilience."
104. Shannon Van Zandt et al., "Mapping Social Vulnerability to Enhance Housing and Neighborhood Resilience," *Housing Policy Debate* 22 (2012): 29–55.

105. Sammy Zahran et al., "Social Vulnerability and the Natural and Built Environment: A Model of Flood Casualties in Texas," *Disasters* (2008): 537–60.
106. Arjen Boin, Louise K. Comfort, and Chris C. Demchak, "The Rise of Resilience," in *Designing Resilience: Preparing for Extreme Events*, ed. Louise K. Comfort, Arjen Boin, and Chris C. Demchak (Pittsburgh: University of Pittsburgh Press, 2010), 11.
107. Cutter et al., "A Place-Based Model."
108. Smith, *Planning*.
109. Ibid.
110. James M. Kendra, James M. and Tricia Wachtendork, "Community Innovation and Disasters," in *Handbook of Disaster Research*, ed. Havidan Rodriguez, Enrico Quarantelli, and Russell R. Dynes (New York: Springer, 2007), 320.
111. Paton, "Disaster Resilience: Integrating," 314.
112. Paton and Jang, "Disaster Resilience," 83; Monica Schoch-Spana et al., "Community Engagement: Leadership Tool for Catastrophic Health Events," *Biosecurity and Bioterrism: Biodefense Strategy, Practice, and Science* 5 (2007): 14; and Smith, *Planning*, 267.
113. Cutter et al., "A Place-Based Model."
114. de Bruijne, Boin, and van Eeten, "Resilience: Exploring the Concept," 28.
115. Cutter et al., "A Place-Based Model."
116. Ibid, 599.
117. Ibid, 603.
118. Ibid.
119. Ibid.
120. Ibid.
121. Norris et al., "Community Resilience," 130.
122. Ibid.
123. Ibid, 136.
124. Ibid, 134.
125. Ibid, 134.
126. Ibid.
127. Ibid, 130.
128. Ibid.
129. Ibid, 143.
130. Ibid, 144.
131. Ibid, 132.
132. Ibid, 143.
133. Ibid.
134. Paton, "Disaster Resilience: Building," 8.
135. de Bruijne, Boin, and van Eeten, "Resilience: Exploring the Concept," 28.
136. Elaine Enarson and Betty Hearn Morrow, "Women Will Rebuild Miami: A Case Study of Feminist Response to Disaster," in *The Gendered Terrain of Disaster: Through Women's Eyes*, ed. Elaine Enarson and Betty H. Morrow (Wesport, CT: Praeger Publishers, 1998), 185–198.
137. Betty Hearn Morrow, "Disaster in the First Person," in *Hurricane Andrew: Ethnicity, Gender, and the Sociology of* Disasters, ed. Walter G. Peacock, Betty Hearn Morrow, and Hugh Gladwin (College Station: Hazard Reduction and Recovery Center, Texas A&M University, 2000), 4.
138. Morrow, *Hurricane Andrew*, 6.
139. Godschalk et al., *Natural Hazard*, 104.
140. Ibid, 114.
141. Enarson and Morrow, "Women," 185.
142. Ibid.

143. Ibid.
144. Betty Morrow and Walter G. Peacock, "Disasters and Social Change: Hurricane Andrew and the Reshaping of Miami?," in *Hurricane Andrew: Ethnicity, Gender, and the Sociology of Disasters*, ed. Walter G. Peacock, Betty Hearn Morrow, and Hugh Gladwin (College Station: Hazard Reduction and Recovery Center, Texas A&M University, 2000), 232.
145. Enarson and Morrow, *Gendered Terrain*, 191.
146. Ibid, 190.
147. Ibid, 191.
148. Ibid, 192.
149. Ibid, 197.
150. Karen DeSalvo, "Delivering High-Quality, Accessible Health Care: The Rise of Community Centers," in *Resilience and Opportunity: Lessons from the U.S. Gulf Coast after Katrina and Rita*, ed. Amy Liu, Roland V. Anglin, Richard M. Mizelle Jr., and Allison Plyer, (Washington, DC: The Brookings Institution, 2011), 45–63.
151. Ibid, 47.
152. Ibid, 49.
153. Ibid, 47.
154. Ibid, 45.
155. Ibid, 50.
156. Ibid, 49.
157. Ibid, 46.
158. Ibid, 49.
159. Ibid, 49–50.
160. Ibid, 50.
161. Ibid, 51.
162. Ibid, 53.
163. Ibid.
164. Peacock et al., *Advancing the Resilience*, 22.
165. Ibid, 23.
166. Ibid, 24.
167. Ibid, 25.

3 Studying Disaster Resilience of the Gulf Coast

The Gulf Coast region of the United States is an ideal setting for the study of resilience. The region's history tells a story of people and communities able to withstand adversity, rebuild after devastation, and navigate uncertainty. Woven into this narrative is a series of focusing events that contributed to the development of emergency management in our nation, including the Hurricane of 1900 in Galveston, Hurricane Andrew in Florida, and Hurricane Katrina, which affected the entire Gulf Coast region. Most recently the region has managed the biggest environmental disaster in history—the BP *Deepwater Horizon* oil spill. These events have not only defined and reframed the role and purpose of our federal government in disaster management; they have shown that if resilience is to be found in tangible, meaningful forms, it is in the Gulf Coast.

GULF COAST FOCUSING EVENTS IN THE DEVELOPMENT OF U.S. EMERGENCY MANAGEMENT

Focusing events are "phenomena that profoundly shape public and elite attitudes about issues that demand immediate attention by government."[1] A focusing event is "sudden; relatively uncommon; can be reasonably defined as harmful or revealing the possibility of potentially greater future harms; has harms that are concentrated in a particular geographical area or community of interest; and known to policy makers and the public simultaneously."[2] Natural disasters fit the definition of focusing events. Political scientist Richard Sylves contends that hurricanes in particular have shaped American perceptions regarding how disasters are defined. In turn, these perceptions have influenced federal, state, and local emergency management.[3]

The Gulf Coast region, unlike any other region in the United States, has been at the heart of focusing events that have influenced the development of emergency management in our country. The hurricanes that hit the Gulf Coast revealed the weaknesses of disaster response and relief; the area has also been a representative example of our national framework for disaster recovery—both what to do and *not* to do. And unlike any other natural disaster in

American history, the catastrophe that unfolded across the Gulf Coast as a result of Hurricane Katrina rocked the foundation of emergency management in our country, shifting institutional bounds and calling attention to a new disaster management strategy: *resilience.* This strategy has been put into action with recent disasters, including the *Deepwater Horizon* oil spill.

Early Disaster Management

During the first 150 years of our nation's history, disaster assistance from the federal government was sporadic. In a study of early disaster relief, political scientist Peter May counted 128 legislative acts related to disasters, dating from 1803 to 1947.[4] Each piece of legislation was event-specific since no federal guidelines existed for disaster assistance. Moreover, it was the norm for the federal government to offer no assistance.[5] Disaster relief responsibilities, then, were carried by local government and volunteer agencies including the American Red Cross.[6] This was the case with the Galveston Hurricane of 1900.

The Galveston Hurricane of 1900

At the turn of the 20th century, the City of Galveston, in line with trends across the Gulf Coast region, was growing in population and economic prosperity. The city was one of the wealthiest in the nation[7] and had become an important regional and national port.[8] This came to an abrupt halt on September 8, 1900 when a hurricane of Category 4 strength hit the low-lying island, inundating the city with storm surges of over 15 feet.[9]

The Galveston Hurricane of 1900 is still today the deadliest natural disaster in U.S. history, claiming an estimated 6,000 to 12,000 lives.[10] In addition to the lives lost, 3,600 homes were destroyed by the storm surge, and damage costs exceeded $20 million, an approximate $700 million today.[11] Immediate response to the storm fell on the shoulders of Galvestonians themselves. Only a day after the storm, citizens met to elect members of the Central Relief Committee choosing the mayor, state senator, and various businessmen and financiers to lead the city's recovery efforts.[12] The committee quickly organized to manage the most urgent needs, and citizens came together to provide needed shelter, medical care, food, and clothing.[13] Outside disaster assistance soon reached Galveston with the arrival of a team of American Red Cross workers, including founder 78-year-old Clara Barton.[14] The U.S. Army also sent soldiers, tents, and food,[15] and as news spread of the disaster, donations poured in from all over the nation and the world.[16] With external financial assistance, clean-up efforts were supported, utilities restored, and the immediate needs of food, shelter, and clothing for survivors were met.[17] In addition, the Central Relief Committee used the funds to rebuild Galveston, paying for the construction of nearly 500 new homes and providing partial financial aid for the rebuilding of more than 1,000 houses.[18] Galveston officials also got to work rebuilding the city, pursuing what was considered an engineering marvel—the construction of seawall.

The Galveston seawall, financed by the county through a bond issue, took two years to complete, and when finished stood 17 feet above mean low tide, was 15 feet thick at the base, and reached 3.5 miles in length.[19] The federal government was not involved in this initial construction except through technical advisement provided by the Army Corps of Engineers.[20] However, realizing value of mitigation the federal government built an additional section of the wall the following year. Similar mitigation efforts were undertaken in response to large-scale disasters in the following decades.

Expansion of the Federal Role with Flood Mitigation

The Great Mississippi Flood of 1927 inundated 20,000 square miles of land with water including the Gulf Coast states of Louisiana[21] and Mississippi and left an estimated 700,000 people homeless.[22] In response the Flood Control Act of 1928 was passed to create a partnership between federal and local governments in the construction and maintenance of flood control structures. It also marked a broad shift in the role and obligations of the federal government with regards to disaster management, which did not take long to materialize. Hazards scholars David Butler notes that Congress appropriated $10 million for relief and reconstruction related to the 1927 flood but spent thirty times this amount the following year on flood mitigation projects along the lower Mississippi River.[23]

Federal government involvement in emergency management continued over the next two decades with considerable investment in mitigation projects.[24] In 1935 President Franklin D. Roosevelt signed the Emergency Relief Appropriation Act, which set aside $4.8 million for public assistance programs.[25] These programs required aid recipients to work on public projects, many of which were aimed at reducing future vulnerabilities to drought.[26] The next year Congress responded to a series of flood events by passing the Flood Control Act of 1936, which effectively enacted a national policy of flood control.[27] The legislation also set into motion numerous public works programs headed by the U.S. Army Corp of Engineers, which included the construction of dams, dikes, and levees to reduce vulnerability to floods.[28] Additional flood control acts were passed in 1938 and 1941, and $11 billion was appropriated for flood control during 1936 and 1952.[29]

Civil Defense & the Emergence of Federal Emergency Management Framework

Emergency management took a turn in the 1940s and 1950s as focus shifted from domestic issues to foreign threats of attack and nuclear warfare. Civil defense became the overriding concern of policy-makers and citizens alike. Legislative acts passed at this time to provide for civil defense on the federal, state, and local levels became the model for modern emergency management. At the same time Congress initiated the first programmatic federal disaster assistance. During the following decades a series of severe natural disasters prompted policy-makers to vastly expand these relief policies.

Civil Defense Act of 1950

In response to World War II, many state and local governments established civil defense organizations to develop protection plans and involve citizens in the war effort.[30] While this early civil defense legislation was not aimed at dealing with natural disasters, the local agencies and volunteer networks it engendered proved to be effective during the 1944 Cuba–Florida Hurricane, a Category 3 storm that struck southern Florida then traveled northeast, going back out to sea south of Jacksonville near St. Augustine.[31] *The St. Augustine Record* noted that the local defense council was instrumental during this storm in coordinating efforts to alert, evacuate, and shelter citizens.[32]

While local civil defense organizations might effectively coordinate a response to an emergency situation such as a hurricane evacuation, many contended that state and local governments were not equipped to handle nuclear threats associated with enemy attacks—threats that grew more pressing with the Soviet Union's successful test of an atomic bomb in 1949 and the initiation of U.S. military action in Korea during the summer of 1950.[33] On the other hand, there were concerns that the federal government post–World War II was growing too big and becoming too paternalistic.[34] To address these conflicting pressures, President Harry S. Truman worked with Congress to pass the Civil Defense Act of 1950, which provided a framework for civil defense to guide states' efforts without placing the focus of responsibility—administrative or fiscal—on federal government.[35] Instead, the act set up the Federal Civil Defense Administration as a coordinating agency responsible for preparing civil defense plans, organizing federal and state activities, promoting interstate mutual aid agreements among states, and providing a limited amount of grants to states for civil defense activities, primarily for the construction of shelters.[36] The Civil Defense Act also authorized the president to proclaim, or Congress to establish, a state of emergency, which was and still is required for the president to direct federal aid to the states.[37]

Under the Civil Defense Act much of the burden for civil defense fell on the states.[38] Consequently, the states moved to establish their own institutions for civil defense to oversee and distribute responsibility to regional and local councils. In the Gulf Coast region, Louisiana was the first state to act by passing legislation in 1950 to create a state civil defense agency.[39] Florida and Texas established similar institutions headed by their governors the following year, and Alabama adopted state legislation to accomplish the same in 1955.[40] These state agencies were supported with funding from the Federal Civil Defense Administration.[41] Even though state civil defense frameworks progressed as a result of the Civil Defense Act and were facilitated by federal funding, many local officials remained concerned that the federal government did not lead in the area of civil defense relying instead on a decentralized framework.[42] In 1958, Congress changed this by passing legislation that held federal, state, and local governments jointly responsible for civil defense while charging the federal government with a greater role in guiding and coordinating these efforts.[43]

The Federal Disaster Relief Act of 1950

In conjunction with the Civil Defense Act, Congress passed the Federal Disaster Relief Act in 1950. It outlined three key provisions for disaster assistance: 1) Congressional action is not needed to direct assistance following each disaster; 2) Decisions regarding assistance are made by the president; and 3) Federal government aid can be extended if a state's governor requests it and if the state can certify that federal aid is supplemental[44] to a reasonable amount of state and local funds allocated for response and recovery effort.[45] The act initially authorized federal aid for emergency assistance and repairs only—construction that replaced damaged buildings would not be funded.[46] Yet within a year of its enactment, Congress expanded the Federal Disaster Relief Act granting the president authority to approve temporary housing and shelter for disaster victims and authorizing an increase in the mortgage insurance limit related to rebuilding homes post-disaster.[47] Congress continued to revise the act in the following decade, expanding its scope.

Disaster relief following the passage of the Federal Disaster Relief Act was fairly modest in comparison to appropriations made for civil defense. Keith Bea, former specialist in American national government in the Government and Finance Division of the Congressional Research Service, notes that from 1950 to 1964, the federal government spent $275 million on disaster relief for 174 disaster declarations while Congress appropriated more than $450 million in half that amount of time (from 1951 to 1958) for civil defense planning.[48] The need for assistance beyond the scope of the Federal Disaster Relief Act was realized, unfortunately through severe disaster events.

Expanding the Federal Role in Disaster Management

Hurricanes across the Gulf Coast during the 1960s and 1970s contributed to a series of focusing events that pushed policy-makers to expand federal disaster assistance.[49] In 1965, Hurricane Betsy made landfall in Key Largo, Florida as a Category 3 hurricane then turned northwest, gained in intensity to a Category 4 hurricane, and struck Grand Isle, Louisiana the next day.[50] The storm caused 76 deaths and resulted in more than $1 billion in damages ($7.5 billion in current US dollars).[51] In 1969, Hurricane Camille, one of the most intense hurricanes to ever hit the United States, landed on the Mississippi coast causing 143 deaths in the Gulf Coast region and $1.42 billion in damages (over $10 billion in current US dollars).[52] In 1972, Hurricane Agnes made landfall as a Category 1 hurricane on Florida's Panhandle near Cape San Blas causing flooding and spawning, by some counts, 28 tornadoes[53] that caused over $12 million of property damage.[54] The hurricane caused greater damage when it traveled along the East Coast, moved over the Atlantic Ocean, then struck New York City where it dumped 10 to 14 inches of rain over Virginia, Maryland, Pennsylvania, and New York. Resultant severe flooding caused 50 deaths and created $2 billion of property damages.[55] These events underscored that the Federal Disaster Relief Act was insufficient for damages on this scale. As a result, Congress passed several pieces of legislation that expanded disaster assistance.[56]

Increased Disaster Relief Aid

In 1968, a Congressional act established the National Flood Insurance Program that set up a system where property owners pay for future (hypothetical) disaster losses through premiums.[57] In 1969, legislative revisions to the Disaster Relief Act of 1966 established a formalized program of individual benefits; prior to this, disaster relief was primarily aimed at state and local governments.[58] Aid to individuals increased further with the Disaster Relief Act of 1970, including provisions for temporary housing and legal assistance for low-income families. Relief aid was expanded again with the Disaster Relief Act of 1974 which authorized individual grants to replace past loan forgiveness programs.[59] It also shifted emergency management focus to an all-hazards approach and made federal disaster assistance to states and localities conditional on the evaluation and implementation of hazard mitigation measures.[60]

The expansion of federal government disaster programs and assistance largely followed major disasters during the 1950s to 1970s. Many of these focusing events were hurricanes that struck the Gulf Coast, as shown in Figure 3.1. Federal disaster assistance peaked with Hurricanes Camille and Agnes, and subsequent to the passage of the Disaster Relief Act in 1974, levels of assistance continued to rise.

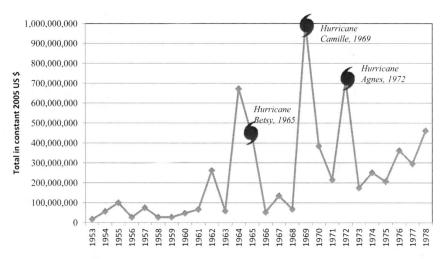

Figure 3.1   Gulf Coast Focusing Events & Disaster Expenditures, 1953–1978

Source: Expenditure data adapted from Keith Bea, "The Formative Years: 1950–78" in *Emergency Management: The American Experience 1900–2005.*

The Creation of FEMA in 1979

Despite appeasing public calls for relief following severe disasters, new concerns emerged regarding the administration of emergency management in the country. Central to these concerns was the lack of clarity of the federal disaster framework which Sylves blames on "presidential and congressional failure to recognize the need for cohesiveness and sound organization in federal disaster management."[61] Studies of emergency preparedness in the late 1970s concluded: "[G]overnment activity in this area . . . suffers from the lack of high-level attention, organizational diffusion, inadequate foresight and coordination, weak or misdirected funding, and the absence of a comprehensive approach to what is basically a homogenous group of planning and programmatic functions."[62]

These findings were echoed in the frustrations of state and local officials, who saw a need for a more centralized federal emergency management framework.[63] In response, President Jimmy Carter established the Federal Emergency Management Agency (FEMA) in 1979 as an independent agency charged with the responsibility for emergency preparedness, civil defense, disaster relief, flood and crime insurance, fire prevention, and continuity of government.[64] Disaster loan programs were not transferred to FEMA but instead operated by the Department of Commerce Small Business Administration.[65] Since not all federal disaster and emergency functions were consolidated under FEMA, federal agencies continued to compete for jurisdiction over these issues and, consequently, issues of the cohesiveness of the federal emergency management framework persisted.[66]

Until the 1980s disaster management overlapped with civil defense and national security. The two had been coupled since the 1950 Civil Defense and Disaster Relief Acts, and the federal government further entrenched them by implementing "dual use" policy in the 1960s and 1970s.[67] Civil defense and focus on nuclear attacks were reprioritized toward the end of President Ronald Reagan's administration as U.S.–Soviet relations improved.[68] In 1994 the Civil Defense Act was repealed, and most of its provisions were reenacted in Title VI of the Stafford Act, whose purpose is to provide a comprehensive system of emergency preparedness in the face of *all* hazards and across all phases of emergency management—mitigation, preparedness, response, and recovery.[69] FEMA was given the statutory responsibility for coordinating this comprehensive emergency preparedness system, a change so important that many consider the Stafford Act as marking the beginning of modern emergency management.[70]

The Stafford Act of 1988

The Stafford Act was passed in 1988 under President Reagan. In addition to establishing an all-hazards approach to emergency management, it set the parameters for how federal disasters are declared, establishing two incident levels: emergencies[71] and major disasters.[72] It also determined the types of federal disaster assistance provided including public assistance to local governments for emergency work, repair and restoration, and debris removal as well as mitigation grants for reducing vulnerabilities pre-disaster. Provisions were also made to define a cost-sharing program, breaking the share of public assistance programs into 75 percent the federal government and 25 percent state and local governments. FEMA was charged with carrying out the provisions of the Stafford Act, including the distribution of the majority of the federal disaster assistance provided by the legislation, which averages $2 billion a year.[73]

Hurricane Andrew

FEMA and the Stafford Act were soon tested by a series of mega-disasters that hit the Gulf Coast including Hurricane Hugo that struck the Caribbean and eastern United States in 1989 and Hurricane Andrew that hit the Gulf Coast in 1992. Hurricane Andrew, a Category 5 storm, made landfall at Homestead, Florida then traveled across the Gulf to strike near Morgan City, Louisiana. In all it caused $26.5 billion in damages—all but $1 billion associated with destruction in Florida—and resulted in 23 fatalities.[74] The aftermath of the storm revealed total devastation—trees uprooted, homes in complete disarray.[75] It was described by one individual who experienced it as looking like "a bomb had gone off."[76]

Response to this disaster was highly criticized as being uncoordinated and inadequate. Political scientist Saundra Schneider notes that the federal response was slow as FEMA waited on state and local officials to assess damage and identify needs before sending assistance.[77] This delay meant that the immediate needs of those affected by the hurricane were largely neglected. Moreover, failures in communication among government levels and relief organizations added to the lack of coordination and confusion post-disaster. In all, the response was deemed a failure, revealing "significant flaws in the nation's system of disaster management."[78]

Criticism was also aimed at Florida's mitigation policies. Structural damage from Andrew was largely due to wind gusts that peaked at 164 miles per hour during the storm. At the time code violations and shoddy construction practices were blamed; however estimations now report that these contributed to less than one-tenth of the total losses suffered.[79] Regardless, the state of Florida did not have a mitigation plan in place when Andrew struck. It developed one post-disaster, and 21 months after the storm FEMA approved it.[80] Additionally, Florida significantly revised its building codes and state emergency management framework. On the federal level, Congress amended the Stafford Act to increase federal funding for hazard mitigation activities and projects.[81]

Expanded Federal Role in Disaster Mitigation

In the wake of Hurricane Andrew, the federal government looked to strengthen mitigation efforts aimed at reducing vulnerabilities to hazards prior to a disaster event.[82] FEMA under the leadership of Director James Lee

Witt was able to make mitigation "the foundation of emergency management and the primary goal of the agency."[83] This was accomplished through programs including Project Impact that increased local mitigation efforts through collaboration partnerships.

Mitigation efforts continued with the passage of the Disaster Mitigation Act of 2000. This act amended the Stafford Act to give FEMA the authority to establish a technical and financial assistance program aimed at improving pre-disaster mitigation on state and local levels.[84] Additionally, this legislation required that states provide a comprehensive program for pre-disaster mitigation before receiving post-disaster mitigation funds. Local governments were also required to identify potential mitigation measures to incorporate into repairs such as improved building codes before receiving federal funding. These mitigation efforts were the result of concerted efforts to comprehensively approach natural disasters, a focus that dramatically shifted back to national defense with the terrorist attacks of September 11, 2001.

The Terrorist Attacks of 9/11 and the Institution of a New Emergency Management Framework

The response to the 9/11 attacks on the World Trade Center in New York City was led by the city's fire and police departments, emergency medical systems, and office of emergency management with the assistance of the New York/New Jersey Port Authority police and FEMA search and rescue teams.[85] Emergency management practitioner and researcher, John Harrald, assessed the initial response as "exceptional," noting that the state and local authorities were not overwhelmed; however, federal, state, and local coordination was "impeded by the inability of different agencies to communicate with one another during the immediate response."[86]

Part of the coordination issues experienced in the response to 9/11 stemmed from the federal approach to emergency management at the time that vested responsibility for classes of hazards among different federal agencies and specified varying relationships among federal, state, and local governments. Harrald notes that under the Federal Response Plan, the state has the lead role in responding to natural disasters with support by the federal government; on the other hand, under the Interagency Domestic Terrorism Concept of Operations Plan, the federal government leads the response to terrorist attacks.[87] The 9/11 attacks exposed this weakness of the federal emergency management framework, and reaction to the event included a congressional push for creation of a national response system that more fully integrated local, state, federal, civilian, and military response forces.[88]

The Creation of the Department of Homeland Security

In response to growing political pressure, President George W. Bush signed the 2002 Homeland Security Act that reorganized government to establish the Department of Homeland Security (DHS).[89] This reorganization incorporated all or part of 22 federal agencies, including FEMA, with "very diverse organization structures, missions, and cultures, and, importantly, diverse ideas about the management of domestic threats and emergencies."[90] Sylves argues that this reorganization effectively "expand[ed] the role of defense and law enforcement-oriented activities concerned exclusively with terrorism while diminishing the role and decreasing the prestige of organizations conducting all-hazards emergency management."[91]

Of particular importance is FEMA's loss of agency independence, visibility, and resources because it is the only organization within DHS responsible for disasters not linked to terrorism.[92] Sociologist and hazards scholar Kathleen Tierney notes that this loss of influence caused considerable concern among emergency management experts including former FEMA director James Lee Witt. Witt cautioned in Congressional testimony: "I assure you that we could not have been as responsive and effective during disasters as we were during my tenure as FEMA director had there been layers of federal bureaucracy between myself and the White House."[93]

In addition to creating the DHS, President Bush further revised federal emergency management by passing the Homeland Security Presidential Directive-5 (HSPD-5), which established the National Response Plan (NRP) and the National Incident Management System (NIMS).[94] The objective of these was to integrate all levels of government under one unified framework with a "core set of concepts, principles, terminology, and technologies covering the incident command system, multiagency coordination systems, unified command, training, qualification, certification, and incident information collection, tracking, and reporting."[95] All federal agencies as well as state and local governments that receive federal assistance were required to adopt and adhere to these measures. Similarly, requirements for funding contingent on FEMA-approved state mitigation plans were put into place. In all, this directive established "for the first time both the structure and doctrine to effectively and consistently apply federal capability and resources in preparation for, response to, and recovery from incidents of national significance."[96] But it also significantly modified "the 'bottom-up' emergency management and 'shared governance' policies that had existed before."[97] While the federal framework was in transition during the years following this legislation, multiple hurricanes, including Hurricane Katrina, hit the Gulf Coast and stressed this new system of emergency management to a breaking point.

Reinventing FEMA Post-Katrina
In 2004 five major storms—Tropical Storm Bonnie, Hurricane Charlie, Hurricane Frances, Hurricane Ivan, and Hurricane Jeanne—made landfall in Florida and affected parts of Alabama, Mississippi, and Louisiana, cumulatively causing 117 deaths, over $20 million in damages, and 10 million

evacuees.[98] In 2005, Hurricane Dennis made landfall near Pensacola, Florida, affecting areas still recovering from Hurricane Ivan.[99] Dennis caused 15 fatalities and created more than $2 billion in losses. A month later, Hurricane Katrina, with a radius of 25–30 nautical miles, made landfall at the Mississippi–Louisiana border.[100]

Fatalities associated with Hurricane Katrina have been estimated to be 1,833, and more than one million people were displaced due to the storm.[101] Katrina affected 90,000 square miles across the states of Louisiana, Mississippi, and Alabama causing more than $125 billion in damages.[102] Katrina's storm surge hit Mississippi the hardest; homes and buildings in Waveland, Bay St. Louis, Pass Christian, and Long Beach were flattened by surge heights of 24–28 feet.[103] The surge, reaching heights of 17–22 feet in Biloxi and Gulf Shores, also destroyed parts of these towns.[104]

New Orleans was severely impacted by Katrina. The storm caused a surge that traveled up the Mississippi River Gulf Outlet and brought heavy rains which, combined with levee failures, caused 80 percent of the city to flood with water reaching a height of 20 feet in some areas.[105] Efforts to drain the city were not achieved until after Hurricane Rita which flooded the city again but caused even more extensive damage in western Louisiana, leveling Cameron Parish.[106] A month after Hurricane Rita, Hurricane Wilma hit Florida causing five deaths and $12 billion in damages. Collier County, Florida was particularly affected with storm surges over 8 feet.[107]

Federal disaster aid reached all-time highs with this series of events. In 2004 and 2005, FEMA public assistance grants totaled over $22 billion. As shown in Figure 3.2, nearly all of these funds—an average of 87 percent for this two year period—were poured into the Gulf States of Texas, Louisiana, Mississippi, Alabama, and Florida.

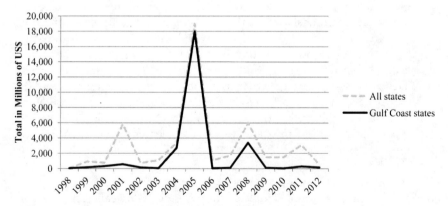

Figure 3.2   Gulf Coast States' Share of FEMA Public Assistance Grants, 1998–2012

Source: Author's calculations based on FEMA Public Assistance Funded Projects Detail, available at http://www.fema.gov/library/viewRecord.do?id=6295

Although the Gulf Coast storms of 2004 and 2005 were collectively a devastating—and costly—blow to the region, Hurricane Katrina called into question our nation's emergency management system like no other natural disaster in American history. By many estimates the response to Katrina was in itself a disaster. Hazards scholars Melanie Gall and Susan Cutter describe it:

> In communities all along the Gulf Coast, but particularly in New Orleans, organizational breakdowns added to the desperate plight of residents. Roads leading out of the area were clogged with traffic—and later made impassable by rising floodwaters. Search and rescue operations were understaffed and ill prepared. Elderly and sick residents were stranded in hospitals and nursing homes, and living conditions in the Superdome and shelters of last resort were deplorable. For days, the entire disaster area was without food, potable water, power, medication, sanitation, sheltering, and any form of organizational help.[108]

The bipartisan Senate committee on Homeland Security and Government Affairs concluded in the report titled "Hurricane Katrina: A Nation Still Unprepared" that the human suffering following the storm was a result of "the failure of government at all levels to plan, prepare for, and respond aggressively to the storm."[109] Furthermore, the committee noted that these failures were "not just conspicuous" but "pervasive," occurring "against a backdrop of failure, over time, to develop the capacity for a coordinated, national response to a truly catastrophic event. . ." Four factors were identified as a cause of these failures: "1) Long-term warnings went unheeded and government officials neglected their duties to prepare for a forewarned catastrophe; 2) Government officials took insufficient actions or made poor decisions in the days immediately before and after landfall; 3) Systems on which officials relied on to support their response efforts failed; and 4) Government officials at all levels failed to provide effective leadership."[110] FEMA's 2006 review of state and urban emergency plans echoed these conclusions pointing to needed improvements in evacuation, command structure, resource management, and attention to special needs populations.[111] Similar points and recommendations have been made by academic studies focused on the emergency management and public administration failures of Hurricane Katrina.[112]

In response, Congress passed the Post-Katrina Emergency Management Reform Act of 2006 which effectively reorganized DHS to expand FEMA's authority and responsibilities.[113] The act reestablished FEMA's mission to "lead and support efforts to reduce the loss of life and property and protect the nation from all hazards."[114] FEMA was charged with the additional responsibilities of "ensuring first responder effectiveness, supervising grants, administering and implementing the National Response Plan, preparing and implementing federal continuity of government and operations plans . . . and maintaining and operating the response coordination center."[115] The act also provided for additional positions, a Disability Coordinator and Small State and Rural Advocate as well as a National Advisory Council.[116] Further, the act created regional advisory councils, regional emergency communications working groups, and ten regional offices[117] as well as consolidated regional assistance teams staffed with full-time personnel.[118] FEMA Director Craig Fugate noted in a 2011 congressional hearing that these regional resources "proved invaluable" during the response to Hurricane Irene that struck the east coast of the U.S. in 2011.[119] Fugate went on to say that the Post-Katrina Reform Act has given FEMA the authority needed to successfully "leverage the entire emergency management team in response and recovery efforts" including government, private and nonprofit partners, and citizens.[120]

The Emergence of Resilience as a New Frame for Emergency Management

In addition to fundamentally shifting the authority and responsibilities of FEMA through the Post-Katrina Reform Act, Hurricane Katrina spurred the introduction of a new term to the Department of Homeland Security: *resilience*. Resilience formally became a part of the DHS lexicon in January 2006 with the recommendations of the Homeland Security Advisory Council's Critical Infrastructure Task Force Report.[121] In this report, the Critical Infrastructure Task Force promoted resilience as a strategic objective, noting: "While protection forms a sound foundation, in the post September 11 environment and in the wake of the critical infrastructure failure that made Katrina a national tragedy, it has become obvious that critical infrastructure resiliency is a regional and national imperative."[122] Protection, the task force asserted, is a "brittle strategy" when used alone; resilience, on the other hand, is dynamic, flexible, and can "maintain its function and structure in the face of internal and external change."[123] Resilience was touted as a "bottom-up" strategy that can empower local solutions to emergency management problems. The focus on resiliency, therefore, became an attractive frame, and community resilience has been widely adopted as a guiding principle for emergency management by the federal government. Despite that this has been applied imprecisely; recent disaster events along the Gulf Coast highlight how federal response and community perceptions now see emergency management through the lens of resilience.

Hurricane Ike first made landfall in Cuba on September 7, 2008 as a category 4 storm; it then traveled over the Gulf of Mexico to strike Galveston Island, Texas on September 13.[124] Ike was the third costliest storm in U.S. history, behind Andrew in 1992 and Katrina in 2005.[125] Much of the public reaction to Ike considered the event in terms of resilience as evidenced by this news headline "Texas Rebuilds after Hurricane Ike with Resilience and Resolve."[126] Research following the event also approached it through the framework of resilience. For example, an initiative by the Hazards Reduction and Recovery Center team at Texas A&M University organized a community workshop in

Galveston to determine which resilience issues were most important to local stakeholders; they found high priorities for disaster reduction, infrastructure development, land-use planning, and environmental protection.[127]

The BP *Deepwater Horizon* oil spill has also been largely interpreted in terms of resilience. On April 20, 2010 the BP-operated Macondo 252 oil well exploded off the coast of Louisiana; its drilling rig, *Deepwater Horizon*, also set fire, causing 11 causalities.[128] Over 200 million gallons of crude oil (20 times the volume associated with the Exxon *Valdez* tanker accident of 1989) was released into the Gulf of Mexico as a result of the spill.[129] The oil spill contaminated 250 square miles of the ocean; damaged fragile ecosystems along the coast of Louisiana; polluted beaches in Mississippi, Alabama, and Florida; and negatively impacted regional economies including the fishing and shrimping industries and coastal tourism. Immediate response to the spill expressed concern for community resilience. Local initiatives such as the Alabama Coastal Recovery Commission's "Roadmap for Resilience" emerged with a focus on community engagement to develop effective solutions to the oil spill.[130]

The strategy of resilience, however, proved to be difficult in response to the oil spill because state and local community leaders were constrained by the emergency management protocols that put the federal government, namely the Coast Guard, in charge. Conflicts of authority emerged among state governors and mayors with federal agencies,[131] and local communities were confused and frustrated about the management of the spill.[132] This draws attention to the tension that exists between the localized nature of resilience and the centralized nature of our federal emergency management.[133] It also highlights that much more study is needed to fully understand disaster resilience on the local level.

Assessing Community Disaster Resilience of the Gulf Coast

Broadly, disaster resilience can be defined as *a set of capacities that imbue a community with the strengths needed to respond, cope, and recover from a disaster event as well as a process of collective action enabled by these capacities to adapt to the post-disaster environment.* Therefore, resilience is both a set of adaptive capacities and a process of adaptation. A resilient community is one that has the capacity to respond to disaster events in innovative, flexible, and collaborative ways. While these theoretical tenants seem straightforward, the reality of resilience is much more muddled and presents the opportunity to study how resilience is understood and applied in the context of disaster management.

Resilience in Theory

Resilience as adaptive capacities is a set of qualities that represent the strengths or weaknesses a community has in managing disaster events. Adaptive capacities can be categorized into the following components:

- *Social Capacity:* Populations that have low vulnerability to hazards—well-educated, adequate provisions for special needs, and access to transportation and health care—generally fare better in disasters.
- *Community capital:* Citizens who are more connected to one another can more easily work collectively to deal with disaster events.
- *Economic Capacity:* A robust, diverse economy can rebound from interruptions caused by disasters.
- *Institutional and Infrastructure Capacity:* Disaster mitigation plans and sound infrastructure facilitate response and recovery efforts.
- *Ecological Capacity:* Preservation of natural hazard barriers such as wetlands and dunes boost resilience.

These capacities imbue a community with the attributes needed to prevent a disaster or, in the event of disaster, effectively respond and recover. The adaptive process is set into motion by a disaster event, and how it develops, particularly in the response stage, depends largely on the adaptive capacities of a community. If a disaster completely devastates a community, fully engaging in action that promotes resilience is very difficult, especially if the population is displaced. Typically, capacities are temporarily overwhelmed and once restored enable a community to engage in the adaptive process of resilience.

The adaptive process of resilience is largely characterized by four qualities: improvisation, coordination, engagement, and endurance. Improvisation is marked by adaptable, impromptu action taken to meet local needs following a disaster. This action requires coordination linking available resources with response and recovery needs post-disaster, and collaboration among stakeholders is critical for sustainable solutions to be implemented. Engagement of broad community groups produces better solutions as a diverse set of interests and knowledge is represented. The goal is to make decisions and put into action policy that not only achieves the rebuilding of a community but also improves it by addressing pre-event vulnerabilities. To ensure that the outcomes created within this impromptu, collaborative, and inclusive environment last beyond the disaster event, the lessons learned must take on some quality of endurance.

Resilience Puzzles

While resilience in the abstract is relatively straightforward, in reality it is much more complicated and presents a few issues that should be examined. The first is how it is understood. Resilience has been adopted as an overarching goal of national defense and emergency management without a clear meaning. On this, the Homeland Security Advisory Council Community Resilience Task Force noted in a June 2011 report of recommendations:

> . . . '[R]esilience' is seen as jargon in that it too often is used imprecisely. References to resilience are increasingly heard from White House and

other federal officials, but the descriptions of what is meant remain both varied and abstract. Regionally-focused resilience initiatives are gaining momentum, yet a common understanding and standard measures that would enable assessment of the current state of resilience have not emerged.[134]

The same sentiment is echoed by Mark de Bruijne, Arjen Boin, and Michel van Eeten in the book *Designing Resilience*. They note that "the definition of resilience has become so broad as to render it almost meaningless."[135] In addition to a lack of a clear meaning, resilience has failed to be "converted into an operational tool." Also concerned with the lack of measurement, the Subcommittee on Disaster Reduction of the National Science and Technology Council Committee on Environment and National Resources called for "effective standards and metrics for assessing disaster resilience" that can "support comparability among communities and provide a context for action to further reduce vulnerability" in their 2005 Grand Challenges Report.[136]

The second issue is that resilience poses a conundrum to modern emergency management. The federal government's promotion of resilience as an overarching strategy that "acknowledges the use of local knowledge and experimentation and flexibility to deal with local circumstances"[137] conflicts with the centralized national disaster policy that has developed over time. Disaster scholar Thomas Birkland argues our national disaster policy works to undermine resilience because it operates in a top-down manner with "feds know best" tendencies. Moreover, resilience is undercut by the emphasis on post-disaster action. In the past two decades, the distribution of post-disaster relief aid has reached unprecedented amounts; funding that often encourages continued development in high risk areas.[138] Therefore, resilience presents a challenge for emergency management to reconcile—the promotion of a localized, bottom-up strategy within the context of a centralized, top-down institutional framework.

The promotion of resilience as an overarching strategy for emergency management values local action to disasters, but what is meant by resilience and how resilience fits into our national disaster policy framework remains unclear. While studies of hazards and disasters have contributed to the development of the conceptual meaning and measurement of resilience, there remains a need to understand how resilience is perceived and practiced on the local level—where it is purported to develop and make the most impact. This study attempts to address this by answering a series of research questions focused on deepening our understanding of disaster resilience on the local level.

Questions to Frame the Study of Resilience
There are four research questions this study seeks to answer in exploring disaster resilience. The first is: *How is community resilience understood?* Resilience has been criticized as being broad, imprecise, and simply jargon.[139]

Yet, resilience continues to be promoted as an overarching strategy of federal emergency management. It is commonly referred to by federal agencies and is part of disaster management plans and programs. Given its predominance in modern emergency management, assessment of the meanings associated with the term resilience is warranted.

The second question is: *What trends are evident in adaptive capacities?* Adaptive capacities encompass an array of community attributes, ranging from social to economic to ecological. Assessments of adaptive capacities reflect a community's ability to respond to and recover from a disaster event. While this information is useful in mapping resilience, it is also important to explore the factors associated with trends in adaptive capacities and to identify commonalities among groups.

The third question is: *How has the adaptive process been evident in recovery to recent disasters?* Unlike adaptive capacities, which are amenable to measurement by objective means, the adaptive process of resilience can be difficult to assess. Therefore, examining how it has played out on the local level as well as identifying the factors associated with its attributes can go far in tracing how resilience develops. This is particularly important for understanding how resilience unfolds as a localized, bottom-up process within the context of a centralized, top-down emergency management framework.

Finally, the fourth question is: *How community adaptive capacities and the adaptive processes align?* Given that theory links adaptive capacities to adaptive processes in building disaster resilient communities, it is important to examine how trends in these overlap. Assessing patterns in community level adaptive capacities and processes can help identify the factors related to local disaster resilience.

Systematically answering these questions can shed light on how resilience develops on the local level. Comparing and contrasting the meaning, adaptive capacities, and adaptive processes associated with disaster resilience clarifies how resilience in principle is translated to practice. The findings of these analyses can enhance our understanding of resilience for the cases studied and also contribute to our broader knowledge of disaster resilience.

Gulf Coast Counties and Municipalities: A Laboratory of Resilience

The best place to study community disaster resilience is in the context in which it is thought to develop—local settings. While local can be defined in a myriad of ways, according to our federal emergency management framework, local refers to counties. Counties are the responsible level of government for disaster management, and county emergency managers as agents of this local government unit work with a multitude of different groups to plan for, respond to, and recover from disasters. Municipal governments are one of the groups heavily involved in local emergency management, and as component units of counties, it is important to include municipalities in the analysis of Gulf Coast resilience.

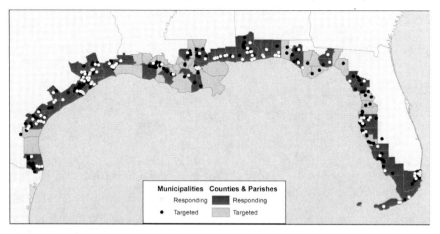

Figure 3.3 Research Sample[1]

[1]All the counties shown are included in the study sample for adaptive capacities. Responding counties and municipalities are included in the survey sample that analyzes the adaptive process.

The sample selected for this study includes counties and municipalities within 25 miles of the Gulf of Mexico in the states of Alabama, Florida, Louisiana, Mississippi, and Texas. The 25 mile criterion was established to make the sample as comparable as possible. Certainly, counties and municipalities further inland also face coastal hazards, but their location means that they most likely balance a different set of issues in managing disaster impacts. Based on this criterion, the research sample targeted 75 counties and over 300 municipalities, shown spatially in Figure 3.3. Adaptive capacities for all 75 counties are analyzed in this study, and a subsample of 56 counties and 122 municipalities who participated in the study surveys are examined. Appendix A provides a list of this sample. This group of cases shares vulnerability to hazards, especially hurricanes but also oil spills, flooding, and tornadoes. Moreover, this sample shares a collective history and culture—dynamics that are not directly studied in this analysis but that do impact the development of community disaster resilience and, therefore, are important to hold constant.

In addition to the commonalities among the cases, the sample exhibits considerable social and economic variation. These differences are important as they may produce conditions that influence to varying degrees the development of resilience. Figure 3.4[140] illustrates the variation in population size and income per capita across the cases included in the sample. Seventy-five percent of the cases have municipal populations lower than 16,500 or county populations of 250,000 or less. However, populations among the cases studied reach values as high as 2,191,400 for municipalities and 4,092,459 for counties. Regarding wealth, 75 percent of municipal income per capita is $30,800 or lower while 75 percent of county income per capita is $38,536 or lower. The spread of income values are tighter for the county cases, indicating a smaller range of income per capita for the county cases.

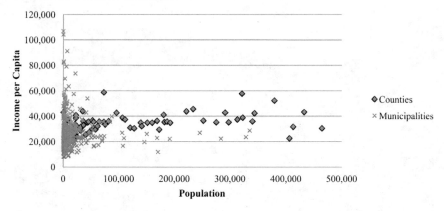

Figure 3.4   Variation in Economic and Social Factors across Survey Sample

Sources: County population data were taken from the U.S. Census of Demographic Profile Data 2010; county income per capita data were obtained from the Bureau of Economic Analysis 2010; municipal population data and income estimates were taken from the U.S. Census Bureau 2010 redistricting data and 2005–9 American Community Survey, respectively.

However, the maximum value of income per capita for the county sample is $58,799. Overall, there is substantial variation in the cases sampled in terms of population size and wealth. This sets up a natural laboratory to study resilience as these factors are representative of broad trends including the supply and demand for local emergency services that may affect the way resilience develops.

Data and Measurement

To explore resilience on the county and municipal level in a manner that addresses the research questions posed requires an assessment of local adaptive capacities as well as resilience perceptions and experiences on the local level. Measuring and comparing adaptive capacities is undertaken in this study on the county level but not on the municipal level. The measurement and creation of an adaptive capacity index in this study replicates and improves upon Disaster Resilience of Place (DROP) index[141] devised by geologist and hazards scholar Susan Cutter and her colleagues. Secondary sources are used to measure adaptive capacities across six areas: social resilience, social capital, economic resilience, institutional resilience, infrastructure resilience, and ecological resilience. The data sources include the U.S. Census Bureau, FEMA, and the National Oceanic and Atmospheric Administration. The majority of the data is taken from 2010 sources although the range of the data sources years is 2000–12.

The choice to exclude the municipal level from the assessment of adaptive capacities is driven by three considerations. First, disaster response and recovery unfold on the county level since this is the level of government responsible for disaster management. Under this framework, the county largely "calls the shots" and is the link between local needs and resources higher up the chain of command. Therefore, measuring the adaptive capacity of municipalities would not provide meaningful information since it cannot not be connected to distinct disaster response efforts. Second, existing models of adaptive capacities focus on the county. To contribute to this research, a focus on county adaptive capacities is needed so that comparisons can be made among the findings of existing studies and this one. Third, municipal data is not available on all the components of adaptive capacities. Proceeding with limited information is problematic because it could misrepresent realities. Adaptive capacities should be measured on the county level where secondary data sources are widely available.

In addition to evaluating county adaptive capacities, this study addresses perceptions of resilience held by administrative and political elites. On the county level, emergency management directors or deputy directors were surveyed. Elected officials, including mayors and city council members, were surveyed on the municipal level. The county survey was administered during the months of May and June of 2012; the municipal survey responses were collected during the months of June and July 2011.

While there are numerous public officials and community leaders that are involved in the development of resilience on the local level, county emergency managers and municipal officials are central to community efforts. This is largely due to the authority and responsibility vested in these positions that make them legally responsible for governance in this regard. County emergency managers are charged with disaster management; it is their job. Local elected officials are electorally responsible to municipal citizens to develop priority policy areas, including those related to hazards and disaster events. Although both are involved in disaster management, they undoubtedly have different perspectives. County emergency managers tend to be more focused on administrative issues while municipal elected officials are typically focused on local economic development. Taken together, this group of administrative and political elites should provide valuable perspectives on Gulf Coast resilience.

County Survey Questionnaire

The county survey was targeted to county emergency managers. Before administering the survey to counties and parishes across the Gulf Coast, the instrument was piloted in three Texas counties with varying populations and past disaster experience. The survey focused on six areas: resilience perceptions, county disaster experiences, role and activity of emergency management directors, emergency management capacities and planning, coordination with various groups in disaster response, and background characteristics. The full county survey questionnaire is available in Appendix B.

The first set of questions in the survey was intended to capture general perceptions of disaster resilience. The first question asked was: *What does the term community resilience mean to you?* The format of this question was open-ended to allow participants to reply with any meaning they assign to the term. The second question asked participants to rate the hypothetical resilience of their county by answering the following question: *If your county experienced a severe disaster this year, how easy would you say it would be to bounce back from the damages incurred?* Possible responses to this question included: very easy, somewhat easy, average—not difficult or easy, somewhat difficult, and very difficult.

The second set of questions asked participants to assess their county's disaster experience. Participants were asked to identify the worst disaster the county has ever experienced, rate the severity of the disaster on a four point scale, and evaluate county resilience following the event (how easy it was to "bounce back"). The same was asked for the worst disaster experienced in the past decade.

The third set of questions explored perceptions of the county emergency manager's role and activities. Participants were asked the open-ended question: *What would you say is the primary role of emergency managers when dealing with disasters?* This was followed with a set of questions that asked participants to rate how frequently they took part in seven activities. These included: 1) grant writing, paperwork, and record keeping; 2) design standard operating procedures and other guidelines for various disaster scenarios; 3) develop communication with citizens, first responders, public and private entities; 4) work on collaboration with public and private partners; 5) examine county vulnerabilities to assess risk; 6) generate public awareness for disaster preparedness; 7) work on zoning ordinances and other policies that steer development away from areas at high risk for flooding and wind damage; and 8) engage the public or community organizations in disaster planning. Possible responses ranged from "very often (almost daily)" to "often (weekly)" to "sometimes (monthly or quarterly)" to "once in a while (yearly)" to "almost never."

The fourth set of questions asked in the county survey included assessments of emergency management resources and planning. Participants were asked to rate the disaster response capabilities of the municipalities within their jurisdiction. They were also asked to list the number of public entities (i.e. municipalities, law agencies, EMS service districts) with whom they coordinate efforts. Participants were also asked if their county has mutual aid agreements with neighboring counties.

The fifth set of questions explored coordination with various groups in disaster response. Participants were asked to rate the communication and coordination with the following groups in past disaster response: 1) average citizens and citizen groups; 2) private partners; 3) nonprofit partners; 4) municipal elected officials; 5) county elected officials; 6) neighboring county emergency management directors; 7) state emergency management officials; and 8) federal emergency management officials. Possible responses ranged from "poor" to "adequate" to "good" to "excellent" and also included "no experience."

The final set of questions gathered information on the background of the participant and the county emergency management office. Participants were asked to list the number of staff employed in their office and to cite if their position was full-time or part-time. Additionally, participants were asked to name how many years' experience they have in emergency management and the highest level of education they have obtained.

The county survey was administered during May and June 2012 by the author and twelve student research assistants from multiple universities across the Gulf Coast, including Texas A&M University-Corpus Christi, Texas A&M University at Galveston, Louisiana State University, Tougaloo College, and Florida Atlantic University. The interviews were recorded by hand. Of the 75 counties included in the survey sample, county emergency managers from 56 counties chose to participate—a 75 percent response rate.[142]

Municipal Survey Questionnaire
The municipal survey was constructed to capture the disaster experiences and resilience perceptions of mayor and city council members. Before distributing the survey, the instrument was piloted in 14 cities across the Gulf States that varied in population size and experience with disasters. The survey focused on four areas: 1) disaster experience, 2) municipal characteristics, 3) disaster management, and 4) personal background. The municipal survey questionnaire is available in its entirety in Appendix C.

The first set of questions regarding disaster experience asked respondents to rate the severity of the worst disaster the municipality had experienced in the last 10 years; following this, respondents were asked how easy it was for the community to "bounce back" from this as a proxy for resilience. Respondents were also asked if they have been involved in disaster response and/or recovery as an elected official and to specify which actions they have undertaken as part of these efforts. Possible responses included: coordination with state/federal government, collaboration with neighboring municipalities, applying for disaster relief funding, developing a post-disaster recovery plan, grants administration, and meeting with citizens.

The second set of survey questions explored municipal characteristics. These questions asked respondents to give subjective assessments of their community's social capital and economy. To assess community social capital, the question posed is: "To what degree do you regularly observe neighbors helping neighbors in your municipality?" To evaluate their municipal economy, respondents were asked to identify the approximate percentage of their community is financially vulnerable. Respondents were also asked to identify the most critical parts of their municipality's economy in terms of sector, ranging from tourism and service to fishing and oil/gas.

The third set of questions focused on disaster management. Respondents were first asked to rate the training and expertise of their municipality's disaster responders as well as the sufficiency of fiscal and human resources devoted to disaster response. Following this, questions regarding the existence of a municipal disaster plan and methods of communication with citizens during disasters were posed.

Respondents were also asked how they would characterize the collaboration and coordination of their local government with the following entities during past disaster response: the federal government, state government, county emergency officials, neighboring municipalities, volunteer and faith-based groups, and municipal citizens. Following this, respondents were asked about how they would characterize working with the following entities to secure disaster funding for recovery projects: federal government, state government, nonprofit groups, and corporations.

In addition to experience with past disaster response and recovery, two questions were asked with the intention to capture decision-making dynamics. Respondents were asked how they would characterize their municipality's autonomy in making decisions during past disasters. Also, they were asked to identify which level of government they perceive to have the most responsibility and decision-making power with regards to disasters.

To conclude the section on disaster management, respondents were asked to specify what critical lessons their municipal government has learned from past disasters. Possible responses included: pre-disaster risk and analysis is important, communication must be improved, municipal government autonomy must be preserved, coordinate with other local governments is important, collaborate with federal/state agencies is important for response and recovery efforts, involving volunteer groups/citizens is important, advising citizens to make more extensive preparations, providing citizens with incentives for disaster preparation is needed, transportation and evacuation routes must be well planned and executed, proper records must be kept post-disaster, recover planning is important, control of information must be maintained, and/or mental health concerns cannot be overlooked.

The final set of survey questions asked respondents to give information about their personal and professional backgrounds. Questions were asked about past leadership positions in community organizations. Respondents were also asked to identify their highest level of education completed.

The municipal survey was administered during June and July of 2011 in three stages: 1) initial contact with municipalities, 2) invitation to participate online, and 3) follow-up communication. Initial contact was made via a letter sent through traditional mail to each municipality's mayor and council office to introduce them to the research project and alert them to an upcoming invitation to participate.[143] E-mail invitations to participate in the survey were sent directly to mayors and council members where individual e-mail addresses were publicly available; other e-mails were sent to city clerks, secretaries, and administrative staff for distribution to the mayor and council. The e-mail invitation identified the project scope and goals and provided a weblink to participate in the survey; the e-mail also assured respondent anonymity.[144] Follow-up e-mails were sent shortly after the initial invitation e-mail to encourage participation. In all, approximately 1,500 local government officials were invited to participate; 209 individuals responded from 122 municipalities—a response rate of nearly 12 percent.

Roadmap to the Study of Resilience

The following chapters empirically analyze the four questions posed in this study using secondary source data and information collected in the original surveys detailed above. Chapter 4 examines perceptions of the meaning of resilience by analyzing county emergency managers' survey responses. Chapter 5 explores in depth the adaptive capacities of the 75 counties included in the sample. An adaptive capacity for resilience index is constructed using secondary source data, and patterns among the cases are spatially and statistically analyzed to determine which factors are correlated with trends in adaptive capacities. Chapter 6 analyzes the adaptive process by assessing county emergency managers' and municipal elected officials' coordination efforts. This statistical analysis relies on the county and municipal survey data. Finally, Chapter 7 tackles the question of how these perceptions overlap with resilience realities by comparing survey data with the adaptive capacity for resilience index created from secondary sources.

CHAPTER SUMMARY

The nation's emergency management framework has transformed considerably over the past century; this evolution can be tied to events that occurred in the Gulf Coast region. In the early 1900s, the federal government had no direct role in disaster response. Recovery and mitigation efforts following the Galveston Hurricane of 1900, however, opened the opportunity for the federal government to advise and fund, in part, the building of a seawall. Federal involvement in mitigation efforts such as these expanded in the 1920s with the Flood Control Act of 1928, passed in response to the Great Mississippi Flood which severely impacted the Gulf Coast states of Louisiana and Mississippi. The federal government's role grew even more in subsequent decades as there was a call for federal coordination of state and local civil defense and emergency management efforts. In 1950, the federal government passed the first disaster relief legislation. In the following decade, hurricanes across the Gulf Coast including Hurricanes Agnes, Camille, and Betsy, tested this relief program and found it to be lacking. The severe property damages associated with these disaster events spurred federal action resulting in the creation of the National Flood Insurance Program in 1968 and the Disaster Relief Act of 1969, which provided the first provisions for individual benefits.

Despite the growth in federal government disaster assistance, concerns grew regarding the cohesiveness and coordination of the national emergency management framework. In response, Federal Emergency Management Agency was created in 1979 as an independent agency reporting to the president tasked with emergency preparedness, civil defense, and disaster relief. Less than a decade later the Stafford Act was passed in 1988, establishing a comprehensive system of emergency preparedness in the face of *all* hazards. This new framework was tested when Hurricane Andrew struck the Gulf Coast of Florida in 1992. The federal response to this disaster was highly criticized as being too slow, and lax building codes across the state and region were exposed. As a result, FEMA improved its local mitigation efforts and programs. In 2000 the Disaster Mitigation Act was passed to provide grants for local mitigation projects.

The federal government's focus on local emergency management shifted to defense and security following the terrorist attacks of September 11, 2001. The Department of Homeland Security was created by merging multiple federal agencies including FEMA. In this reorganization FEMA lost much of its prestige, visibility, and resources. This became important with the series of hurricanes that struck the Gulf Coast in 2004 and 2005, the biggest being Hurricane Katrina. The response to Hurricane Katrina called into question the federal emergency management as it represented a failure on all levels of government to be prepared and coordinate an effective response to a severe disaster event. The following year, Congress passed the Post-Katrina Emergency Management Reform Act of 2006, which expanded FEMA's authority and responsibilities.

In the aftermath of Hurricane Katrina, the term resilience emerged on the federal level and stuck as a guiding principle for emergency management. This has resonated with policy-makers, community leaders, and the public as evidenced by the framing of action in response to Hurricane Ike and the BP *Deepwater Horizon* oil spill. Despite this, it remains unclear what the term means and how it is applied, particularly on the local level where it is thought to develop and make the most impact. To address these issues, this book poses four questions: How is community resilience understood? What trends are evident in adaptive capacities? What factors are correlated with the adaptive process of resilience? How do meanings of resilience, adaptive capacities, and adaptive processes align?

Data from secondary sources and original survey of county emergency managers and municipal elected officials are used to empirically answer these questions. The cases chosen for the analyses are counties and municipalities within 25 miles of the Gulf of Mexico. The Gulf of Mexico is an ideal setting for the study of resilience because of its shared history of disaster experience coupled with the social and economic diversity among its localities.

DISCUSSION QUESTIONS

1. In addition to the focusing events detailed in this chapter, what else may have contributed to the expanded role the federal government has assumed in disaster relief and emergency management?

2. In your opinion, have disaster focusing events across the Gulf Coast created sound policy outcomes or simply government reaction to public outcry?

3. Thinking about how emergency management has been shaped by the events of September 11, what factors are important to consider in

balancing homeland security and defense with emergency management for disasters?

4. In addition to the Gulf Coast, which other settings might be suitable for the study of resilience? Why?

5. If you were to construct a survey to assess resilience, what questions would you include? Whom would you survey? And how would this contribute to our understanding of community disaster resilience?

NOTES

1. Thomas A. Birkland, *After Disaster: Agenda Setting, Public Policy, and Focusing Events* (Washington, DC: Georgetown University Press, 1997). Quoted in Alasdair Roberts, "Building Resilience: Macrodynamic Constraints on Governmental Response to Crises," in *Designing Resilience: Preparing for Extreme Events*, ed. Louise K. Comfort, Arjen Boin, and Chris C. Demchak (Pittsburg: University of Pittsburg Press, 2010), 87.

2. Thomas A. Birkland, "Focusing Events, Mobilization, and Agenda Setting," *Journal of Public Policy* (1998): 54.

3. Richard T. Sylves, "Federal Emergency Management Comes of Age: 1979–2001," in *Emergency Management: The American Experience 1900–2005*, ed. Claire B. Rubin (Fairfax, VA: Public Entity Risk Institute, 2007), 143.

4. Peter J. May, *Recovering From Catastrophes: Federal Disaster Relief Policy and Politics* (Westport, CT: Greenwood Press, 1985).

5. David Moss, "Courting Disaster? The Transformation of Federal Disaster Policy since 1803," in *The Financing of Catastrophe Risk,* ed. Kenneth A. Froot (Chicago: University of Chicago Press, 1999), 307–62.

6. According to David Butler, "Focusing Events in the Early Twentieth Century: A Hurricane, Two Earthquakes, and a Pandemic," in *Emergency Management: The American Experience 1900–2005*, ed. Claire B. Rubin (Fairfax, VA: Public Entity Risk Institute, 2007), 14: The Red Cross was founded in 1881 by Clara Barton then chartered by Congress in 1900 with the legal status of "a federal instrumentality," a designation indicating the organization is bound to carry out responsibilities assigned by the federal government. The federal government relied (and still relies) on the Red Cross to coordinate immediate assistance to victims following a disaster. It was instrumental in aiding victims of the Galveston Hurricane of 1900, and today it remains the only nonprofit to be mentioned in federal disaster legislation.

7. Butler, "Focusing Events," 16.

8. Patricia B. Bixel and Elizabeth H. Turner, *Galveston and the 1900 Storm* (Austin: University of Texas Press, 2000).

9. Butler, "Focusing Events," 15.

10. Ibid.

11. "The Great Galveston Hurricane of 1900," last accessed June 30, 2013, *http://celebrating200years.noaa.gov/magazine/galv_hurricane/welcome.html#intro*

12. "Galveston's Response to the Hurricane of 1900," last accessed June 30, 2013, *http://www.texasalmanac.com/topics/history/galvestons-response-hurricane-1900.*

13. Butler, "Focusing Events," 18.

14. "Galveston's Response."

15. Butler, "Focusing Events," 18.

16. "Galveston's Response."

17. Ibid.

18. Ibid.
19. Ibid.
20. Rutherford H. Platt, *Disasters and Democracy: The Politics of Extreme Natural Events* (Washington, DC: Island Press, 1999), 1.
21. For an account of how New Orleans elites responded to the flood, further entrenching socioeconomic and racial inequalities, see David Butler, "The Expanding Role of the Federal Government: 1927–1950," in *Emergency Management: The American Experience 1900–2005*, ed. Claire B. Rubin (Fairfax, VA: Public Entity Risk Institute, 2007), 52–4.
22. Butler, "The Expanding Role," 51.
23. Ibid, 55.
24. Saundra K. Schneider, *Dealing with Disaster: Public Management in Crisis Situations* (New York: M.E. Sharpe Inc, 2011), 19.
25. Butler, "The Expanding Role," 64.
26. Ibid.
27. Ibid, 55.
28. Thomas E. Drabek, "The Evolution of Emergency Management," in *Emergency Management: Principles and Practice for Local Government*, ed. Thomas E. Drabek and Gerard J. Hoetmer (Washington, DC: International City Management Association, 1991), 3–29.
29. Butler, "The Expanding Role," 55.
30. Keith Bea, "The Formative Years: 1950–1978," in *Emergency Management: The American Experience 1900–2005*, ed. Claire B. Rubin (Fairfax, VA: Public Entity Risk Institute, 2007), 81–110.
31. "Storm Surge and Coastal Inundation," last accessed June 30, 2013, *http://www.stormsurge.noaa.gov/event_history_1940s.html*.
32. *The St. Augustine Record* also notes that these efforts were segregated, and that the "colored units of the Defense Council" provided "excellent" services. See "1944: A Dangerous Year," last accessed June 30, 2013, *http://staugustine.com/news/local-news/2010–11–01/1944-dangerous-year*.
33. Bea, "The Formative Years," 82.
34. Richard Sylves, *Disaster Policy & Politics: Emergency Management and Homeland Security* (Washington, DC: CQ Press, 2008), 48.
35. Bea, "The Formative Years," 82, and Sylves, *Disaster Policy*, 48.
36. Ibid.
37. Ibid, 82.
38. Sylves, *Disaster Policy*, 48.
39. "Civil Defense Control Center," last accessed June 30, 2013, *http://neworlean-shistorical.org/items/show/274#.Udi_Dazlf2x*.
40. "Emergency Operations Plan," last accessed June 30, 2013, *http://www.ema.alabama.gov/filelibrary/Alabama_EOP.pdf*; "Our History," last accessed June 30, 2013, *http://www.fepa.org/index.php/about-fepa*; "Emergency Management: Handbook of Texas Online," last accessed June 30, 2013, *http://www.tshaonline.org/handbook/online/articles/mze01*.
41. "Annual Statistical Report," last accessed June 30, 2013, *http://training.fema.gov/EMIWeb/edu/docs/HistoricalInterest/FCDA%20-%201955%20-%20%20Annual%20Statistical%20Report.pdf*.
42. Bea, "The Formative Years," 85.
43. Ibid.
44. Platt refers to this as the "supplemental myth" because no federal laws and regulations have detailed how to assess the aid state and local governments can render themselves. See Platt, *Disasters*, 17.
45. Bea, "The Formative Years," 85, and Sylves, *Disaster Policy*, 49.
46. Platt, *Disasters*, 16.
47. Bea, "The Formative Years," 86.

48. Ibid, 87.
49. The Alaskan earthquake of 1964 was also critical at focusing attention on the need for federal government expansion of assistance, according to Bea, "The Formative Years," 88.
50. "1965—Hurricane Betsy," last accessed June 30, 2013, *http://www.hurricane science.org/history/storms/1960s/betsy/*.
51. Bea, "The Formative Years," 90.
52. "1969—Hurricane Camille," last accessed June 30, 2013, *http://www.hurrica nescience.org/history/storms/1960s/camille/*.
53. Initial reports counted 15 tornadoes, but recent work has corrected that count to 28. See "Thirty Years After Hurricane Agnes—The Forgotten Florida Tornado Disaster," last accessed June 30, 2013, *http://www.srh.noaa.gov/media/ mlb/pdfs/Agnes30.pdf*.
54. "1972—Hurricane Agnes," last accessed June 30, 2013, *http://www.hurrica nescience.org/history/storms/1970s/agnes/*.
55. Ibid.
56. According to Bea, "The Formative Years," 92–5, these included: the Southeast Hurricane Disaster Relief Act of 1965 (P.L. 85–339), the Disaster Relief Act of 1966 (P.L. 89–796), the National Flood Insurance Act of 1968 (P.L. 90–448), 1969 expansion of the 1966 Disaster Relief Act (P.L. 91–79), the Disaster Relief Act of 1970 (P.L. 91–606), the 1971 legislation following the San Fernando Valley earthquake (P.L. 92–209), and the 1972 legislation following Hurricane Agnes (P.L. 92–385).
57. Bea, "The Formative Years," 92.
58. Platt, *Disasters*, 16.
59. Bea, "The Formative Years," 93–4 and 99–101.
60. Sylves, *Disaster Policy*, 55.
61. Sylves, *Disaster Policy*, 58.
62. Bea, "The Formative Years,"102.
63. This is in reference to a proposal put forward by the National Governors Association in the late 1970s. See Sylves, *Disaster Policy*, 56.
64. Bea, "The Formative Years,"103.
65. Sylves, *Disaster Policy*, 57.
66. Ibid.
67. Ibid, 50.
68. Ibid, 60.
69. Sylves, *Disaster Policy*, 66 notes that FEMA Director James Lee Witt, appointed by President Bill Clinton, implemented the shift to all-hazards approach, creating three functional directorates corresponding to the major phases of emergency management: Mitigation; Preparedness, Training, and Exercises; and Response and Recovery.
70. Ibid, 60.
71. Emergencies are defined as "any occasion or incident for which, in the determination of the President, federal assistance is needed to supplement State and local efforts," Mitchell Moss, Charles Schelhamer, and David A. Berman, "The Stafford Act and Priorities for Reform," *Journal of Homeland Security and Emergency Management*, 6 (2009): 2.
72. Moss, Schelhamer, and Berman, "The Stafford Act," 2.
73. Ibid, 3.
74. Sylves, "Federal Emergency Management," 148–9.
75. Betty Morrow, "Disasters in the First Person," in *Hurricane Andrew: Ethnicity, Gender, and the Sociology of Disasters*, ed. Walter G. Peacock, Betty Hearn Morrow, and Hugh Gladwin (College Station: Hazard Reduction and Recovery Center, Texas A&M University, 2000), 3.

76. "Hurricane Andrew's Legacy: 'Like a Bomb' in Florida," last accessed June 30, 2013, *http://www.npr.org/2012/08/23/159613339/hurricane-andrews-legacy-like-a-bomb-in-florida*.
77. Schneider, *Dealing*, 121–4.
78. Sylves, *Disaster Policy*, 61.
79. Morrow, "Disasters," 8.
80. David R. Godschalk et al., *Natural Hazard Mitigation: Recasting Disaster Policy and Planning* (Washington, DC: Island Press, 1999), 128.
81. According to Sylves, *Disaster Policy*, 68: The Volkmer Amendment, passed in 1993, amended parts of the Stafford Act to increase FEMA funds dedicated to hazard mitigation activities from a subsidy of 10 percent (in the Stafford Act) to 15 percent. Additionally, the federal share of specific mitigation activities was increased from 50 percent to 75 percent.
82. Godschalk et al., *Natural Hazard*, 4.
83. Sylves, *Disaster Policy*, 68.
84. Ibid, 69.
85. John R. Harrald, "Emergency Management Restructured: Intended and Unintended Outcomes of Actions Taken Since 9/11," in *Emergency Management: The American Experience 1900–2005*, ed. Claire B. Rubin (Fairfax, VA: Public Entity Risk Institute, 2007), 166.
86. Ibid, 165.
87. Ibid, 163.
88. Ibid, 166.
89. Sylves, *Disaster Policy*, 70.
90. Kathleen Tierney, "Recent Developments in U.S. Homeland Security Policies and Their Implications for the Management of Extreme Events," paper presented at First International Conference on Urban Disaster Reduction, Kobe, Japan, January 18–20, 2005, 2.
91. Sylves, *Disaster Policy*, 70.
92. Tierney, "Recent Developments," 2.
93. James Lee Witt, "Testimony before the Subcommittee on National Security, Emerging Threats and International Relations and the Subcommittee on Energy Policy, Natural Resources and Regulatory Affairs," March 24, 2004. Quoted in Tierney, "Recent Developments," 3.
94. These were passed into law through the Homeland Security Presidential Directive–5, according to Sylves, *Disaster Policy*, 72.
95. Sylves, *Disaster Policy*, 72.
96. Harrald, "Emergency Management," 172.
97. Sylves, *Disaster Policy*, 73.
98. Harrald, "Emergency Management," 175.
99. Melanie Gall and Susan L. Cutter, "2005 Events and Outcomes: Hurricane Katrina and Beyond," in *Emergency Management: The American Experience 1900–2005*, ed. Claire B. Rubin (Fairfax, VA: Public Entity Risk Institute, 2007), 187.
100. Gall and Cutter, "2005 Events," 188.
101. Ibid, 189.
102. Ibid, 188.
103. Ibid, 189.
104. Subject #10, Personal Interview by Ashley D. Ross, Biloxi, Mississippi, February 20, 2011.
105. Gall and Cutter, "2005 Events," 189.
106. Ibid, 191.
107. Ibid.
108. Ibid, 189.
109. U.S. Senate, Committee on Homeland Security and Government Affairs, *Hurricane Katrina: A Nation Still Unprepared* (Washington, DC: U.S. Government

Printing Office, 2006), accessed June 30, 2013, *http://www.gpo.gov/fdsys/pkg/ CRPT-109srpt322/pdf/CRPT-109srpt322.pdf.*

110. Ibid.
111. Gall and Cutter, "2005 Events," 193.
112. See, for example: Louise K. Comfort, Namkyung Oh, Gunes Ertan, and Steve Scheinert, "Designing Adaptive Systems for Disaster Mitigation," in *Designing Resilience: Preparing for Extreme Events,* ed. Louise K. Comfort, Arjen Boin, and Chris C. Demchak (Pittsburgh: University of Pittsburgh Press, 2010), 33–61; Beverly A. Cigler, "The Big Question of Katrina and the 2005 Great Flood of New Orleans," *Public Administration Review,* 67 (2007): 64–76; Jeanne-Marie Col, "Managing Disasters: The Role of Local Government," *Public Administration Review,* 67 (2007): 114–24; Louise K. Comfort, "Crisis Management in Hindsight: Cognition, Communication, Coordination, and Control," *Public Administration Review,* 67 (2007): 189–97; James L. Garnett and Alexander Kouzmin, "Communicating Throughout Katrina: Competing and Complementary Conceptual Lenses on Crisis Communication," *Public Administration Review,* 67 (2007): 171–88; William Lester and Daniel Krejci, "Business 'Not' as Usual: The National Incident Management System, Federalism, and Leadership," *Public Administration Review,* 67 (2007): 84–93; Ivor Ll. Van Heerden, "The Failure of the New Orleans Levee System Following Hurricane Katrina and the Pathway Forward," *Public Administration Review,* 67 (2007): 24–35; William L. Waugh Jr., "EMAC, Katrina, and the Governors of Louisiana and Mississippi," *Public Administration Review,* 67 (2007): 107–13.
113. Congressional Research Service, *Federal Emergency Management Policy Changes After Hurricane Katrina: A Summary of Statutory Provisions,* Keith Bea, Elaine Halchin, Henry Hogue, Frederick Kaiser, Natalie Love, Francis X. McCarthy, Shawn Reese, and Barbara Schwemle, RL33729 (Washington, DC: CRS, 2006), last accessed June 30, 2013, *http://www.tisp.org/index .cfm?cdid=10986&pid=10261.*
114. *Federal Emergency,* 7.
115. Ibid, 9.
116. Ibid, 7.
117. Gall and Cutter, "2005 Events," 194.
118. "Written Statement of Craig Fugate, Administrator, Federal Emergency Management Agency, before the House Committee on Homeland Security, Subcommittee on Emergency Preparedness, Response, and Communications, Five Years Later: An Assessment of the Post Katrina Emergency Management Reform Act," last accessed June 30, 2013, *http://www.dhs.gov/news/2011/10/25/written-testimony-fema-house-homeland-security-subcommittee-emergency-preparedness.*
119. Ibid.
120. Ibid.
121. U.S. Department of Homeland Security, Homeland Security Advisory Council, *Community Resilience Task Force Recommendations,* (Washington, DC: DHS, 2011), last accessed June 30, 2013, *http://www.dhs.gov/ xlibrary/assets/hsac-community-resilience-task-force-recommendations -072011.pdf.*
122. U.S. Department of Homeland Security, Homeland Security Advisory Council, *Report of the Critical Infrastructure Task Force,* (Washington, DC: DHS, 2006), last accessed June 30, 2013, *http://www.dhs.gov/xlibrary/assets/HSAC_ CITF_Report_v2.pdf,* 43.
123. Ibid, 5.
124. "Hurricane Ike," last accessed June 30, 2013, *http://www.nhc.noaa.gov/pdf/ TCR-AL092008_Ike_3May10.pdf.*

125. The State of Texas, Department of Emergency Management, *Hurricane Ike Impact Report* (Austin: Office of the Governor, 2008), last accessed June 30, 2013, *http://www.fema.gov/pdf/hazard/hurricane/2008/ike/impact_report.pdf.*

126. "Texas Rebuilds After Hurricane Ike with Resilience and Resolve," last accessed June 30, 2013, *http://www.telegraph.co.uk/expat/5201437/Texas-rebuilds -after-Hurricane-Ike-with-resilience-and-resolve.html.*

127. Hazard Reduction and Recovery Center, *Advancing the Resilience of Coastal Localities: Developing, Implementing and Sustaining the Use of Coastal Resilience Indicators: A Final Report,* Walter G. Peacock et al. (College Station: Texas A&M University, 2010).

128. John R. Harrald, "The System Is Tested: Response to the BP Deepwater Horizon Oil Spill," in *Emergency Management: The American Experience 1900–2010 2nd Edition,* ed. Claire B. Rubin (Fairfax, VA: Public Entity Risk Institute, 2007), 213–215.

129. Ibid.

130. Coastal Recovery Commission of Alabama, *Roadmap for Resilience: Toward a Healthier Environment, Society and Economy for Coastal Alabama,* 2011, accessed June 30, 2013, *http://crcalabama.org/wp-content/uploads/2011/02/ CRC-Report-02-2011.pdf.*

131. Harrald, "The System."

132. Subject #30, Personal Interview by Ashley D. Ross, Gulf Shores, Alabama, March 19, 2011.

133. Thomas A. Birkland, "Federal Disaster Policy: Learning, Priorities, and Prospects for Resilience," in *Designing Resilience: Preparing for Extreme Events,* ed. Louise K. Comfort, Arjen Boin, and Chris C. Demchak (Pittsburgh: University of Pittsburgh Press, 2010), 107.

134. *Community Resilience Task Force,* 12.

135. Mark de Bruijne, Mark, Arjen Boin, and Michel van Eeten, "Resilience: Exploring the Concept and Its Meanings," in *Designing Resilience: Preparing for Extreme Events,* ed. Louise K. Comfort, Arjen Boin, and Chris C. Demchak (Pittsburgh: University of Pittsburgh Press, 2010), 28.

136. *Grand Challenges,* 2.

137. de Bruijne, Boin, van Eeten, "Resilience," 28.

138. Birkland, "Federal Disaster," 107.

139. *Community Resilience Task Force;* de Bruijne, Boin, van Eeten, "Resilience," 28.

140. County cases are marked with triangles while municipal cases are denteod by x's. Seven cases with very high values were excluded for presentation purposes. This included: Lee County, Florida (population—618,754 and income per capita—$41,094); Pinellas County, Florida (population—916,542 and income per capita—$41,964); Hillsborough County, Florida (population—1,229,226 and income per capita—$36,869); Miami-Dade County, Florida (population— 2,496,435 and income per capita—$36,520); Harris County, Texas (population 4,092,459 and income per capita—$44,757); Miami, Florida (population—419,490 and income per capita—$22,216); and Houston, Texas (population—2,191,400 and income per capita—$25,625).

141. Susan L. Cutter, Christopher G. Burton, and Christopher T. Emrich, "Disaster Resilience Indicators for Benchmarking Baseline Conditions," *Journal of Homeland Security and Emergency Management,* 7 (2010): 1–22.

142. Note that Kleberg and Kenedy Counties, Texas jointly employ one emergency manager who participated in the survey.

143. Due to time constraints we were only able to send letters to Texas and Louisiana municipalities.

144. The survey responses were not tracked by email or individual respondent. However, we did ask respondents to identify which city and state they belonged so that we could match municipal data with these individual level responses.

4 Resilience Meanings and Perceptions

The definition and use of the term resilience in the field of disaster management has been criticized as being "so broad as to render it almost meaningless."[1] Certainly there are varied applications of the term that make its meaning unclear. However, resilience is too valuable a resource for emergency management to toss it out. Rather, a careful examination of its meaning (and perceptions of its meaning) is warranted. This chapter traces the application of the term resilience to federal emergency management frameworks and explores the way resilience is understood on the local level by county emergency managers.[2] Examination of assigned meanings to the term resilience is critical to fully assessing how the strategy of resilience has developed on the local level where it is purported to make the most impact.

RESILIENCE IN HOMELAND SECURITY AND EMERGENCY MANAGEMENT FRAMEWORKS

Resilience is a term that emerged among policy circles in the aftermath of Hurricane Katrina and has since become a guiding principle of the federal emergency management framework. It was formally introduced to the Department of Homeland Security lexicon in January 2006 as part of a report put forth by the Homeland Security Advisory Council's Critical Infrastructure Task Force to offer recommendations in improving critical infrastructure across the nation—an issue that was at the forefront of failures linked to the tragedy resulting from Hurricane Katrina.[3] Since the discussion of resilience in this report, the term has been widely adopted by federal government agencies and applied in various formats to emergency management. This has created multiple definitions or implied meanings of resilience, which undoubtedly generates varied understandings or perceptions of the term on the local level.

Federal Government and Resilience

Resilience formally became a part of the Department of Homeland Security (DHS) lexicon in January 2006 with the recommendations of the Homeland Security Advisory Council's Critical Infrastructure Task Force Report.[4] In

Table 4.1 Federal Government Usage of Resilience

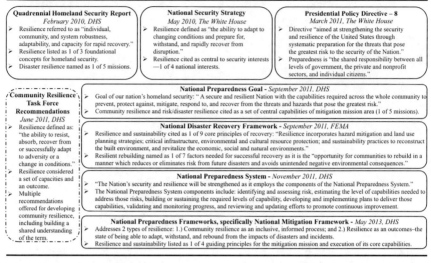

Quadrennial Homeland Security Report *February 2010, DHS*	National Security Strategy *May 2010, The White House*	Presidential Policy Directive – 8 *March 2011, The White House*
➤ Resilience referred to as "individual, community, and system robustness, adaptability, and capacity for rapid recovery." ➤ Resilience listed as 1 of 3 foundational concepts for homeland security. ➤ Disaster resilience named as 1 of 5 missions.	➤ Resilience defined as "the ability to adapt to changing conditions and prepare for, withstand, and rapidly recover from disruption." ➤ Resilience cited as central to security interests —1 of 4 national interests.	➤ Directive "aimed at strengthening the security and resilience of the United States through systematic preparation for the threats that pose the greatest risk to the security of the Nation." ➤ Preparedness is "the shared responsibility between all levels of government, the private and nonprofit sectors, and individual citizens."

Community Resilience Task Force Recommendations *June 2011, DHS*	*National Preparedness Goal - September 2011, DHS*
➤ Resilience defined as: "the ability to resist, absorb, recover from or successfully adapt to adversity or a change in conditions." ➤ Resilience considered a set of capacities and an outcome. ➤ Multiple recommendations offered for developing community resilience, including building a shared understanding of the term.	➤ Goal of our nation's homeland security: " A secure and resilient Nation with the capabilities required across the whole community to prevent, protect against, mitigate, respond to, and recover from the threats and hazards that pose the greatest risk." ➤ Community resilience and risk/disaster resilience cited as a set of central capabilities of mitigation mission area (1 of 5 missions). **National Disaster Recovery Framework** - *September 2011, FEMA* ➤ Resilience and sustainability cited as 1 of 9 core principles of recovery: "Resilience incorporates hazard mitigation and land use planning strategies; critical infrastructure, environmental and cultural resource protection; and sustainability practices to reconstruct the built environment, and revitalize the economic, social and natural environments." ➤ Resilient rebuilding named as 1 of 7 factors needed for successful recovery as it is the "opportunity for communities to rebuild in a manner which reduces or eliminates risk from future disasters and avoids unintended negative environmental consequences." **National Preparedness System** - *November 2011, DHS* ➤ "The Nation's security and resilience will be strengthened as it employs the components of the National Preparedness System." ➤ The National Preparedness System components include: identifying and assessing risk, estimating the level of capabilities needed to address those risks, building or sustaining the required levels of capability, developing and implementing plans to deliver those capabilities, validating and monitoring progress, and reviewing and updating efforts to promote continuous improvement. **National Preparedness Frameworks, specifically National Mitigation Framework** - *May 2013, DHS* ➤ Addresses 2 types of resilience: 1.) Community resilience as an inclusive, informed process; and 2.) Resilience as an outcomes–the state of being able to adapt, withstand, and rebound from the impacts of disasters and incidents. ➤ Resilience and sustainability listed as 1 of 4 guiding principles for the mitigation mission and execution of its core capabilities.

Notes: Quotes taken from original documents; see discussion in text for page numbers.

this report, the Critical Infrastructure Task Force promoted resilience as a strategic objective, noting that protection is a "brittle strategy" when used alone; resilience, on the other hand, is dynamic, flexible, and can "maintain its function and structure in the face of internal and external change."[5] Resilience, therefore, became an attractive frame, and it was widely adopted as a guiding principle for emergency management by the federal government. However, its application has not been consistent as shown in Table 4.1, which summarizes the use of the term resilience in key homeland security and emergency management directives and plans put forth by the White House and federal agencies. The following discussion reviews each in turn.

Quadrennial Homeland Security Review

Resilience was identified in the Quadrennial Homeland Security Review, released in February 2010 by DHS, as one of three foundational concepts for a comprehensive approach to homeland security which included: 1) Security—protect the United States and its people, vital interests, and way of life; 2) Resilience—foster individual, community, and system robustness, adaptability, and capacity for rapid recovery; and 3) Customs and Exchange—expedite and enforce lawful trade, travel, and immigration.[6] In addition, ensuring resilience specifically to disasters was named as one of five homeland security missions in the report. This resilience mission was described as a vision for "a Nation that understands the hazards and risks we face; is prepared for disasters; can withstand the disruptions disasters may cause; can sustain social trust, economic, and other functions under adverse conditions; can manage itself effectively during a crisis; can recover quickly and effectively; and can adapt to conditions that have changed as a result of the event."[7]

To achieve disaster resilience the Quadrennial Homeland Security Review calls for two broad changes in the emergency management framework. One, more emphasis should be placed on mitigation and preparedness to balance response and recovery efforts. This should be accompanied by fully incorporating "a comprehensive understanding of risk to establish priorities and inform decision-making."[8] Two, achieving resilience necessitates "a shift from a reliance on top-down emergency management to a process that engages all stakeholders—local, tribal, territorial, and State governments, Federal departments and agencies as well as nongovernmental organizations, the private sector, and individuals, families, and communities."[9] These changes require local emergency management to expand disaster mitigation and preparedness activities to include a more holistic approach that engages the broader community.

National Security Strategy

Following the Quadrennial Homeland Security Review in May 2010 the White House released the National Security Strategy, which identified four national interests: 1) Security—domestic and international, 2) Prosperity—human and fiscal capital, 3) Values—democracy and human rights, and 4) International order—alliances and cooperative institutions. Resilience was cited as a central component to ensure and enhance security.[10] It was defined as "the ability to adapt to changing conditions and prepare for, withstand, and rapidly recover from disruption."[11] Multiple factors were named as part of a strategy to strengthen domestic resilience including effectively managing emergencies, increasing public-private partnerships, and engaging with communities and citizens.[12] The White House emphasized the linkages between these efforts by noting that continued collaboration with communities ensures "preparedness efforts are integrated at all levels of government with the private and nonprofit sectors."[13]

Presidential Policy Directive 8

Echoing the National Security Strategy's emphasis on collaborative emergency management, Presidential Policy Directive 8, released March 30, 2011, asserted that strengthening national resilience to terrorist threats and national disasters requires systematic preparation that is "the shared responsibility between all levels of government, the private and nonprofit sectors, and individual citizens."[14] This directive focused specifically on preparedness for emergencies. It called on federal agencies to develop a national preparedness goal along with a system of integrated programs and plans to guide achievement of the goal.

The directive has resulted in the development of five products by federal agencies: 1) the National Preparedness Goal which outlines the objectives of homeland security and emergency management; 2) the National

Preparedness System to expound on the core capabilities needed to achieve the preparedness goal; 3) National Planning Frameworks to detail the execution of the national preparedness system; 4) a campaign to promote the development of national preparedness on the individual and community level; and 5) an annual National Preparedness Report to assess the progress made toward achieving the national goal.[15] Some of these efforts have been undertaken by DHS while others have been promoted by its subsidiaries, namely the Federal Emergency Management Agency (FEMA). Since the release of Presidential Policy Directive 8, FEMA has heavily promoted shared responsibility for preparedness with the concept of "whole community" involvement in disaster preparations.[16]

Community Resilience Task Force Recommendations

In response to Presidential Policy Directive 8, DHS released a set of recommendations from the Homeland Security Advisory Council, Community Resilience Task Force (CRTF) in June 2011. The purpose of the task force was to review resilience in concept and application with regards to how it fits into the national homeland security framework. This was undertaken prior to developing the products specified in Presidential Policy Directive 8.

The CRTF defined resilience according to the 2008 DHS Risk Lexicon as the "ability to resist, absorb, recover from or successfully adapt to adversity or a change in conditions."[17] Further, it delineated resilience as the "ability of systems, infrastructures, government, business and citizenry to resist, absorb, recover from, or adapt to an adverse occurrence that may cause harm, destruction, or loss of national significance."[18] The CRTF asserted that resilience best serves as a unifying goal for the homeland security framework but that the lack of a common understanding of the term impedes its usage.

The CRTF contended that resilience is often used "imprecisely" and perceived as "jargon"; despite its increased use by the White House and federal agencies, descriptions of resilience are "varied and abstract."[19] The task force recognized that perceptions of resilience may vary across geographical units and stakeholder groups. Nonetheless, they maintained that there is "value in identifying the common ground for shared objectives in terms of stakeholder-specific models that illustrate what constitutes resilience within the operational context of particular groups. Such models could build a shared understanding while also facilitating development of common measures of resilience."[20]

In addition to building a shared understanding of resilience, the CRTF proposed the following initiatives to the Department of Homeland Security: 1) develop a campaign to strengthen and sustain national resilience; 2) organize for effective execution by establishing a National Resilience Office; 3) build the knowledge and talent base for resilience through education and training programs; 4) update ready.gov to disseminate information on resilience; 5) build public awareness about social resilience; 6) motivate and enable community engagement through inventive programs; 7) leverage existing federal assets to develop a resilience initiative; 8) align federal grant program related to infrastructure to support the development of plans for improvement of operational resilience; 9) enable community-based resilient infrastructure initiatives; and 10) enable community-based resilience assessments through the development of methods and measures of resilience.[21]

National Preparedness Goal

Following the CRTF report, DHS released the first National Preparedness Goal in September 2011 which fulfilled the mandate of Presidential Policy Directive 8. DHS identified the goal as: "A secure and resilient nation with the capabilities required across the whole community to prevent, protect against, mitigate, respond to, and recover from the threats and hazards that pose the greatest risk."[22] To achieve this goal, "core capabilities" were enumerated to be developed across five interdependent mission areas representing the disaster phases of prevention, protection, mitigation, response, and recovery.

Community resilience as well as risk and disaster resilience emerged as a set of core capabilities within the mitigation mission area. The report connected mitigation and resilience as follows: "Mitigation requires an understanding of the threats and hazards that, in turn, feed into the assessment of risk and disaster resilience in the community. The whole community, therefore, has a role in risk reduction by recognizing, understanding, communicating, and planning for a community's future resilience. Mitigation links the long-term activities of the whole community to reduce or eliminate the risk of threats and hazards from developing into disasters and lessen the impacts of the disasters that occur."[23]

National Disaster Recovery Framework

FEMA released a National Disaster Recovery Framework in the same month as DHS' National Preparedness Goal. Nine core principles for recovery were identified by FEMA including "resilience and sustainability." This principle was described as: "Resilience incorporates hazard mitigation and land-use planning strategies, critical infrastructure, environmental and cultural resource protection, and sustainability practices to reconstruct the built environment, and revitalize the economic, social and natural environments."[24] Additionally, "resilient rebuilding" was named as one of the seven factors needed for successful recovery. Resilient rebuilding referred to the "opportunity for communities to rebuild in a manner which reduces or eliminates risk from future disasters and avoids unintended negative environmental consequences" including such measures as stronger building codes, land-use ordinances, and retrofitted structures.[25]

National Preparedness System and Frameworks

In addition to a national goal for preparedness, Presidential Policy Directive 8 also called for a national system of preparedness and plans to guide execution of this system. DHS released a National Preparedness System in

November 2011. The National Preparedness System provided the instrument by which the core capabilities identified in the National Preparedness Goal for prevention, protection, mitigation, response, and recovery can be achieved. Six components were presented as part of the National Preparedness System: 1) identifying and assessing risk; 2) estimating the level of capabilities needed to address those risks; 3) building or sustaining the required levels of capability; 4) developing and implementing plans to deliver those capabilities; 5) validating and monitoring progress; and 6) reviewing and updating efforts to promote continuous improvement. Resilience was not specifically incorporated into these components. Rather, resilience was referred to as an end goal—these components should enable a collaborative, whole community approach to strengthening national security and resilience.

National Planning Frameworks

The National Planning Frameworks released by DHS in May 2013 detailed the execution of the National Preparedness Goal and System by summarizing the roles and responsibilities of each part of the whole community. Whole community approach recognizes that "everyone can contribute to and benefit from national preparedness efforts" including families, businesses, nonprofit and faith-based organizations, and all levels of government.[26] The frameworks also defined the core capabilities needed to meet the goal of strengthening the security and resilience of the United States through systematic preparation for the threats that pose the greatest risk to the security of the nation.

Five planning frameworks were offered to align with the five mission areas put forth by the National Preparedness Goal—prevention, protection, mitigation, response, and recovery. Consistent with the National Preparedness Goal, the only mission area that involves resilience is mitigation. The National Mitigation Framework addresses two types of resilience: 1) community resilience as an "inclusive, informed process that involves social, economic, natural and cultural, technical, and organizational dimensions within a community—preparing a community to consciously mitigate rather than ignore risks;" and 2) resilience as an "outcome—the state of being able to adapt to changing conditions and then withstand and rebound from the impacts of disasters and incidents."[27] Additionally, "resilience and sustainability" are identified as one of four guiding principles for achieving the mitigation mission and executing its core capabilities. "Community resilience" and "assessing risk and disaster resilience" were also designated as two of seven core capabilities needed to meet mitigation goals.

Federal Usage of Resilience

When taken as a whole, the federal government's treatment of resilience is varied. It is evident that resilience is considered to be a set of capacities for adaption and recovery in the face of a disaster and that it requires community engagement and collaboration to develop. Yet aspects of this are emphasized to varying degrees, and there is a lack of a central definition of resilience.

Resilience is referred to inconsistently by federal agencies. The Quadrennial Homeland Security Report listed resilience as one of three *foundational concepts* for homeland security and disaster resilience as one of five *missions;* the National Security Strategy cited resilience as central to national security *interests;* the National Preparedness Goal identified community resilience and risk/disaster resilience as a set of *central capabilities* of the mitigation mission area; the National Disaster Recovery Framework cited resilience and sustainability as one of nine *core principles* of recovery and resilient rebuilding as one of seven *factors* needed for successful recovery; and the National Mitigation Framework names resilience and sustainability as one of four *guiding principles* for the mitigation mission and execution of its *core capabilities*, which included community resilience and risk/disaster resilience. Incorporation of resilience in this manner communicates that resilience is important, but the varied and inconsistent usage of the concept does not convey specifics.

Not only are the labels assigned to resilience inconsistent, definitions are varied as well. The federal directives examined were released within a span of three years by three interdependent agencies—the White House, the Department of Homeland Security, and the Federal Emergency Management Agency. Given the short amount of time and the close institutional relationship of the agencies, it is remarkable that multiple definitions of resilience are offered in these documents. Within these policies and reports, resilience is referred to as:

- "individual, community, and system robustness, adaptability, and capacity for rapid recovery"[28]
- "the ability to adapt to changing conditions and prepare for, withstand, and rapidly recover from disruption"[29]
- "the ability to resist, absorb, recover from or successfully adapt to adversity or a change in conditions"[30]
- "the state of being able to adapt, withstand, and rebound from the impacts of disasters and incidents."[31]

On first glance, these definitions seem similar. However, there are inconsistencies that muddle the concept of resilience. It is unclear, for example, if "system robustness" is analogous to the "ability to absorb adversity." Moreover, there are inconsistent assumptions among these definitions of resilience. For example—is *rapid* recovery necessary for resilience? The nuances of these definitions are significant because they have varied implications when translated into practice.

Adding to these issues is the common treatment of resilience as an interchangeable term with security and sustainability. For example, Presidential Policy Directive 8 was aimed at "strengthening the security and resilience of the United States," and the National Preparedness Goal put forth by DHS for our nation's homeland security involves "a secure and resilient nation." Substitution of the terms resilience and security—without defining either—is also common in FEMA training and educational materials.[32] Additionally, resilience was coupled with sustainability in the context of mitigation and recovery by DHS and FEMA with the idea that resilience involves land-use and mitigation activities. Certainly resilience is linked to sustainability, but interchanging resilience with these terms adds to definitional inconsistencies because it muddles the distinctions between these complex concepts.

Despite these issues all of the definitions given by federal agencies cited capacity for adaptation and recovery as a central attribute of resilience. Moreover, the majority of these documents referred to engagement of the community and/or a whole community approach as essential to the development of resilience. The Quadrennial Homeland Security Review asserted that resilience involves "a process that engages all stakeholders."[33] Presidential Policy Directive 8 took engagement a step further by emphasizing that disaster preparedness is "the shared responsibility" of "all levels of government, the private and nonprofit sectors, and individual citizens."[34] This "whole community" approach carves out a role for all members of the community in disaster preparedness and was incorporated into the National Preparedness Goal and System released by DHS as well as FEMA's National Recovery Framework. Clearly, there is a consensus among federal agencies that engagement of the community and collaboration among the community/stakeholder groups is a key aspect of developing resilience. How the concept of resilience is perceived by members of the community however, is not as clear.

GULF COAST PERCEPTIONS OF RESILIENCE

Given the varied meanings of and approaches to resilience on the federal level, it is not surprising that the first recommendation posed by the Homeland Security Advisory Council Community Disaster Resilience Task Force regarding resilience was building a "shared understanding" across stakeholder groups.[35] The task force noted that despite the differences that may exist in perceived meanings of resilience across groups, evaluating resilience perceptions can contribute to our broader understanding, measurement, and development of community disaster resilience. With this in mind, this study surveyed one key stakeholder group—county emergency managers—to assess their perceptions of resilience. There is considerable value in assessing the perceptions county emergency managers hold because they are responsible for local disaster management, directly interact with all levels of government, and are one of the primary liaisons to the community in dealing with disaster preparedness, response, and recovery, particularly in small, rural areas. These perceptions are analyzed to identify common meanings of resilience, and the factors related to these shared understandings are examined.

Survey of Emergency Managers

Emergency managers in counties and parishes located within 25 miles of the Gulf Coast were asked to participate in an interview to assess perceptions of local disaster resilience. A total of 56 counties participated. The surveys were conducted in-person during the months of May and June, 2012.[36] To assess perceptions of county emergency managers, the question was asked: *What does the term community resilience mean to you?* To avoid bias this question was the first asked in the interview. It was also open-ended, allowing for unrestricted responses.

Figure 4.1 illustrates the responses given by county and parish emergency managers across the Gulf Coast states to the question: *What does the term community resilience mean to you?*[37] Word clouds indicate the frequency of the response by the size of the word; more frequently used words are larger in size while those mentioned less often are smaller in size. The most commonly referenced words and phrases in response to the survey question were: ability, prepare, recover, bounce back, respond, withstand, and return to normal. Putting these together we get an idea that Gulf Coast emergency managers have the collective perception that community resilience is *the ability to prepare for, withstand, respond to, and recover from a disaster in a way that bounces back and returns the community to normal.* However, the figure also underscores that there are multiple understandings of resilience among Gulf Coast emergency managers. Therefore, it is important to qualitatively and quantitatively assess these to identify the factors that explain these differences.

To qualitatively evaluate emergency managers' perceptions of resilience, the responses to the survey question—*What does the term community resilience mean to you?*—were grouped into common themes. Each response was reviewed and labeled with a central meaning; this approach collapsed a pool of 54 varied survey responses to eight common themes.[38] These themes were then systematically analyzed—first for the distribution of the themes across the states, and second for the factors that may influence county emergency manager perceptions of resilience. The factors included in the regression analysis were county urban-rural character and disaster experience. The qualitative analysis involving grouping the responses into common themes is presented first, and then the quantitative analysis of factors related to these responses is discussed.

Common Themes of Resilience

There are eight common themes among the group of survey responses related to the meaning of community resilience: 1) bounce back, 2) preparedness, 3) continuity, 4) recovery, 5) self-sufficiency, 6) community responsibility, 7) disaster phases, and 8) adaption. The tabulation of these for the entire group and among the states analyzed including Alabama, Florida, Louisiana, Mississippi, and Texas is presented in Table 4.2. The following discussion explores each theme in turn.

Figure 4.1 Meanings of Community Resilience[1]

Source: Author's original interviews with county emergency managers across the Gulf Coast.

[1] Word size in the cloud is indicative of the frequency of response. Larger words represent responses that many interview participants gave while smaller words indicate less commonly cited responses.

Table 4.2 Meanings of Community Resilience among Gulf Coast Emergency Managers

Response given emphasizes . . .	Response Rate of Total	Response Rate within State				
		Alabama	Florida	Louisiana	Mississippi	Texas
BOUNCE BACK *"Bouncing back to the way things were before."*	25.9% (14)	0% (0)	21.1% (4)	17.6% (3)	33.3% (1)	42.9% (6)
PREPAREDNESS *"To be as prepared as we can be to be able to avoid or manage any disaster event."*	16.7% (9)	0% (0)	31.6% (6)	5.9% (1)	33.3% (1)	7.1% (1)
CONTINUITY *"How well a community's government and other decision makers can continue to function after a disaster."*	14.8% (8)	0% (0)	5.3% (1)	23.5% (4)	0% (0)	21.4% (3)
RECOVERY *"Community resilience is a quick recovery to all disasters."*	12.9% (7)	100% (1)	15.8% (3)	17.6% (3)	0% (0)	0% (0)
SELF-SUFFICIENCY *"To be able to withstand a disaster event without outside assistance."*	9.3% (5)	0% (0)	10.5% (2)	17.6% (3)	0% (0)	0% (0)
COMMUNITY RESPONSIBILITY *"Our people's eagerness and willingness to rebuild and repair."*	9.3% (5)	0% (0)	5.3% (1)	5.9% (1)	33.3% (1)	14.3% (2)
DISASTER PHASES *"The ability of the government to prepare, prevent, respond and mitigate for a disaster."*	7.4% (4)	0% (0)	5.3% (1)	11.8% (2)	0% (0)	7.1% (1)
ADAPTATION *"Having a motto of 'be flexible' and willingness to change before and after disaster."*	3.7% (2)	0% (0)	5.3% (1)	0% (0)	0% (0)	7.1% (1)

Notes: Percentage of total responses reported with frequency of responses in parentheses. Responses categorized by primary theme by the author. Examples of responses given under each theme heading.

Source: Author's original survey of county emergency managers.

Bounce Back

Describing resilience as the ability to "bounce back" was the most common response given by county and parish emergency managers. Nearly 26 percent of interview participants gave a response that resilience is bouncing back. This is not surprising as resilience is often described as such by federal government agencies and scholars alike. This harkens to the origins of the term in physics where it is used to refer to the quality of material that can spring back to its original state after being subjected to stress.

Examples of responses in this category described community resilience as: "the ability to bounce back and/or resist disasters, and how prepared are you and how quickly can you recover;" "the ability of community to rebound after catastrophe (manmade or natural) and start rebuilding process;" and "the level, ability and speed to which a community can bounce back after a major disaster. . . . based on physical—buildings, roads—and human ability—inner strength and belief based on self-empowerment."

Preparedness

The second most common meaning assigned to the term community resilience was disaster preparedness. Nearly 17 percent of the survey respondents gave an answer to the survey question that focused on preparing for disaster events. This closely aligns with the importance placed on preparedness by Presidential Policy Directive 8 and the accompanying National Preparedness Goal, System, and Frameworks released by the Department of Homeland Security. This also reflects the traditional emergency management role of preparing for disaster response—making plans for emergency personnel, deployment of equipment, evacuation of residents, and communications during an emergency incident.

Examples of responses given in this category included defining community resilience as: being "as prepared as we can be to be able to avoid or manage any disaster event;" "to have plans and procedures in place to bring community back to normal;" and "folks and businesses are prepared for disasters and work together as a team during all phases of emergency management."

Continuity

Continuity was the third most commonly referenced theme among the survey responses. Nearly 15 percent of the survey participants used phrasing that indicated continued functioning and/or a return to normal or pre-disaster conditions as part of their understanding of resilience. References to resilience as continuity described community resilience as: "the ability to resume normal economic and social activity," "the ability for systems we rely on to restore themselves—social, economic, physical systems—that make everyday living normal," and "how well a community's government and other decision makers can continue to function after a disaster."

Recovery

Recovery was another theme present in the survey responses with nearly 13 percent of answers to the survey question involving some mention of recovering from a disaster. Responses in this category considered community resilience to be: a "community's ability to rapidly recover from a disaster," "how quick you can recover (and how well prepared you are to recover)," and "ability for community to survive and recover from a disaster."

Self-Sufficiency

Nine percent of the survey responses given regarding the meaning of community resilience cited self-sufficiency or independence. This is a classic idea of resilience and conjures ideas of communities and families that are able to "batten the hatches" and "weather the storm" on their own.[39] Examples of responses in this category ranged from community resilience is "self-sufficiency—how prepared each individual family is to deal with a disaster" to community resilience is to "be able to withstand a disaster event without outside assistance."

Community Responsibility

A portion of the responses regarding understandings of community resilience focused on the community. Nine percent of responses cited the community in a predominant way in their response, including: Community resilience is "people helping people" or "the ability of community to withstand and respond to any typed of manmade/natural disaster." Another response given was: Community resilience is "our people's eagerness and willingness to rebuild and repair and to get back to the way things were before." Yet another proposed: Community resilience is the "community response to commands given by Emergency Management."

Understanding resilience as "community" seems at first glance fitting and promising. Community is, after all, at the heart of resilience. However, careful consideration of the responses given highlights that the connection of resilience to community focused on placing responsibility for disaster response and recovery on the community. There is a seeming disconnect in some of the responses between the community and emergency management, and an emphasis on engagement of the community in disaster management is lacking. This is troubling because integrating the community into collaborative decision-making is a key aspect of the adaptive process of resilience.[40]

Disaster Phases

Other survey responses to perceptions of resilience were distinguishable by their reference to the disaster phases. Coupling resilience with mitigation, preparedness, response, and recovery aligns with the Department of Homeland Security's views of emergency management and resilience, particularly expressed in the Quadrennial Homeland Security Review and the Homeland Advisory Council Community Resilience Task Force's recommendations.

Seven percent of survey responses tied resilience to the disaster phases, namely preparation, response, recovery. Only two responses explicitly mentioned mitigation. These included defining community resilience as "the ability for a community to conduct the necessary mitigation and preparation activities to minimize the impact of an incident in order to improve and expedite the response and recovery time for a community to return to normal activities" and "the ability of government to prepare, prevent, respond, and mitigate for a disaster." Other responses in this category incorporated the disaster phases by proposing community resilience is "the ability for a community to prepare, respond, and recover from a disaster" and "takes the whole community to prepare, respond, and recover from a disaster."

Adaptation

Finally, two survey responses—less than 4 percent of the total—involved mention of adaptation and change following a disaster. These included: community resilience is having "a motto of 'be flexible'—willing to change before and after disaster" and is "adapt[ing] to different situations." Adaption is considered a hallmark of resilience by most scholars studying the topic.[41] Central to the scholarly conceptualization of resilience is the adaptive process which involves the community coming together post-disaster to collaborate and innovatively solve problems.[42] The lack of mention of adaption is also a shortcoming of federal government directives and programs. As evident from the discussion of federal homeland security and resilience initiatives at the beginning of this chapter, adaption is rarely explicitly addressed as part of resilience, although, federal resilience meanings do focus on collaboration and community engagement—components of many scholarly treatments of resilience.

State Differences in Meanings of Resilience

Across the themes identified regarding the meaning of resilience, there are distinct patterns among the states in the frequency of the responses given. In Alabama, the meaning of resilience focused on recovery. In Florida, most responses focused on preparedness, bouncing back, and recovery. In Louisiana, parish emergency managers had varied understandings of resilience including the most common themes of continuity, recovery, self-sufficiency, and bouncing back. The same was true in Mississippi where the emergency managers referenced resilience in terms of bouncing back, preparedness, and community. Finally, in Texas the majority of emergency managers understood resilience as bouncing back, although resilience was also frequently described as continuity and community.

This underscores that similar to federal government agencies there are varied meanings to resilience. *What factors explain the differences in these perceptions?* The following section explores through quantitative analysis the urban-rural characteristic and disaster experience of counties as possible explanations for this variation.

Factors Related to Community Resilience Perceptions

County context may shape emergency managers' perceptions of community resilience. Urban-rural county characteristics are important to consider because they represent the resources and demands placed on emergency managers for disaster management. In urban settings, emergency managers have a larger population to coordinate in disaster preparation, response, and recovery; however, they are typically afforded greater fiscal and human resources as well. Rural emergency managers usually face challenges of limited resources,[43] which may mean that they juggle multiple job duties in addition to disaster management. Further complicating this is the tendency for rural communities to have higher levels of social vulnerability—less education, lower income, and higher unemployment.[44] However, rural communities have been found to have greater levels of social capital and cooperation based on communal ties.[45] Although it is unclear if this eases emergency management demands. Therefore we may expect:

Proposition 4.1: The urban-rural context of the county or parish should influence the emergency manager's perceptions of the meaning of resilience.

In addition to a county's urban-rural character, the disasters collectively experienced may influence emergency manager's perceptions of community resilience. Severe disasters derail a community. Populations are displaced, and local economies are halted. The emotional and psychological toll of the disaster aftermath can be overwhelming and devastating for some. Considerable property damage requires extensive rebuilding efforts that can take years to complete. In all, experience with a severe, highly destructive disaster could profoundly shape perspectives of emergency management and, subsequently, community resilience.

Proposition 4.2: The severity of past disasters experienced in the county or parish should influence the emergency manager's perceptions of the meaning of resilience.

Data and Methods

To estimate the effects of county context on emergency managers' perceptions of community resilience, data was collected to capture the urban-rural composition and disaster experience of each county. A variable was constructed to measure the urban-rural character of counties using the Rural-Urban Continuum or Beale Codes from the U.S. Department of Agriculture.[46] The Rural-Urban Continuum Codes range from one to nine and distinguish counties based on population size and adjacency to metropolitan areas. Because of the small number of cases analyzed, this was collapsed into a variable with six categories, coded one to six.

The value of one corresponds to metropolitan counties. This is defined as "one urbanized area of 50,000 or more population plus adjacent territory and have a high degree of social and economic integration"[47] with a population of one million or more. Twenty-two percent of the counties in the analysis fall into this group. The same percentage of cases falls into in category two which included metropolitan counties with a population of 250,000 to one million. The third category is comprised of metropolitan counties with a population less than 250,000; 18.5 percent of the cases analyzed belong to this category. The fourth group includes nonmetropolitan but urban counties with populations of 20,000 or more while the fifth category includes urban counties with a population of 2,500 to 19,999. Seventeen percent of the counties analyzed are categorized in the fourth group while 18.5 percent belong to the fifth group. The sixth category includes completely rural counties with population less than 2,500; only 2 percent of the cases in the analysis fall into this group. The resultant variable ranges from one to six; as the values of the categories increase, the population of the county decreases and indicates a more rural context.

In addition to the urban-rural context of the county, two variables are used to measure disaster experience on the county in an effort to capture the disaster events that have most profoundly affected the Gulf Coast. The first variable measures the impact of the *Deepwater Horizon* oil spill in terms of economic loss. Each county along the Gulf Coast was assigned by BP specific economic loss claim zones based on the impact of the spill on local economies.[48] These claim zones were averaged and converted to a scale of 0, indicating no economic loss because the county was not affected by the spill, to 5, representing the highest level of economic loss as the entirety of the county was severely impacted by the spill. Appendix E describes in detail the coding scheme used to create this scale.

County experience with hurricanes is also considered. It is measured as the maximum property damage caused by hurricane events from 2002–2011 in millions of dollars. This data was obtained from SHELDUS.[49] For some counties this variable reflects damages incurred by Hurricane Katrina; for others this reflects damages from Hurricane Irene, Hurricane Dennis, and other tropical cyclone events.

The dependent variables include six of the eight themes identified among county and parish emergency managers' responses to the interview question: *What does the term community resilience mean to you?* As discussed in the previous section the most common response involved mention of bouncing back. Other themes frequently cited were preparedness, continuity, and recovery. Self-sufficiency and community responsibility were regular mentions in responses as well. Less frequently mentioned were the themes of disaster phases and adaptation. Given the small number of cases in less frequent categories they were excluded from the statistical analyses.

Because the dependent variables are binary, coded 1 if the emergency manager's definition of resilience fell into that category and 0 otherwise, logistic regression analyses were conducted. A separate regression was conducted for each of the six dependent variables. Given the distinct patterns of survey responses among the states, as discussed in the previous section, the observations were clustered by state.

Regression Results

The results of the statistical analyses are reported in Table 4.3.[50] Because the coefficients of logit analyses are difficult to interpret, predicted probabilities for each independent variable are reported in the table as well.[51] The results are also discussed in terms of predicted probabilities. The findings for each dependent variable or resilience theme is considered in turn.

The variables urban-rural and hurricane maximum damage are negatively and significantly associated with the theme of *bouncing back*. This indicates that more urbanized, metropolitan counties as well as those that have experienced severe hurricane events are more likely to say community resilience is bouncing back. The predicted probabilities for the variable urban-rural report that an emergency manager in a metropolitan county with a population of one million or more has a 37 percent likelihood of citing bouncing back when describing community resilience while an emergency manager in a rural county with a population less than 2,500 has an 11 percent chance of the same. Additionally, the predicted probabilities for the variable hurricane maximum damage indicate that an emergency manager in a county that has little experience with severe hurricanes—the minimum value of hurricane property damage—has a higher likelihood (35 percent) of saying community resilience is bouncing back compared to a 10 percent likelihood with an emergency manager in a county that has experienced the maximum damage of a very severe hurricane.

Experience with severe hurricanes, measured by hurricane property damage, has the opposite effect on the likelihood of describing community resilience as *preparedness*. The regression results show that hurricane maximum property damage is the only variable significantly related to preparedness. The predicted probabilities for this variable report that an emergency manager in a county that has experienced the least hurricane property damage has a 10 percent likelihood of citing preparedness in reference to resilience while an emergency manager in a county with the most hurricane property damage has a 33 percent likelihood of naming preparedness. This underscores that emergency managers in counties that have a history of severe hurricane events prioritize preparedness in relation to resilience.

Disaster experience also emerges as significantly correlated to the responses of *continuity* and *recovery*. The variable BP oil spill economic loss claim zones is negatively associated with continuity but positively associated with recovery. The predicted probabilities for this variable indicate that emergency managers in counties with the minimum value of no economic loss have a 22 percent likelihood of focusing on community resilience as continuity compared to 6 percent likelihood in counties with the maximum value of economic loss. On the other hand, emergency managers in counties with no economic loss have a 4 percent likelihood of citing recovery in reference to community resilience while their counterparts in counties that have experienced the most economic loss have a 39 percent likelihood of saying the same.

Table 4.3 Factors that Explain Differences in Perceptions of Community Resilience

	Common Themes among Responses to the Question: "What does community resilience mean to you?"					
	Bounce Back	Preparedness	Continuity	Recovery	Self-Sufficiency	Community Responsibility
Urban-Rural	-0.302***	-0.229	-0.040	0.248	0.334**	0.327***
	(0.050)	(0.144)	(0.106)	(0.233)	(0.170)	(0.031)
Predicted 1: Metro >1 million pop	0.37	0.21	0.15	0.07	0.05	0.05
Probabilities 2	0.30	0.18	0.14	0.09	0.06	0.06
3	0.24	0.15	0.14	0.11	0.09	0.09
4	0.19	0.12	0.13	0.13	0.12	0.12
5	0.15	0.10	0.13	0.17	0.15	0.15
6: Rural < 2,500 pop	0.11	0.08	0.12	0.20	0.20	0.20
BP Oil Spill Economic Loss Zones	0.063	-0.083	-0.328**	0.551**	0.112	0.003
	(0.165)	(0.063)	(0.158)	(0.252)	(0.467)	(0.247)
Predicted Minimum value	0.22	0.17	0.22	0.04	0.07	0.08
Probabilities Maximum value	0.28	0.12	0.06	0.39	0.11	0.08
Hurricane Max Property Damage	-0.001*	0.001**	-2.98e-04	-0.001	-1.48e-04	-1.85e-04
	(0.001)	(0.001)	(6.94e-04)	(0.001)	(0.001)	(0.001)
Predicted Minimum value	0.35	0.10	0.15	0.13	0.09	0.09
Probabilities Maximum value	0.10	0.33	0.11	0.06	0.07	0.07

Constant	0.156	−1.398***	−1.017**	−3.505**	−3.503**	−3.272
	(0.386)	(0.518)	(0.443)	(1.463)	(1.469)	(0.496)
N	54	54	54	54	54	54
Pseudo R²	0.05	0.06	0.03	0.09	0.04	0.04

Notes: Logit analysis conducted for each model with observations clustered by state. Coefficients reported for the variables urban-rural, BP economic loss claim zone, hurricane maximum property damage, and the constant with robust standard errors in parentheses. Statistical significance denoted as: *** $p \leq 0.01$; ** $p \leq 0.05$; * $p \leq 0.10$ (all two-tailed tests). Significant variables are also shown in bold. Predicted probabilities (chance of responding to the question with the response shown) are reported across the values of the independent variables; in calculating predicted probabilities all variables were held at their means. Dependent variable data are taken from author's original interviews conducted with county and parish emergency managers. The themes of all disaster phases and adaptation were excluded from the logit analysis because of the limited number of positive outcomes (less than 5) associated with these variables.

The BP *Deepwater Horizon* oil spill was a devastating disaster that severely damaged the health and well-being of beaches, ecosystems, local economies, and citizen populations. Those counties and parishes assigned claim zones representing the most economic loss are located across the Gulf Coast primarily in the states of Louisiana, Mississippi, and Alabama where oil washed ashore on beaches, covered protected marshlands, and coated wildlife. These are the areas where fishing and shrimping were halted due to health hazards and where families had to be treated for depression as a result of the economic, social, and psychological effects of the spill.[52] Given the experiences associated with this disaster, it is not surprising to find that emergency managers in counties that experienced the worst of the spill associated community resilience with recovery and not continuity. Continued "normal" functioning was not possible for many citizens, businesses, and local governments in the face of the oil spill. Commercial fishermen were forced to stop their operations; restaurants had no choice but to close their doors when tourists stopped visiting the area.[53] Even local governments were not permitted in the initial response to clean their beaches. On the other hand, these counties do identify with recovery—the long process of restoring social and economic systems following a disaster event. This has been and continues to be, three years later, the focus for many severely impacted by the oil spill.[54]

While disaster experience (or lack of) accounted for responses of continuity and recovery, the urban-rural context of the county are positively and significantly related to the responses of *self-sufficiency* and *community*. This signifies that emergency managers in rural counties are more likely to describe community resilience as self-sufficiency or focus on their response on community responsibility. The predicted probabilities indicate that an emergency manager in a metropolitan area with a population greater than one million has a 5 percent likelihood of citing self-sufficiency or community responsibility in reference to community resilience. On the other hand, an emergency manager in a rural county with a population less than 2,500 has a 20 percent likelihood of saying the same. Independence and self-sufficiency is often a necessity of everyday living in rural areas with dispersed populations. Therefore, it follows that emergency managers in this rural context highlight the role of individuals, families, and communities in providing for and directing the development of their own abilities to manage disaster events.

In summary, these analyses have shown that the context in which emergency managers operate does influence their perceptions of community resilience. Emergency managers in urban contexts are more likely to cite bouncing back while those in rural contexts are more likely to reference self-sufficiency and community responsibility. Emergency managers in counties that have experienced very severe hurricane events are more likely to describe community resilience in terms of preparation while those in counties that have been severely impacted by the BP *Deepwater Horizon* oil spill are most likely to cite recovery in relation to resilience. In the context of little disaster experience with hurricanes and the oil spill, emergency managers are more likely to define community resilience in terms of bouncing back or continuity.

CONCLUDING THOUGHTS ON A SHARED UNDERSTANDING OF RESILIENCE

Resilience is abstract. We cannot touch, taste, or see it; we cannot contain it in a defined space. It is not a thing; rather, it is a concept. It is the idea that despite the bad, uncontrollable events that happen, we can persevere and even improve our conditions. As such, resilience is incredibly promising. But for it to be an effective guiding principle of our national homeland security and emergency management framework, it must be more.

What is needed is a common understanding of resilience and of its attributes in terms that can be translated into action. The White House and federal agencies have attempted to provide this, but their efforts to delineate the role of resilience in emergency management has muddled its meaning. Federal policy directives and programs have complicated what is meant by resilience and have compartmentalized it in ways that detract from its value as a unifying concept. Moreover, federal references of resilience have reduced it to an outcome synonymous with security as compared to scholars who consider it to be a complex, adaptive process rather than an end point.[55]

Despite the varied meanings of and references to resilience, there is some alignment on the local level with federal resilience directives. Based on the survey conducted in Gulf Coast counties and parishes, a considerable portion of emergency managers identify resilience as bouncing back, preparedness, continuity, and recovery—all aspects highlighted by federal agencies in efforts to develop resilience. The question remains, however, whether this constitutes a shared understanding of the term. By what criteria do we assess a common meaning of resilience? How shared must an understanding of resilience be and how specific should the common meaning be for it to create effective results on the local level? These are questions that policy-makers, practitioners, and scholars should ask and flesh out as we continue to use resilience as a guiding principle and strategy for emergency management.

SUMMARY

There are multiple meanings assigned to the term resilience by the White House and federal agencies in using resilience as a guide for our national homeland security and emergency management framework. Common among the federal usage of the term is defining resilience as a set of capacities for adaption and recovery in the face of a disaster. Community engagement and collaboration are also emphasized. However, the concept of resilience is treated differently by federal agencies with a variety of labels and contexts assigned to the term. In all, there is a lack of a central message or meaning being put forth by the federal government.

Survey responses of county emergency managers indicate that there are also varied meanings of community resilience on the local level. Responses to the question—*What does the term community resilience mean to you?*—were analyzed, and eight themes were identified: bounce back, preparedness, continuity, recovery, self-sufficiency, community responsibility, disaster phases, and adaption. Emergency managers in urban contexts are more likely to cite bouncing back while those in rural contexts are more likely to reference self-sufficiency and community responsibility. Respondents in counties that have experienced very severe hurricane events are more likely to describe community resilience as preparation while those in counties that have been severely impacted by the BP *Deepwater Horizon* oil spill are most likely to cite recovery. Emergency managers in counties with little disaster experience are more likely to define community resilience in terms of bouncing back or continuity. Many of the perceptions of resilience held by county emergency managers overlap with meanings put forth by the federal government. However, it is unclear if this constitutes a sufficiently shared meaning as to effectively develop resilience on the local level.

DISCUSSION QUESTIONS

1. Should the federal government adopt one definition of resilience?
2. Is resilience interchangeable with security and sustainability? What commonalities do these concepts share?
3. What conclusions can be drawn from the word cloud presented in Figure 4.1 other than those presented in this chapter's discussion?
4. What are the pros and cons of framing resilience in terms of self-sufficiency?
5. How might we gain a more collective understanding of resilience?

NOTES

1. Mark de Bruijne, Arjen Boin, and Michel van Eeten, "Resilience: Exploring the Concept and Its Meanings," in *Designing Resilience: Preparing for Extreme Events,* ed. Louise K. Comfort, Arjen Boin, and Chris C. Demchak (Pittsburgh: University of Pittsburgh Press, 2010), 28.
2. The way states have applied resilience in official policy largely reflects federal approaches to resilience because many of these are mandated by federal directives. Therefore, this chapter focuses on federal treatments of resilience.

3. U.S. Department of Homeland Security, Homeland Security Advisory Council, *Report of the Critical Infrastructure Task Force* (Washington, DC: DHS, 2006), accessed June 30, 2013, *http://www.dhs.gov/xlibrary/assets/HSAC_CITF_Report_v2.pd.*

4. Ibid.

5. Ibid, 4.

6. U.S. Department of Homeland Security, *Quadrennial Homeland Security Review* (Washington, DC: DHS, 2010), accessed June 30, 2013, *http://www.dhs.gov/quadrennial-homeland-security-review-qhsr.*

7. Ibid, 31.

8. Ibid.

9. Ibid.

10. The White House, *National Security Strategy.* (Washington, DC: The White House, 2010), accessed June 30, 2013, *http://www.whitehouse.gov/sites/default/files/rss_viewer/national_security_strategy.pdf.*

11. Ibid, 18.

12. Ibid, 18–19.

13. Ibid, 18.

14. The White House, *Presidential Policy Directive/PPD—8* (Washington, DC: The White House, 2010), accessed June 30, 2013, *http://www.dhs.gov/xlibrary/assets/presidential-policy-directive-8-national-preparedness.pdf.*

15. "Learn about Presidential Policy Directive—8," last accessed June 30, 2013, *http://www.fema.gov/learn-about-presidential-policy-directive-8.*

16. "Whole Community," last accessed June 30, 2013, *http://www.fema.gov/national-preparedness/whole-community.*

17. U.S. Department of Homeland Security, Homeland Security Advisory Council. *Community Resilience Task Force Recommendations* (Washington, DC: DHS, 2011), 8, last accessed June 30, 2013, *http://www.dhs.gov/xlibrary/assets/hsac-community-resilience-task-force-recommendations-072011.pdf.*

18. Ibid.

19. Ibid, 12.

20. Ibid, 13.

21. Ibid.

22. U.S. Department of Homeland Security, *National Preparedness Goal* (Washington, DC: DHS, 2011), 1, last accessed June 30, 2013, *http://www.fema.gov/pdf/prepared/npg.pdf.*

23. Ibid, 9.

24. U.S. Department of Homeland Security, Federal Emergency Management Agency, *National Disaster Recovery Framework: Strengthening Disaster Recovery for the Nation* (Washington, DC: DHS, 2011), 11, last accessed June 30, 2013, *http://www.fema.gov/national-disaster-recovery-framework.*

25. Ibid, 16.

26. "National Planning Frameworks," last accessed June 30, 2013, *http://www.fema.gov/national-planning-frameworks.*

27. U.S. Department of Homeland Security, *National Mitigation Framework,* (Washington, DC: DHS, 2013), 4, last accessed June 30, 2013, *http://www.fema.gov/library/viewRecord.do?id=7363.*

28. *Quadrennial,* 15.

29. *National Security,* 18.

30. *Community Resilience Task Force,* 8.

31. *National Mitigation,* 4.

32. For example, see FEMA training: "Improving Preparedness and Resilience through Public-Private Partnerships," last accessed June 30, 2013, *http://training.fema.gov/EMIWeb/IS/courseOverview.aspx?code=is-662.*

33. *Quadrennial,* 31.
34. *PPD-8,* 1.
35. *Community Resilience Task Force,* 13.
36. See chapter 3 for a full discussion of the sample and county survey. The county questionnaire is available in Appendix B.
37. The full list of responses is given in Appendix D. To protect the anonymity of the survey participants, no identifiers—county or individual—are provided along with the responses.
38. The number of observations was reduced due to missing (nonresponse) survey data.
39. Arjen Boin, "Designing Resilience: Leadership Challenges in Complex Administrative Systems," in *Designing Resilience: Preparing for Extreme Events,* ed. Louise K. Comfort, Arjen Boin, and Chris C. Demchak (Pittsburg: University of Pittsburg Press, 2010), 138.
40. Douglas Patton and Li-ju Jang, "Disaster Resilience: Exploring All Hazards and Cross-Cultural Perspectives," in *Community Disaster Recovery and Resiliency: Exploring Global Opportunities and Challenges,* ed. DeMond S. Miller and Jason D. Rivera (Boca Raton, FL: Auerback Publications, 2011), 83.
41. Susan L. Cutter et al., "A Place-Based Model for Understanding Community Resilience to Natural Disasters," *Global Environmental Change* 18 (2008): 598–606; Fran H. Norris et al., "Community Resilience as a Metaphor, Theory, Set of Capacities, and Strategy for Disaster Readiness," *American Journal of Community Psychology,* 41: 127–50; Douglas Paton, "Disaster Resilience: Building Capacity to Co-Exist with Natural Hazards and Their Consequences," in *Disaster Resilience: An Integrated Approach,* ed. Douglas Paton and David Johnston (Springfield, IL: Charles C Thomas Publisher Ltd., 2006), 3–10; Julie Ann Pooley, Lynne Cohen, and Moira O'Connor, "Links between Community and Individual Resilience: Evidence from Cyclone Affected Communities in North West Australia," in *Disaster Resilience: An Integrated Approach,* ed. Douglas Paton and David Johnston (Springfield, IL: Charles C Thomas Publisher Ltd., 2006), 161–70.
42. Paton and Jang, "Disaster Resilience," 84.
43. Linda Labao and David S. Kraybill, "The Emerging Roles of County Governments in Metropolitan and Nonmetropolitan Areas: Findings from a National Survey," *Economic Development Quarterly,* 19 (2005): 245–59.
44. Susan L. Cutter, Bryan J. Boruff, and W. Lynn Shirley, "Social Vulnerability to Environmental Hazards," *Social Science Quarterly,* 84 (2003): 242–61; Labao and Kraybill, "The Emerging Roles."
45. Bonnie Erikson, "Social Networks: The Value of Variety," *Contexts,* 2 (2003): 25–31.
46. U.S. Department of Agriculture. Economic Research Service, *2003 Rural-Urban Continuum Codes [Downloadable Data File]* (Washington, DC: USDA, 2004), accessed April 5, 2012, *http://www.ers.usda.gov/data-products/rural-urban-continuum-codes.aspx#.Udj8CKzlf2w.*
47. Metropolitan is defined as "one urbanized area of 50,000 or more population plus adjacent territory and have a high degree of social and economic integration."
48. BP Deepwater Horizon Settlements, "Map of Economic Loss Zones," last accessed June 30, 2013, *http://www.deepwaterhorizonsettlements.com/Documents/Economic%20SA/Ex1A_Map_of_Economic_Loss_Zones.pdf.*
49. Hazards & Vulnerability Research Institute, *The Spatial Hazard Events and Losses Database for the United States, Version 10.0* [Online Database] (Columbia, SC: University of South Carolina, 2013), accessed September 5, 2012, *http://www.sheldus.org.*

50. The reduction in the number of observations is due to missing (nonresponse) data. Two-tailed significance tests were used given the nondirectional nature of the propositions posed to explain resilience perceptions. Descriptive statistics for the variables in this regression are available in Appendix F.

51. In calculating the predicted probabilities, all variables were held at their means.

52. Common observations from interviews conducted by the author with multiple municipal elected officials during the period February 16–March 16, 2011 and with county emergency managers during the period June 4–21, 2012 in the states of Louisiana, Mississippi, and Alabama.

53. Subject #25, personal interview by Ashley D. Ross, Gulf Shores, Alabama, March 16, 2011; Subject #30, personal interview by Ashley D. Ross, Gulf Shores, Alabama, March 19, 2011.

54. Subject #54, personal interview by Ashley D. Ross, Robertsdale, Alabama, June 21, 2012.

55. Norris et al., "Community Resilience."

5   Adaptive Capacities for Disaster Resilience across the Gulf Coast

If resilience is a resource, then adaptive capacities are the well from which the fount flows. Adaptive capacities are the strengths that enable a community to ideally prevent a disaster or to effectively respond and recover if a disaster occurs. They are largely manipulable by a community in that capacity can be shaped by policies and programs if there is the political will to do so. This means that adaptive capacities as a source of resilience can be cultivated locally, which is incredibly promising for emergency management.

ASSESSING DISASTER RESILIENCE THROUGH MEASUREMENT OF ADAPTIVE CAPACITIES

A community's adaptive capacity is its *collective strengths and abilities to prevent, withstand, and manage a disaster event*. Adaptive capacities entail tangible products and observable characteristics of a community. Disaster mitigation plans exist on paper. Flood insurance is traceable through records. Education levels, age groups, and special needs populations are recorded by government agencies. These factors as well as others comprise the components of a community's adaptive capacity for disaster resilience and are measurable through secondary sources such as the U.S. Census Bureau and the Federal Emergency Management Agency (FEMA).

Measurement of adaptive capacities in this chapter builds on the previous work of hazards scholars and focuses on evaluating the resilience of counties across the Gulf Coast along six dimensions:

- *Social capacity for resilience* is the aggregation of a community's characteristics including age, education levels, wealth, and language capacity that translate to able, mobile, and resource-enabled individuals in the event of a disaster.
- *Community capital* refers to the connectedness of community members that enable cooperation and collaboration in disaster planning, response, and recovery.
- *Economic capacity for resilience* refers to the robustness and diversity of a community's economy.

- *Institutional capacity for resilience* concerns the plans and preparations a community has made for disasters.
- *Infrastructure capacity for resilience* refers to a community's basic public service capacity in terms of shelter, roads, and medical facilities that may be needed in the event of a disaster.
- *Ecological capacity for resilience* speaks to how community development has affected natural coastal barriers such as wetlands.

Rating Disaster Resilience

Two important measurement models that have applied a rating system of adaptive capacities are the Disaster Resilience of Place (DROP) index[1] devised by hazards scholar Susan Cutter and her colleagues and the Community Disaster Resilience Index (CDRI)[2] created by scholars at Texas A&M University's Hazard Reduction and Recovery Center, led by Walter Peacock. Both approached the assessment of adaptive capacity on the county level. The DROP model was applied by Cutter et al. to assess disaster resilience of FEMA Region IV which includes 736 counties in the states of Kentucky, Tennessee, North Carolina, South Carolina, Mississippi, Alabama, Georgia, and Florida. The CDRI was applied to the Gulf Coast, including all 144 National Oceanic and Atmospheric Administration (NOAA) designated coastal counties in the states of Texas, Louisiana, Mississippi, Alabama, and Florida.

The DROP and CDRI indices measure the same components of resilience but label these categories somewhat differently. These categories overlap as shown in Table 5.1. The DROP index includes measures of social, economic, institutional, and infrastructure resilience as well as community capital. The CDRI measures resilience as four components: social, economic, physical, and human capital. Social resilience in the DROP index refers to demographic characteristics, education levels, and the transportation and communication capacity of the population. This most closely resembles human capital in the CDRI which measures education and labor characteristics. There are indicators in the human capital category of the CDRI, however, that also correspond to the DROP index category of institutional resilience including percentage of the population covered by a hazard mitigation plan. Measurement of economic resilience in the DROP index corresponds to measurement of economic capital in the CDRI while institutional and infrastructure resilience in the former is largely captured by measurement of physical capital in the latter. Finally, community capital in the DROP index is encompassed as measurement of social capital in the CDRI.

In addition to measurement of resilience across the components of social, economic, physical, and human capital, the CDRI groups indicators within these categories into the four disaster management phases: mitigation, preparedness, response, and recovery. Social and economic capital are identified as affecting all stages of disaster management.[3] Social capital refers to the connectedness of a community, a quality that is valuable in all

Table 5.1   Comparison of DROP and CDRI Indices of Resilience

Disaster Resilience of Place Index Susan Cutter et al. (2010)	Community Disaster Resilience Index Walter Peacock et al. (2010)
Social Resilience	**Human Capital**
Education, age, transportation, language, special needs, and health coverage	*Education, language, special needs transportation, health care, comprehensive plan coverage, building codes and zoning coverage*
Institutional Resilience	
Mitigation plan coverage, Citizen Corps and Storm Ready communities, first responder services	**Physical Capital**
Infrastructure Resilience	*Construction establishments, insurance establishments, housing units, vacant housing, hospitals, fire stations, ambulances, community food service facilities, schools*
Housing type, vacant rental units, schools, hotels/motels, hospital beds, housing age	
Economic Resilience	**Economic Capital**
Homeownership, employment, income inequality, female labor force, business size, healthcare access	*Income per capita, median household income, employment, value of housing, business establishments, health insurance coverage*
Community Capital	**Social Capital**
Net migration, voter participation, religious adherents, civic and social advocacy organizations	*Registered voters, nonprofit groups, civic and religious organizations, recreational centers, business and professional associations*

Notes: Indicators used to measure each category are listed in italics. Not all indicators are reported. For a full list, see Cutter et al. (2010), page 7, and Peacock et al. (2010), pages 33–4.

stages of a disaster ranging from collaborative planning during mitigation to providing support networks that can be drawn upon in disaster response and recovery. Economic capital, too, is important in all stages because it represents the financial resources available for efforts to mitigate, prepare for, respond to, and recover from disasters. Physical capital entails a community's infrastructure and built environment as well as plans that regulate these. The majority of the physical capital indicators are prominent in the mitigation and response stages of disaster management. Finally, indicators of human capital are primarily associated with the mitigation and recovery stages of disaster management. Peacock et al. note that a well-educated, healthy, and productive population can more fully engage in mitigation efforts and recovery activities to prevent disasters and/or manage their impact.[4]

The DROP index and CDRI did not include ecological resilience because of the inconsistency that would be presented by these measures. Many ecological or natural systems features purported to affect resilience vary in their relevance by geographical area. However, both sets of scholars noted the importance of considering this through assessment of factors known to either enhance or promote natural resilience.[5] Such measures for coastal regions include the degradation of wetlands, erosion rate, the percentage of impervious surfaces, and the number of coastal defense structures.

Measuring Gulf Coast Adaptive Capacities for Resilience

Disaster Resilience of Place (DROP)[6] and the Community Disaster Resilience Index (CDRI)[7] serve as blueprints for this study to measure Gulf Coast adaptive capacities. The categories and indicators used to create the DROP index are incorporated with the disaster phases emphasized in the CDRI. Additionally, ecological resilience is considered. Because this study's sample size is restricted to counties within 25 miles of the Gulf of Mexico the assessment of ecological resilience is possible. This area of focus is sufficiently small and homogenous to assume that the factors measured as part of ecological resilience are relevant and comparable.

This study also improves upon the DROP index and CDRI by including recent data. This is made possible by the release of secondary source data, primarily the update of the U.S. Census for the year 2010. Both the DROP and CDRI rely on information from the 2000 census. While accurate, this information predates many of the disaster events that have shaped the Gulf Coast in the last decade, including Hurricane Katrina. More recent data reflects the social, economic, and demographic changes that have developed from these disaster events and subsequent efforts to rebuild and recover. Therefore, the resultant index is a more precise estimation of current adaptive capacities across the region.

Indicators of Adaptive Capacities

Adaptive capacities for resilience were measured across six components: social resilience, community capital, economic resilience, institutional resilience, infrastructure resilience, and ecological resilience. Multiple indicators were aggregated to create an index for each of these components as shown in Table 5.2. These categories and the indicators for all but ecological resilience were adopted from Cutter et al.'s DROP index.[8] The source for most of the indicators is the U.S. Census 2010, but additional secondary sources were used, all of which are noted in the table. Appendix G summarizes the data sources used for the construction of these indices; Appendix H provides the data collected by county.

Social Resilience

Social resilience refers to the education, health, and mobility of a population. It represents the degree of vulnerability that influences the way

Table 5.2 Adaptive Capacity for Disaster Resilience Indicators by Component

Component	Variable	Definition (± Effect on Resilience)	Data Source
Social Resilience	Education	Percent of the population with a college degree (+)	American Communities Survey 2010
	Transportation access	Percent of households with a vehicle (+)	American Communities Survey 2011
	Communication capacity	Percent housing units with a telephone (+)	American Communities Survey 2011
	Language competency	Percent of the population over 5 years of age that speak English "very well" (+)	American Communities Survey 2010
	Non-vulnerable population	Percent non-elderly population (+)	USA Counties 2009
		Percent population without a physical disability (+)	US Census 2000
	Health care coverage	Percent population with health insurance (under 65 years of age) (+)	USA Counties 2007
Community Capital	Place attachment	Net international migration per 1,000 population (–)	American Communities Survey 2009
		Percent of the population born in the state that resides in the state (+)	American Communities Survey 2010
	Political engagement	Percent voter turnout in 2008 presidential election (+)	Secretary of State/Dept. of State 2008
		Religious adherents per 1,000 (+)	ASARB 2010
	Social capital	Civic organizations per 10,000 (+)	County Business Patterns 2009
		Social advocacy organizations per 10,000 (+)	County Business Patterns 2009
Economic Resilience	Housing capital	Percent owner occupied housing (+)	US Census 2010
	Employment	Percent of the population that is employed (+)	American Communities Survey 2010
		Percent of labor force that is female (+)	American Community Survey 2010
	Income equality	Quintiles of Gini Index (higher values = more equal) (+)	American Communities Survey 2012
	Economic diversity	Percent of the population not employed in farming, fishing, forestry, or extractive industries (+)	US Census 2012
	Business robustness	Ratio of large to small business employees (+)	US Census 2009
	Health care access	Total physicians per 10,000 (+)	USA Counties 2009

Category	Indicator	Description	Source
Institutional Resilience	Mitigation plans	Percent population covered by a multi-hazard mitigation plan (–)	FEMA 2012
	Mitigation organizations and activities	Percent population participating in Community Rating System (+)	FEMA 2012
		Percent population covered by Citizen Corps council (+)	Citizen Corps 2012
	Emergency services	Percent population in Storm Ready communities (+)	NOAA 2012
		Percent local government expenditures for health/hospitals, fire and police (+)	USA Counties 2002
	Administrative decentralization	Number of municipalities, school districts, and special districts (–)	US Census 2007
	Disaster experience	Number of Presidential disaster declarations, 2002-2011 (+)	FEMA 2012
Infrastructure Resilience	Housing vulnerability	Percent of housing not mobile homes (+)	American Communities Survey 2010
		Percent housing units built 1970–94 (–)	American Communities Survey 2010
	Evacuation capacity	Primary and secondary road miles per square mile (+)	US Census 2010
	Medical capacity	Number of hospital beds per 10,000 (+)	County and City Data Book 2007
	Shelter capacity	Percent vacant rental units (+)	US Census 2010
		Number of hotels/motels per square mile (+)	County Business Patterns 2009
	Service restoration	Number of public schools per square mile (+)	FEMA Hazus 2.0 2011
Ecological Resilience	Wetland preservation	Net change in percent wetland area between 1996 to 2006 (+)	NOAA 2010
	Impervious surfaces	Percent impervious surface in square miles of land area (–)	National Land Cover Database 2006
	Floodplain development	Index of severe repetitive loss properties (higher values = more loss) (–)	FEMA 2007

Notes: Detailed information on the data sources is given in Appendix G. County-level data for each of these indicators is provided in Appendix H.

communities respond to and recover from disaster events.[9] The index for social resilience was comprised of seven indicators:

- *Education*—Measured as percent of the population with a college education.[10] A population with a high level of education should be knowledgeable and have skills that aid in the development of resilience, particularly planning and preparedness. Moreover, education is generally linked to socioeconomic status, including income. More wealthy households and communities are known to have more resources to prepare for and manage disaster events.
- *Transportation access*—Measured as the percent of households with a vehicle. Mobility is a critical aspect of disaster resilience, especially during the onset of a disaster. In particular, households with vehicles are able to evacuate, which relieves demands on local government to provide these services.
- *Communication capacity*—Measured as the percent of housing units with a telephone. Communication is an essential part of disaster management as it serves as a way for local governments to warn citizens of impending dangers and to update them on disaster events.
- *Language competency*—Measured as the percent of the population over 5 years of age that speak English "very well." Studies have shown that minority populations are often marginalized during disaster events because of language barriers. Therefore, the more English speakers in a community, the higher the collective resilience as English is the language used most often to communicate disaster warnings and information.
- *Nonvulnerable population*—Measured by two factors: 1) the percent of the population under the age of 65 years and 2) the percent of the population without a physical disability. Vulnerable populations need special care during disaster events. The elderly and disabled often need evacuation assistance and can also require medical care. This necessitates careful planning to mobilize resources, including transport and medical specialists, to meet the needs of this population; this may strain limited resources during a disaster.
- *Health care coverage*—Measured as the percent of the population under the age of 65 years with health insurance.[11]

Community Capital

Community capital refers to the connectedness of individuals within a community and the trust that they build with one another. This connectedness and trust is important because it facilitates cooperation and collaboration among community members. The community capital index was measured through six indicators:[12]

- *Place attachment*—Measured by two factors: 1) the net international migration per 1,000 population and 2) the percent of the population born in a state that still resides in that state. A population that has a higher degree of migration has less place attachment. On the other hand, a population that resides in the state in which they were born has a high degree of place attachment. Attachment to place is an important aspect of resilience because it provides motivation for investing in measures to protect buildings and community features from hazards and serves as an impetus for rebuilding in sustainable ways post-disaster.[13] Both enhance a community's disaster resilience.

- *Political engagement*—Measured as the percent voter turnout in the 2008 presidential election. Voting in elections signals general efficacy and engagement which is often associated with involvement in local planning and preparedness pre-disaster and response and recovery efforts post-disaster.

- *Social capital*—Measured by three factors: 1) the number of religious adherents per 1,000 individuals, 2) the number of civic organizations per 10,000 individuals, and 3) the number of social advocacy organizations per 10,000 individuals. Citizens who are active members of a religious, civic, or social advocacy group are part of a network that can be a source of information and support during a disaster event.[14] Moreover, faith-based and nonprofit groups have been a critical part of disaster efforts ranging from preparedness to recovery activities.[15]

Economic Resilience

Economic resilience refers to the health, vitality, and diversity of the local economy. A community with a robust economy has the resources to better prepare for disasters and invest in hazard mitigation; moreover, communities with stable economies can more quickly recover from disaster events.[16] Economic resilience was measured by seven indicators:

- *Housing capital*—Measured as the percent of owner-occupied housing. Housing capital is an indicator of overall economic well-being; higher rates reflect a population that can afford to purchase homes.

- *Employment*—Measured by two factors: 1) the percent of the population that is employed and 2) the percent of labor force 16 years old and older that is female. Employment rates in general and for females specifically represents the vitality and stability of the labor force in a community. Higher employment rates indicate a healthy local economy which facilitates overall capacity for resilience.

- *Income equality*—Measured by the GINI coefficient, a statistical calculation of the dispersion of income. It ranges from zero to one, with zero representing perfect equality—a scenario where everyone has the same income—and one representing perfect inequality—a scenario where one individual holds all the income. This indicator is broken into five categories: Category 1 = a GINI coefficient of 0.461 to 0.645, Category 2 = a GINI coefficient of 0.439 to 0.460, Category 3 = 0.422 to 0.438, Category 4 = a GINI coefficient of 0.402 to 0.421, and Category 5 = 0.207 to 0.401. Higher values of this indicator, therefore, represent higher income equality. Income equality indicates a community's economic health as higher inequalities may diminish a county's economic stability.[17]

- *Economic diversity*—Measured as the percent of the population not employed in farming, fishing, forestry, or extraction. These employment groups represent typical single-sector agriculture economies; therefore fewer individuals employed in these sectors indicate a more diverse economy. Economic diversity is critical for resilience because it facilitates economic functioning and growth post-disaster.[18] A disaster can damage or obstruct the functioning of specific economic sectors; communities that rely on single labor sectors face considerable fiscal difficulty following a disaster event.
- *Business robustness*—Measured as the ratio of large to small business employees. Large businesses are considered to be those that employ more than 500 while small businesses are those with less than 500 employees. Although small businesses benefit local economies and communities in many ways, they are generally at-risk of not having sufficient fiscal robustness to be capable of restoring functions after a disaster event in comparison to large businesses. Therefore, a community with more citizens employed in large rather than small businesses is more likely to be able to "bounce back" post-disaster than a locality with a lower ratio.
- *Health care access*—This is measured as the number of physicians per 10,000 individuals. A higher number of physicians indicates greater access to health care which is critical for the health and functioning of the labor sector and economy.

Institutional Resilience

Institutional resilience refers to the disaster mitigation, planning, and preparedness a community has committed to.[19] A community actively engaged in developing their disaster resilience will invest in emergency services, create and implement hazards plans, and facilitate voluntary citizen groups focused on disaster preparation and response. Seven indicators were used to create the institutional resilience index:[20]

- *Mitigation plans*—This indicator is measured as the percent of the population covered by a multi-hazard mitigation plan. Planning for multiple hazards, for example flooding, tornadoes, hurricanes, and chemical spills, is a critical component of developing disaster resilience.[21] Communities that have adopted a multi-hazard mitigation plan are more likely to be ready for a disaster event.
- *Mitigation organizations and activities*—This is measured by three factors: 1) the percent of the population participating in FEMA's National Flood Insurance Program (NFIP) Community Rating System (CRS) 2) the percent of the population covered by a Citizen Corps council and 3) the percent of the population in a NOAA StormReady community.

FEMA's NFIP CRS is a voluntary program that encourages community floodplain management to exceed minimum NFIP requirements through activities that disseminate public information regarding flood risk and protection, development flood mapping and regulation, enhance flood damage reduction, and promote flood preparation.[22] As a result of participation in CRS, flood insurance premium rates are discounted. Citizen Corps councils are also voluntary organizations that work with the community to promote community participation in disaster preparation by educating the public on safety and disaster prevention, developing emergency plans and training, encouraging volunteerism, and aiding first responders in the event of a disaster.[23] Citizen Corps councils also partner with FEMA Community Emergency Response Teams, FEMA Fire Corps, and Medical Reserve Corps affiliated with the Department of Health and Human Services. Being part of a NOAA Storm-Ready community is another voluntary way to promote local disaster preparedness. To qualify, communities must have established warning systems including National Weather Service receivers and methods to disseminate information to the public, a working emergency operations center, public information weather safety talks, weather spotter training, formal hazardous weather operations plans, and visits by National Weather Service emergency managers and officials.[24]

- *Emergency services*—Emergency services are measured as the percent of local government expenditures on health and hospital services, fire protection, and police protection. Local government resources are generally limited and expenditures made in one area typically mean that they are not being made in another area. Therefore, the higher the percent spent on emergency services indicates a prioritization of investment in areas that are essential during disaster response and recovery, specifically, and disaster resilience, generally.

- *Administrative decentralization*—This indicator is measured as the number of governments and special districts within a county. The more governmental units that are involved in disaster mitigation, planning, preparedness, response, and recovery, the more difficult it is to coordinate effective action. Counties must work with municipal governments, school districts, and water districts in disaster management. By no fault of their own, counties having a greater number of governments and districts to manage have greater hurdles to surpass in developing resilience. Coordination among fewer governmental entities, on the other hand, facilitates activity to enhance resilience.

- *Disaster experience*—This is measured as the number of presidential disaster declarations during the time period 2002–2010. While devastating, disasters can build institutional resilience by calling attention to needed actions and improvements. Citizens are more likely to get involved in disaster planning and preparation after experiencing a recent disaster. Moreover, funds to facilitate recovery after a disaster event often improve disaster mitigation efforts either through conditionality (plans are required for federal funds) or purpose (some funding is set aside specifically for mitigation activities).

Infrastructure Resilience
Infrastructure resilience reflects the availability and robustness of a community's lifelines,[25] including highways to support transportation and critical facilities such as medical centers. It also refers to the vulnerability of housing to hazards and the community's capacity to manage response and recovery needs. Seven indicators were included in the infrastructure resilience index:

- *Housing vulnerability*—Measured by two factors: 1) the percent of houses that are not mobile homes and 2) the percent of houses that are not built from the time period 1970–94. Mobile homes are particularly vulnerable to high winds and flooding. Similarly, houses built during the time period 1970–94 are known to have been developed under lax building codes and, therefore, are at higher risk to experience damages as a result of a disaster event. A greater number of mobile homes and homes built from 1970–94 detract from overall community capacity for resilience.
- *Evacuation capacity*—Evacuation capacity is measured by the primary and secondary roads per square mile. Primary and secondary roads have an important function during disaster response and recovery. A community with a high number of primary and secondary roads has a greater capacity for evacuation pre-disaster and for transport of emergency personnel and goods post-disaster.
- *Medical capacity*—Measured as number of hospital beds per 10,000 individuals, medical facilities are a critical part of disaster response. Counties that have a higher number of hospital beds have a greater capacity to meet the post-disaster needs of their community. This includes treating patients with existing medical conditions as well as those that are injured by the disaster event.
- *Shelter capacity*—Measured by two factors: 1) the percent of vacant rental units and 2) the number of hotels or motels per square mile. Providing shelter after a disaster event is an important part of response and short-term recovery efforts. If a community has vacant rental units and hotels/motels available it can offer housing to first responders and officials that have come into the area to help with response and recovery as well as meet the needs of individuals and families that have been displaced from their homes and require shelter.
- *Service restoration*—This is measured by the number of public schools per square mile. While there are numerous services to restore post-disaster that are essential to community functioning, one of the most critical for returning a community to "normal" are schools. Schools not only provide educational services, they also serve as a link between youth, families, and the community.[26] Post-disaster, this link can help meet physical,

mental, and emotional needs plus provide support and information to students and families that are needed for effective recovery.

Ecological Resilience

Ecological resilience refers to a community's natural environment and how development has affected it. Along coastal regions this includes the preservation and/or restoration of natural defense features such as wetlands and sand dunes that can enhance a community's adaptive capacities.[27] This also addresses development in ways that make it more vulnerable to hazards. The ecological resilience index was calculated using three indicators:[28]

- *Wetland preservation*—This is measured as the net change in percent wetland area between 1996 and 2006. Wetlands are areas where there is shallow water or very soggy soil at least part of the year. They serve as a natural buffer that can diminish storm surges associated with hurricanes.[29] Communities that have chosen to develop in wetland areas lose the natural defense provided by these environments. Recent hurricane events have called attention to this and, as a result, many coastal communities have begun the process of restoring wetlands and barrier islands in efforts to rebuild their ecological resilience.
- *Impervious surface*—This is measured as the percent of impervious surface per square mile of land. Counties that have a high degree of impervious surface are prone to flooding, which makes them more vulnerable and less resilient. Impervious surfaces include concrete and asphalt and reflect the land-use choices a community has pursued.
- *Floodplain development*—This indicator is measured as the number of FEMA designated Severe Repetitive Loss (SRL) properties. FEMA considers a SRL property as one that has had at least four National Flood Insurance Program claim payments over $5,000 each and has had two separate claims payments with the cumulative amount of the building portion exceeding market value of the building.[30] SRL properties have experienced repeated flooding and remain in high risk areas; as such they reflect vulnerable development. The indicator used for FEMA SRLP is coded on a zero to four scale with zero indicating no SRLP properties in the county, one indicates that there were 1 to 20, two indicates that there were 21 to 30, three indicates that there were 31 to 40, and four indicates 41 and more. A high number of SRL properties may increase a community's vulnerability to hazards and detract from its adaptive capacity for resilience.

Index Calculation

To create a score for each of the six components, the indicators were first standardized to make them comparable using a min-max rescaling method.[31] This procedure rescales all the indicators to a range of 0 to 1 where zero corresponds to the lowest (or worse) observation for a specific indicator and one corresponds to the highest (or best) observation. For any factors that were considered to negatively impact resilience, the inverse of the observation was taken, then the indicator was rescaled. Rescaling the indicators creates a ranking of the counties in comparison to one another as to their adaptive capacity in each area measured.

The indicators were then averaged to generate an index for each resilience component.[32] Averaging, rather than summing, the indicators ensures that the component index is not influenced by the number of indicators (e.g., seven indicators for social resilience but only five for ecological resilience) used to measure it. Each component index, therefore, ranges from 0 to 1 with higher values indicating greater adaptive capacities in that component area.

Finally, each component index was summed to generate an overall disaster resilience score. The disaster resilience index ranges from 0 to 6 with higher values indicating greater overall adaptive capacity for resilience. The component indices were also totaled for each disaster phase—mitigation, preparedness, response, and recovery—in line with Peacock et al.'s method for creating the CDRI.

Peacock et al. aggregated specific indicators from each component—social, economic, physical, and human capital—to create the indices for each disaster phase.[33] Following their categorization, the component indices for social resilience, community capital, economic resilience, institutional resilience, and ecological resilience were totaled to indicate mitigation capacity. These should capture capacities for developing mitigation plans and activities since they all focus on reducing hazard impacts such as building codes and land-use. To approximate preparedness capacity, the economic, community capital, and institution component indices were summed. To measure response resilience, the economic resilience, community capital, institutional resilience, and infrastructure resilience component indices were totaled as each of these should reflect the adaptive capacities needed for disaster response—activities including evacuation, search and rescue, and providing emergency food and shelter. Finally, disaster recovery resilience was calculated as the sum of the economic resilience, community capital, social resilience, and ecological resilience component indices to measure recovery capacity. These disaster phase indices were standardized to ensure comparability.

Gulf Coast Disaster Resilience Index of Adaptive Capacities

The disaster resilience index measuring county adaptive capacities was calculated by summing six resilience component indices—social resilience, community capital, economic resilience, institutional resilience, infrastructure resilience, and ecological resilience. Each component index contained multiple indicators so that the aggregate index reflects 37 measures of adaptive capacities. The indicators and methods used to create the index replicates and improves upon Cutter, et al.'s DROP index and is largely informed by Peacock et al.'s CDRI. The resulting disaster resilience index had a mean

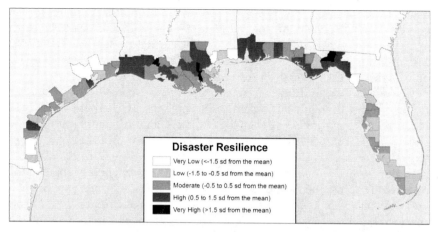

Figure 5.1 Map of Disaster Resilience Index Measuring County Adaptive Capacities

value of 3.26 on a scale that can theoretically range from 0 to 6. The minimum value of the index was 2.54; the maximum value was 3.76. The standard deviation associated with the disaster resilience index is 0.25, reflecting that the county scores cluster close to the mean.

The disaster resilience index is presented spatially in Figure 5.1. The map reports categories of resilience based on transformed disaster resilience index scores (z-scores), calculated as the sum of: social resilience, community capital, economic resilience, institutional resilience, infrastructure resilience, and ecological resilience.[34] The categories of resilience shown on the map are: very low (less than 1.5 standard deviation units below than the mean), low (between 1.5 and 0.5 standard deviation units below than the mean), moderate (between 0.5 standard deviation units lower than the mean and 0.5 standard deviation units above the mean), high (between 0.5 and 1.5 standard deviation units above the mean), or very high (greater than 1.5 standard deviation units above the mean). Darker shading indicates higher resilience.

Overall Patterns of Disaster Resilience

Moving across the Gulf Coast, the map shows that counties in Texas score on the moderate to low end of the resilience index. All the Texas coastal counties studied have moderate to very low resilience with only two exceptions—Galveston and Nueces Counties—which both exhibit high resilience. The opposite is evident in Louisiana. The parish resilience scores in Louisiana range from moderate to very high with one exception—St. Bernard Parish is ranked low. This parish is home to the Ninth Ward and was devastated by Hurricane Katrina. While it has recovered considerably, Katrina has left its mark there which is evident by these data trends.

Similar to Texas, the Mississippi coastal counties fall on the low end of the resilience index while the counties in Alabama score high. The counties in Florida exhibit varied resilience scores. In the panhandle from Escambia

County to Taylor County, the resilience scores are moderate or high with two exceptions—a score of low in Liberty County and a score of very high in Leon County. Moving down the coast of Florida from Dixie County to Miami-Dade County, resilience scores of moderate and low are evident with only Dixie County reporting a resilience score of very low.

The scores of the disaster resilience index vary considerably from the results of the Community Disaster Resilience Index (CDRI) applied to 144 coastal Gulf Coast counties. The CDRI found higher resilience scores in the Greater-Houston region of Texas as well as the coast of Florida but lower scores in Louisiana. These discrepancies may be attributed to the different indicators used to construct each index. They may also reflect changes in the past decade across the Gulf Coast as a result of disaster events experienced; these changes should be represented in the more recent data used in this study. In the next section, the data will be systematically analyzed to determine the county level factors associated with trends in the disaster resilience index scores. Before diving into this analysis, patterns of resilience scores across the component indices and disaster phases are explored.

Patterns of Resilience across the Component Indices
It is important to bear in mind that the disaster resilience index scores are an aggregation of multiple components measured by numerous indicators. What may be more telling is examination of the subcomponents used for this index as they point out areas in which counties exhibit considerable strengths or weaknesses in their adaptive capacities. Any vulnerabilities—even those that are immutable—can be addressed through policy and collective action.

The resilience scores for the component indices are spatially plotted in Figure 5.2.[35] Six maps are presented in this figure, each representing an individual component of capacity for disaster resilience: A. Social Resilience, B. Community Capital, C. Economic Resilience, D. Institutional Resilience, E. Infrastructure Resilience, and F. Ecological Resilience. The same method of standardizing each county disaster resilience score was applied to the component indices so that darker shading indicates higher resilience.

The component index maps reveal a more nuanced story of disaster resilience with considerable variance across the indices. Counties in Alabama and Mississippi scored high on social resilience. The majority of counties in Florida (78 percent) and parishes in Louisiana (88 percent) have moderate to high social resilience while the majority of counties in Texas (83 percent) scored moderate, low, or very low. The counties and parishes with the highest social resilience of the Gulf Coast sample include: Ascension Parish, Louisiana; Baldwin County, Alabama; Santa Rosa County, Florida; St. Charles Parish, Louisiana; and St. Tammany Parish, Louisiana. On the other hand, those with the lowest social resilience scores include: Cameron County, Texas; Dixie County, Florida; Kenedy County, Texas; Miami-Dade County, Florida; and Orleans Parish, Louisiana. Because social resilience includes indicators that reflect the demographics of a county ranging from age to education to special needs, low

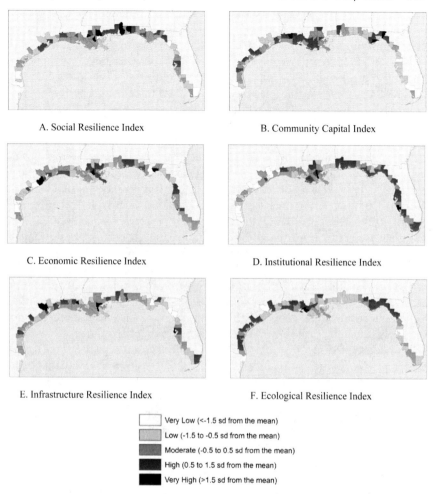

A. Social Resilience Index

B. Community Capital Index

C. Economic Resilience Index

D. Institutional Resilience Index

E. Infrastructure Resilience Index

F. Ecological Resilience Index

Very Low (<-1.5 sd from the mean)
Low (-1.5 to -0.5 sd from the mean)
Moderate (-0.5 to 0.5 sd from the mean)
High (0.5 to 1.5 sd from the mean)
Very High (>1.5 sd from the mean)

Figure 5.2 Map of Adaptive Capacity for Disaster Resilience Component Indices

resilience in this area does not necessarily reflect poor emergency management practices; rather it indicates that the vulnerabilities of the community are high. Therefore, measures should be taken to reduce these vulnerabilities before a disaster event and plan for the management of special population needs during a disaster (i.e. evacuation of the disabled and elderly).

While social resilience includes many immutable characteristics of a county, community capital indicates deliberate actions on the part of community members to be involved in organizations and politics. A highly active and connected community is thought to positively contribute to disaster resilience as it reflects willingness to cooperate and collaborate on communal decisions including those to prepare for, respond to, and recover from disasters. Counties in Alabama and Louisiana demonstrate moderate to high community capital while the majority of counties in Florida (64 percent) and all the counties in Mississippi report low or very low community capital. Counties in Texas are varied; most score moderate (44 percent) while the others score low or high on the community capital index. On this index, the highest scoring cases include: Franklin County, Florida; Jefferson County, Florida; and Jefferson Davis Parish, Louisiana. The lowest scoring cases include: Collier County, Florida; Hancock County, Mississippi; Miami-Dade, Florida; and Pasco County, Florida.

Scores on the third component index, economic resilience, are highly varied within the states. The highest scoring cases on economic resilience are: Brazoria County, Texas; St. Charles Parish, Louisiana; and Wakulla County, Florida. The lowest scoring cases include: Franklin County, Florida; Kenedy County, Texas; Kleberg County, Texas; Liberty County, Florida; and Matagorda County, Texas. Improving low economic capacity requires development of overall economic health to diversify the local economy, increase employment, and decrease income inequality. This cannot be accomplished alone by economic development coordinators, emergency managers, or city planners; rather, improving economic resilience takes a communal effort directed at building a robust local economy. Institutional resilience, on the other hand, is largely dependent on the guidance of local emergency managers.

The scores for institutional resilience reflect county-level efforts to develop disaster mitigation plans and activities. The counties in Alabama demonstrate high institution resilience as do 68 percent of counties in Florida. The state of Florida has made considerable improvements in mitigation since Hurricane Andrew,[36] and this data highlights the payoff of those mandates.

Twenty-five percent of the parishes in Louisiana also score high, but the majority (54 percent) are ranked moderate on the institutional resilience index. Sixty-one percent of the counties in Texas score low or very low, and all of the Mississippi counties are ranked low. The highest-scoring cases include: Jefferson Parish, Louisiana and Sarasota County, Florida. All of the lowest-scoring counties hail from Texas: Cameron County, Chambers County, Jackson County, Kenedy County, Liberty County, Matagorda County, Orange County, and Willacy County.

Infrastructure resilience is similar to economic resilience in that it is highly varied within states and also largely dependent on development driven by agencies and actors outside of the influence of emergency management. Nonetheless, emergency managers can encourage and work with local officials to develop and improve infrastructure and critical facilities in ways that enhance local resilience. The counties that have been most successful at developing infrastructure resilience are: Harris County, Texas; Jefferson Parish, Louisiana; Lafayette Parish, Louisiana; Orleans Parish, Louisiana; and Pinellas County, Florida. Those with the most room for improvement in building institutional resilience include: Dixie County, Florida; Liberty County, Florida; and Levy County, Florida.

Ecological resilience is another area that reflects collaboration among community leaders and members to work together in ways that preserve and restore natural barriers such as wetlands and steer development away from vulnerable areas including floodplains. The majority of counties (61 percent) in Texas exhibit high ecological resilience while the majority of counties in Alabama and Mississippi are ranked low. Although the counties in Florida and parishes in Louisiana are highly varied in their ranking on the ecological resilience index, the highest-scoring case is St. Mary Parish in Louisiana. The cases that score the lowest on ecological resilience are: Harris County, Texas; Hillsborough County, Florida; Orleans Parish, Louisiana; and Pinellas County, Florida.

Clearly there is considerable variation in the component indices of disaster resilience that demonstrate strengths and weaknesses in county adaptive capacities. Some of these capacities including economic, infrastructure, and ecological resilience are dependent on local action and development while others, including social resilience and community capital, reflect population characteristics and social norms. Institutional resilience is the one area most under the influence of local emergency management; although state directives also largely affect capacity in this regard. The next section breaks resilience into the disaster phases; again, variance in resilience scores is revealed among the county cases, which offers another way to approach the development of resilience on the local level.

Patterns of Resilience across the Disaster Phases

Examination of resilience scores across the disaster phases—mitigation, preparedness, response, and recovery—identifies areas in which counties have either strong, moderate, or weak adaptive capacities. This can be helpful in developing policy and directing activities to maintain or improve resilience capacity on the county, state, and regional level. The resilience scores across the disaster phases are presented spatially in Figure 5.3.[37]

Disaster mitigation is an aggregation of five component indices: social resilience, community capital, economic resilience, institutional resilience, and ecological resilience. The score for mitigation reflects county-level capacities for developing mitigation plans and activities that focus on reducing hazard impacts, including building codes and land-use policies. Alabama counties and Louisiana parishes are ranked the highest on the mitigation index with over 50 percent of their cases scoring high. Twenty-five percent of the counties in Florida also rank high on the mitigation index, and Jefferson County, Florida is ranked the highest in the sample. Only two parishes in Louisiana are ranked low while all of the counties in Mississippi counties and 56 percent of the counties in Texas score the same. In line with these trends, the lowest ranking cases include: Cameron County, Texas; Harris County, Texas; Hancock County, Mississippi; Harrison County, Mississippi; Kenedy County, Texas; and Jackson County, Mississippi.

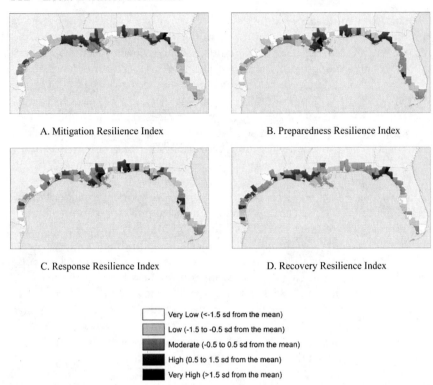

A. Mitigation Resilience Index   B. Preparedness Resilience Index

C. Response Resilience Index   D. Recovery Resilience Index

Very Low (<-1.5 sd from the mean)
Low (-1.5 to -0.5 sd from the mean)
Moderate (-0.5 to 0.5 sd from the mean)
High (0.5 to 1.5 sd from the mean)
Very High (>1.5 sd from the mean)

Figure 5.3   Map of Adaptive Capacity for Disaster Resilience Disaster Phase Indices

Similar patterns across the states emerge for disaster preparedness and response. The preparedness index was the sum of economic, community capital, and institutional resilience; these components reflect economic, social, and planning capacities needed to successfully prepare for disaster events. The response index was the sum of the same plus infrastructure resilience as this is critical for evacuation from hazardous areas and access to disaster-stricken areas. The Alabama counties score high on the preparedness index as do a third of the counties and parishes in Florida and Louisiana. The highest ranking cases for disaster preparedness include Jefferson Parish, Louisiana and St. Charles Parish, Louisiana; the cases with the highest scores for disaster response are: Escambia County, Florida; Jefferson Parish, Louisiana; and Orleans Parish, Louisiana.

On the other hand, two-thirds of the counties from Texas and all of the counties from Mississippi score low or very low on the preparedness index. These rankings are slightly improved for disaster response—56 percent of counties from Texas and two-thirds of the counties from Mississippi score low or very low. The lowest ranked cases for disaster preparedness and response include the following counties: Cameron County, Texas; Chambers County, Texas; Hancock County, Mississippi; Jackson County, Mississippi;

Jackson County, Texas; Kenedy County, Texas; Liberty County, Texas; and Matagorda County, Texas.

Patterns are somewhat different for disaster recovery index which was the sum of economic resilience, community capital, social resilience, and ecological resilience component indices. Alabama, Florida, and Louisiana exhibit slightly lower capacities for recovery than for mitigation, preparedness, and response; Texas ranks slightly higher. Fifty percent of the parishes from Louisiana, 39 percent of the counties from Texas, and 21 percent of the counties from Florida score high or very high. The Alabama counties rank moderate on the response index as do 39 percent of the counties from Texas. On the low end of the index fall all of the counties from Mississippi, 22 percent of counties from Texas, 17 percent of the Louisiana parishes, and 32 percent of Florida counties. The case ranked the highest for recovery capacity is Jefferson County, Florida; the counties scoring the lowest on the recovery index are: Harris County, Texas; Hillsborough County, Florida; Lee County, Florida; Miami-Dade County, Florida; and Pinellas County, Florida.

Comparing the states, these patterns suggest that Alabama, Florida, and Louisiana lead the region in developing capacities for disaster mitigation, preparedness, and response while Mississippi and Texas are weak in these areas. Although some counties exhibit high capacity for disaster recovery, the distribution of the resilience scores indicates a need to improve this across the entire Gulf Coast region. The next section explores state differences in further detail through statistical analyses and also tests if urban-rural characteristics, fiscal resources, and the intensity of disaster experienced affect county-level capacities for disaster resilience.

STATISTICAL ANALYSIS OF GULF COAST RESILIENCE INDEX OF ADAPTIVE CAPACITIES

The descriptive analysis detailed in the previous section underscores that county adaptive capacities across the Gulf Coast region tend to cluster by state. Trends in the data show that parishes and counties in Louisiana, Alabama, and the panhandle of Florida are ranked higher than those in Texas, Mississippi, and the southern coast of Florida. Further variation in resilience scores is highlighted by looking at patterns across the component indices—social resilience, community capital, economic resilience, institutional resilience, infrastructure resilience, and ecological resilience—and disaster phases—mitigation, preparedness, response, and recovery. While this descriptive analysis is useful to understanding how the resilience scores are distributed spatially, it does not explain why resilience patterns emerge in this manner. This section explores four explanations for variance in resilience scores and identifies which factors are statistically correlated with the adaptive capacity for disaster resilience index.

Explaining Resilience Score Variation

Identifying the factors associated with resilience requires that we look beyond its components to broader trends evident on the county level. This includes the urban-rural character of a county. Rural counties with fewer resources and greater geographic isolation may face challenges in developing resilience capacity. Another explanation lies with disaster assistance. Given that funds are largely limited for local emergency management, the external funding and support a county is able to muster to support its functions, purchase new equipment, and develop new programs may be associated with higher resilience. A third factor to examine in relation to resilience is disaster severity. Intense disasters degrade a community's basic capabilities posing challenges to the development of resilience. Finally, assessing state context—institutions for home rule as well as each state's unique set of economic, social, demographic, geographical, and institutional characteristics—is warranted because it can condition the environment in which counties manage disasters and develop resilience capabilities.

Urban-Rural County Context

Urban and rural communities differ in the way they are able to develop adaptive capacities due to the resources—economic and community-based—that are available to them. Sociologist Linda Lobao and agriculture economist David Kraybill assert that rural localities are disadvantaged by their smaller, less diversified economies.[38] Jobs in rural areas tend to be of poorer quality and provide lower incomes, which leads to higher poverty and unemployment rates. Moreover, rural communities have slower-growing, older, and less educated populations. In an analysis of a national sample of counties of with varying urban-rural characteristics, Labao and Kraybill found that rural counties are associated with less expansion of county government activity in the provision of public services (e.g., 911 emergency, housing assistance, health clinics). However, a study by sociologist Bonnie Erickson (2003) found that rural communities have greater social capital due to the diversity of their networks and the smaller size of their communities.[39] High levels of social capital should encourage the development of adaptive capacities, particularly in the area of community capital. Moreover, given the fewer demands on rural counties for development of structures, they should be better positioned to protect their natural features which strengthens ecological resilience. Accordingly, we can expect:

Proposition 5.1A: Rural counties are associated with lower overall resilience.

Proposition 5.1B: Rural counties have higher community capital and ecological resilience.

External Funding and Support

County emergency management budgets are lean. A recent nationwide survey of county governments found the average budget for emergency management offices is $33,000.[40] Another survey reported that lack of funding was cited as the biggest homeland security issue by 52 percent of counties; this was followed by personnel limitations mentioned by 40 percent of county respondents.[41] A central task of emergency managers, therefore, is to enhance their office's fiscal capacity by securing external funding and support.[42] Funding can help support disaster management programs and initiatives. Therefore, we can expect:

Proposition 5.2: Counties with grant funding have higher resilience ratings.

Disaster Severity

Severe disasters disable a community's infrastructure, make the best plans ineffective, displace community members, disrupt economies, and destroy natural barriers. Responding to very intense storms and emergencies often requires external assistance and relies on volunteer and nonprofit group efforts. Once the initial response has been executed communities are left with the task of cleaning up, rebuilding, and recovering economically and emotionally. This task can be daunting and challenging. Many community members chose not to rebuild in New Orleans, Louisiana following Hurricane Katrina;[43] after spending months away from their homes it was not feasible for some to return and restore structures wrecked by flood waters, covered in mold, mildew, and muck. Similarly, entire neighborhoods left Biloxi, Mississippi following Katrina when their homes were washed away by the storm surge.[44] Often financial calculations come into play, but dislocation is also an issue. Once relocated to another city, it is difficult for families to again uproot only to return to unpredictable, unstable situations in their home communities.

Businesses face many of the same decisions as families do in making choices about rebuilding following a severe disaster. Financial feasibility is a critical issue particularly for small organizations. Many small-scale shrimping and fishing operations were severely strained economically as a result of the *Deepwater Horizon* oil spill.[45] Communities also face fiscal challenges with restoring community structures and services. Rebuilding public infrastructure is costly and often requires considerable time to process assistance and execute contracts.[46]

Beyond the hurdles that exist in rebuilding related to financial feasibility, severe disasters negatively impact communities psychologically. Intense disasters can cause deep emotional scars on the individual and collective level. In addition, displacement of individuals and families following a severe disaster erodes community ties and support structures. In all, recovering emotionally, mentally, and psychologically takes time and in the interim can significantly deplete a community's capacities for disaster resilience. Given the negative impact severe disaster events can have on individuals, families, and communities, we can expect:

Proposition 5.3: Severe disaster events are associated with lower disaster resilience index scores.

State Context

The fourth explanation for variance in disaster resilience scores is state context. While the Gulf Coast has a shared history and experience with natural and manmade disasters, each state has a unique set of characteristics that condition the environment in which counties function. These include socioeconomic conditions, home rule institutions, and planning requirements. These are summarized in Table 5.3 and detailed below.

Table 5.3 Variation in State Context

	Alabama	Florida	Louisiana	Mississippi	Texas
Geographic Context					
Population (county average)	297,629	308,084	107,399	123,567	339,463
Land in square miles (county average)	1,410	820	633	590	845
Socioeconomic Conditions					
Income per capita (county average)	$33,456	$34,183	$35,548	$35,203	$35,815
Social vulnerability index (county average)	−2.09	0.39	−1.48	−1.40	0.82
Home Rule Institutions					
Home rule option available or applied to county government	X†	X	X	X	—
Planning Mandates					
Local govt. required to adopt state comprehensive plan	—	X	—	X	X
Local govt. required to create own comprehensive plan	—	X	—	—	—
State provides guidelines for local govt. comprehensive plan	X†	X	X†	X	—
Local govt. comprehensive plan must address natural hazards	—	X	—	—	—

Sources: County population and land data taken from U.S. Census (2010) and refers only to the counties included in the study sample; income per capita data were taken from the Bureau of Economic Analysis (2010); social vulnerability data were taken from the SoVI 2006–2010 developed by Cutter, et al. – higher scores indicate more vulnerability; home rule data were obtained primarily from the National Association of Counties report titled *County Authority* (2010); and the planning data source was the Insurance Institute for Business and Home Safety report titled *Survey of State Land-use and Natural Hazards Planning Laws* (2009).

Notes: The following legend is used: X = yes; — = no; and X† = limited.

Socioeconomic Conditions

Each Gulf Coast state has a unique set of social, economic, and geographic characteristics. These characteristics are indicative of the supply and demand available for the development of resilience capacities. Counties with large populations and geographic areas face greater demands. These demands can be offset by populations that are less vulnerable and have greater resources. As shown in Table 5.3, the states of Louisiana and Mississippi have the lowest average county populations. Not only do the counties in Alabama, Florida, and Texas have larger populations, they also have the greatest average land per square mile which implies that they manage considerable service demands. Alabama, however, is able to offset these demands as it has the lowest average county social vulnerability, but Texas is not because it has the highest average social vulnerability. Income per capita is too similar across the states to make assumptions about resilience capacity.

County Home Rule

In addition to socioeconomic conditions, political institutions including home rule may shape local resilience. Home rule refers to self-governance power given by states to counties and municipalities. States that give local governments the option to declare home rule permit them to make regulations suited to their populations' needs and demands as long as it does not conflict with or is preempted by state law.[47] On the other hand, states that do not grant this authority evoke Dillion's Rule which establishes that local government can exercise no more power than the state government mandates.[48]

Home rule has been applied by the Gulf States to varying degrees. The state of Alabama allows limited home rule for county governments through the Limited Self-Governance Act passed in 2005. If the citizens of a county government in Alabama approve a home rule charter,[49] then the county becomes responsible for and may make laws pertaining to: the abatement of weeds, control of animals and animal nuisances, control of litter and junkyards, the abatement of noise, unsanitary sewage or pollution, and creating a public nuisance.[50] This authority, however, only applies to unincorporated areas of the county. The lack of effective home rule for counties in Alabama has resulted in the proliferation of state legislation regarding local matters.[51]

Since the passage of the Home Rule Powers Act in 1973, the state of Florida permits counties to be governed by home rule charters.[52] Twenty of Florida's 67 counties have adopted home rule including eight in this study.[53] While home rule eases local governance in these counties, fiscal matters remain complicated. Florida retains state authority in taxation, granting limited power to counties to levy taxes including local discretionary sales surtaxes, tourist development taxes, local option food and beverage taxes, local option fuel taxes, municipal resort tax, and tourist impact tax.[54]

Louisiana is another state that allows home rule for parish governments; Dillion's Rule only applies to charter municipalities established prior to 1974.[55] Forty-one of the state's parishes operate as police juries; 23 parishes are governed by a home rule charter.[56] All but five of the 24 parishes included in this analysis have adopted home rule and have either a council-president, consolidated, or city-parish form of local government.

Home rule was made applicable to county governments in Mississippi with the County Reorganization Act of 1988, which amended the state code as follows: "The Board of Supervisors of *any* County shall have the power to adopt any orders, resolutions or ordinances with respect to County affairs, property and finances, for which no specific provision has been made by general law and which are not inconsistent with the Mississippi Constitution . . . "[57]

Texas, unlike the other Gulf Coast states, does not apply or offer the option of home rule to its county governments. Texas voters approved a constitutional amendment in 1933 to extend home rule authority to counties, but no county established home rule governance prior to the amendment's repeal in 1969.[58] Since 1912, municipalities in Texas with a population of 5,000 or more have the option to adopt a home rule charter which cannot contain provisions that conflict with state statutes.[59] This means that county governments in Texas have considerably less authority and power than municipal governments.

Home rule directly affects how local governments manage emergencies and disasters. Home rule provisions stipulate the authority counties have in hazard mitigation, particularly in the passage of zoning and building ordinances.[60] Additionally, home rule authority has influenced the development of local agencies involved in disaster management including criminal justice agencies and their role in emergency response and management.[61] Counties with authority to self-govern should be able to better manage disaster events and develop capacities for community disaster resilience.

Planning Requirements

In addition to socioeconomic conditions and home rule, there is wide variation in state directives for county planning. Given that planning is a critical aspect of emergency management and has been linked to the development of disaster resilience,[62] these differences may matter for county adaptive capacities. As shown in Table 5.3, Florida is the only state in the Gulf Coast that has extensive plan requirements of local governments. It mandates that local governments officially adopt the state comprehensive plan, create their own comprehensive plan, and include a hazards component in the local comprehensive plan.[63] To accomplish this, the state of Florida does offer detailed guidelines for local governments. These mandates, while considerable, have improved local planning. Hazards scholar Samuel Brody compared local comprehensive plans in Florida from 1991 and 1999 and found that local comprehensive plan quality improved due to "policy-making momentum" or the policy legacy of a good plan precedent which is largely influenced by state mandates for planning.[64]

Planning mandates in Texas and Mississippi require that local government adopt the state comprehensive plan, but no guidelines are given.

Detailed guidelines, however, are provided to local governments in the state of Mississippi. Alabama and Louisiana also offer planning guidelines to local governments, but these guidelines are not as detailed and simply list a set of required or suggested components.[65]

Consideration of these three sets of state dynamics—socioeconomic conditions, home rule, and planning requirements—point to Florida as being the most conducive to the development of local capacities for resilience. While Florida may face considerable service demands, its planning requirements and home rule institutions may enable capacity-building. Additionally, Alabama seems favorable with low social vulnerability and some planning mandates. On the other hand, Texas seems to have an environment that may hinder the development of capacity as it has large service demands, few planning requirements, and no home rule for counties. Accordingly, we can expect:

Proposition 5.4A: State context will have varying effects on disaster resilience with counties in Alabama and Florida having the highest and Texas the lowest resilience scores.

Proposition 5.4B: Counties with home rule are associated with higher disaster resilience scores than those that do not have home rule.

Data and Methods

Data from multiple sources were collected to test the four propositions posed: 1) urban-rural context, 2) external assistance, 3) disaster severity, and 4) state context. The following discussion details all of the variables included in the regression model, including measurement, coding, and sources.

Urban-Rural County Context

To measure the urban-rural character of counties, variables were constructed using the Rural-Urban Continuum or Beale Codes from the United State Department of Agriculture.[66] The Rural-Urban Continuum Codes range from 1 to 9 and distinguish counties based on population size and adjacency to metropolitan areas. Because of the small number of cases analyzed, some of the categories were collapsed for the analysis resulting in six categories to represent the urban-rural character of counties. The first includes metropolitan counties[67] with a population of one million or more. Seventeen counties in the sample fall into this group. The second category includes metropolitan counties with a population of 250,000 to one million; 18 counties fall in this class. The third group is comprised of metropolitan counties with a population less than 250,000 which is characteristic of 13 counties in the sample. The fourth group includes nonmetropolitan but urban counties with populations of 20,000 or more while the fifth category includes urban counties with a population of 2,500 to 19,999. There are 10 counties that fall into the fourth category and 14 in the fifth group. The final category includes completely rural counties with population less than 2,500; there are three counties that fit this description in the sample.

Five of the six urban-rural categories are included in the model as dummy variables to determine if a county's urban-rural character influences its resilience. Given that the second category of counties with a population of 250,000 to one million is most common in the sample analyzed—18 counties have populations in this range, it is the category excluded for comparison. The coefficients of the other categories, therefore, will indicate higher or lower resilience in comparison for this category of metropolitan counties.

External Assistance and Support

While there are multiple channels of external assistance and support available to county governments, FEMA grant programs are some the most widely utilized and, therefore, comparable across the cases. FEMA has multiple grant programs to assist county-level governments including Public Assistance (PA) grants to aid counties after a disaster event as well as the Hazard Mitigation Grant Program (HMGP) to promote mitigation measures following a disaster declaration. Both the PA and HMGP grant programs are authorized under the Stafford Act and Disaster Mitigation Act of 2000. PA grants may be used for emergency work including debris removal and emergency protective measures such as warning devices, search and rescue, security forces, temporary levee construction, emergency repairs, and provision of shelters, food, water, and ice.[68] They can also be used for permanent work which involves the repair or replacement of roads and bridges, water control such as dams and levees, buildings, utilities including power generation and distribution facilities as well as water treatment plants, and parks including beaches. Most repairs and replacement under public assistance grants stipulate "pre-disaster" condition or capacity, but some upgrades are eligible to be in compliance with building codes and standards.[69] HMPG funding, however, can be used to enhance properties or pursue projects that enhance long-term mitigation, including the wind retrofitting of building structures and the acquisition of high-risk property.

To measure external assistance, a variable was constructed to report the total number of projects funded by FEMA PA grants by county from the time period 1998–2012.[70] This covers disaster projects from Storm Charley (1998) to Hurricane Isaac (2012) and includes permanent work projects only—those that do not involve debris removal and emergency response. This should capture those projects completed to improve the capacity of the community, not simply to respond to the disaster event. A second variable is included to represent the total number of Hazard Mitigation Grant Program projects awarded to each county.[71] This variable represents the total number of HMGP projects from 1989 to 2011.

Disaster Intensity

Two variables are used to measure disaster intensity.[72] The first is hurricane maximum property damage caused by hurricane events from 2002–2011 in millions of dollars. This data was obtained from SHELDUS.[73] For some counties this variable will reflect damages incurred by Hurricane Katrina; for others this reflects damages from Hurricanes Irene and Dennis as well as other tropical cyclone events.

Tornado maximum intensity is the second measure of disaster intensity. This variable is measured as the maximum Fujita-scale (F-scale) value recorded for tornado events during the time period 2002–2011. The F-scale ranges from 0 to 5 and indicates the degree of intensity of the storm and its associated property damage. Zero corresponds to a storm with winds less than 73 miles per hour and light damage while five refers to a storm with winds 261 to 318 miles per hour and incredible property damage.[74] This information was obtained from NOAA's National Weather Service Storm Prediction Center.[75]

State Context

It was proposed above that a state's home rule institutions as well as its socioeconomic, geographical, and institutional context should influence the development of adaptive capacities on the county level. A variable for home rule is included in the analysis. It is measured as a dummy variable, coded as 1 for those counties with home rule and 0 for those without home rule. Data was obtained from the National Association of Counties and supplemented with information from the Police Jury Association of Louisiana[76] and the Florida Association of Counties.[77] Because Alabama allows only a very limited form of home rule, the counties from this state are not considered home rule in the analysis.[78]

While measuring home rule is fairly straightforward, capturing state context is more difficult. The state differences detailed in Table 5.3 do not directly translate into analyzable variables. This is largely because many of these factors do not vary by county but by state. Therefore, state dummies are included in the model to represent these dynamics. While rudimentary, these variables should reflect the varied socioeconomic and institutional climate in which counties operate.[79] Because Florida is relatively more advanced institutionally due to its planning mandates than the other states in the sample, it is excluded from the model. All of the coefficients of the state variables, therefore, are relative to the state of Florida.

Method

There are 11 dependent variables analyzed in separate regression analyses. These include the adaptive capacities for disaster resilience index, which ranges from 0 to 6, as well as its components—social resilience, community capital, economic resilience, institutional resilience, infrastructure resilience, and ecological resilience—that range from 0 to 1. Also analyzed are combinations of these components to represent the capacities most critical to each disaster stage, ranging 0 to 6. All of the dependent variables are interval level,[80] therefore, ordinary least squares regression analyses were conducted. Given the importance of state context in explaining variation in the environments in which counties function, the observations are not assumed independent but instead are clustered by state.

Results of Regression Analyses

The results of the regression analyses demonstrate some degree of support for each of the propositions indicating that the variation in resilience scores across the counties is explained by their urban-rural character, the number of grants they have been able to secure, the disaster intensity they have faced, and the state context in which counties exist. The results of the analyses are reported in Table 5.4.[81] The first column details the results of the analysis focused on the overall adaptive capacities for disaster resilience. Columns two through seven report the results of the analyses conducted to examine the individual components of the index, and columns eight through 11 list the results of the analyses focused on resilience capacities specific to each of the disaster phases.

Urban-Rural Context

As asserted in the first set of expectations, the regression analyses indicate that rural counties are associated with lower overall resilience. The results show that rural and smaller counties are significantly associated with resilience and its subcomponents. In the first model—adaptive capacities for disaster resilience—rural counties with populations less than 2,500 are statistically correlated with low resilience. The coefficient for this variable signifies that rural counties score 0.40 points lower than metro counties with populations of 250,000 to one million. In terms of predicted values this equates to a disaster resilience score of 2.87 for a rural county compared to a score of 3.27 for a nonrural county. This difference is the same as a one category gap in resilience ratings—for example, a rating of low for the rural county compared to moderate for counties not of this category.

The counties falling into the smallest three categories—rural with population less than 2,500, urban with a population of 2,500–19,999, and urban with populations less than 250,000—are statistically associated with lower economic, institutional, and infrastructure resilience. Social resilience is also lower among rural counties and those with populations less than 20,000. Moreover, the results indicate that these counties are associated with lower resilience capacities for disaster preparedness and response. Given that one-third of the counties in the sample fall into these categories, the challenges that smaller counties face in developing adaptive capacities is an important consideration in understanding disaster resilience.

Rural counties were expected to have higher community capital and ecological resilience. The regression results indicate that the urban-rural character of the county is not significantly related to community capital, but smaller and rural counties do have higher ecological resilience. The coefficients for all the counties with populations less than 250,000 signify

Table 5.4 Factors Associated with Adaptive Capacity for Disaster Resilience Scores

	Disaster Resilience Index	Adaptive Capacity for Resilience Index Components						Resilience Capacities Across Disaster Stages			
		Social	Comm. Capital	Economic	Institutional	Infrastructure	Ecological	Mitigation	Prep.	Response	Recovery
Urban/Rural County — Metro: ≥1 million pop	-0.111 (0.061)	0.016 (0.038)	-0.079 (0.048)	0.059 (0.028)	-0.016 (0.061)	3.07e-04 (0.054)	-0.090 (0.064)	-0.133 (0.134)	-0.072 (0.070)	-0.054 (0.077)	-0.142 (0.238)
Metro: <250,000 pop	0.091 (0.053)	-0.008 (0.029)	-0.003 (0.040)	0.008 (0.044)	0.029 (0.025)	0.005 (0.024)	0.061 (0.025)*	0.104 (0.078)	0.068 (0.052)	0.057 (0.027)*	0.087 (0.130)
Urban: ≥20,000 pop	-0.041 (0.073)	-0.039 (0.035)	0.000 (0.055)	-0.073 (0.025)*	-0.065 (0.024)*	-0.012 (0.013)	0.149 (0.035)**	-0.034 (0.073)	-0.276 (0.059)**	-0.225 (0.057)*	0.055 (0.112)
Urban: 2,500–19,999	-0.062 (0.093)	-0.040 (0.018)*	0.048 (0.039)	-0.060 (0.019)*	-0.125 (0.006)**	-0.042 (0.041)	0.158 (0.020)**	-0.024 (0.063)	-0.275 (0.088)*	-0.269 (0.126)*	0.157 (0.082)
Rural: <2,500 pop	-0.400 (0.099)**	-0.083 (0.009)**	0.022 (0.024)	-0.221 (0.052)**	-0.125 (0.021)**	-0.173 (0.014)**	0.180 (0.038)**	-0.271 (0.136)	-0.647 (0.164)**	-0.745 (0.103)**	-0.153 (0.148)
Grants — Public assistance	1.00e-04 (4.22e-05)*	4.10e-05 (-2.84e-05)	3.20e-05 (1.38e-05)*	-1.49e-05 (1.09e-05)	2.42e-05 (3.84e-05)	9.46e-05 (5.77e-05)	5.29e-06 (6.45e-05)	6.75E-06 (1.08e-04)	8.26e-05 (9.57e-05)	2.03e-04 (1.07e-04)	-2.79e-05 (1.49e-04)
Hazard mitigation	-0.002 (0.002)	3.57e-04 (7.58e-04)	-6.21e-04 (3.68e-04)	-1.09e-04 (3.16e-04)	6.07e-04 (2.07e-04)*	-5.44e-04 (8.15e-04)	-0.002 (0.001)*	-0.002 (0.003)	-2.46e-04 (0.002)	-0.001 (0.001)	-0.004 (0.003)
Disaster — Hurricane max	-1.07e-04 (3.76e-05)*	-1.78e-05 (1.25e-05)	-6.16e-05 (2.00e-05)	4.85e-06 (3.44e-06)	-1.43e-05 (1.89e-05)	-2.23e-05 (1.66e-05)	4.22e-06 (3.74e-05)	-1.02e-04 (6.00e-05)	-1.42e-04 (1.88e-05)**	-1.40e-04 (2.03e-05)**	-1.06e-04 (1.01e-04)
Tornado max	0.011 (0.006)	0.004 (0.003)	0.003 (0.008)	-0.017 (0.014)	0.001 (0.007)	0.016 (0.017)	0.004 (0.020)	-0.006 (0.024)	-0.026 (0.010)*	0.005 (0.028)	-0.009 (0.040)

(Continued)

Table 5.4 (Continued)

	Disaster Resilience Index	Adaptive Capacity for Resilience Index Components						Resilience Capacities Across Disaster Stages			
		Social	Comm. Capital	Economic	Institutional	Infrastructure	Ecological	Mitigation	Prep.	Response	Recovery
Home rule county	0.043 (0.036)	-0.008 (0.007)	0.005 (0.011)	-0.015 (0.008)	0.025 (0.027)	0.051 (0.027)	-0.014 (0.011)	-0.009 (0.059)	0.030 (0.072)	0.098 (0.051)	-0.049 (0.043)
Alabama	**0.160 (0.047)***	**0.065 (0.010)****	**0.084 (0.016)****	**0.035 (0.007)****	**0.065 (0.006)****	**0.059 (0.026)***	**-0.147 (0.043)***	0.121 (0.074)	**0.366 (0.033)****	**0.363 (0.024)****	0.054 (0.101)
Louisiana	0.088 (0.049)	0.024 (0.015)	**0.120 (0.023)***	-0.005 (0.011)	**-0.092 (0.014)****	**0.025 (0.009)***	0.014 (0.024)	0.074 (0.069)	0.047 (0.053)	**0.073 (0.027)***	**0.231 (0.085)***
Mississippi	**-0.487 (0.050)****	**0.092 (0.019)****	**-0.107 (0.026)***	-0.013 (0.032)	**-0.382 (0.041)****	0.016 (0.016)	**-0.094 (0.019)****	**-0.604 (0.050)****	**-1.003 (0.091)****	**-0.727 (0.063)****	-0.183 (0.083)
Texas	**-0.212 (0.018)****	**-0.031 (0.007)****	0.023 (0.011)	**-0.050 (0.005)****	**-0.267 (0.008)****	**0.038 (0.015)***	**0.074 (0.013)****	**-0.300 (0.032)****	**-0.586 (0.028)****	**-0.382 (0.007)****	0.025 (0.033)
Constant	**3.370 (0.041)****	**0.731 (0.016)****	**0.476 (0.034)****	**0.609 (0.023)****	**0.684 (0.026)****	**0.266 (0.009)****	**0.605 (0.010)****	**3.726 (0.039)****	**3.537 (0.065)****	**3.051 (0.060)****	**3.630 (0.052)****
N	75	75	75	75	75	75	75	75	75	75	75
R²	0.48	0.37	0.58	0.59	0.60	0.48	0.58	0.55	0.58	0.55	0.58

State Context comprises the rows Alabama, Louisiana, Mississippi, and Texas.

Notes: Ordinary least square regression analyses conducted; observations are clustered by state. Coefficients reported with robust standard errors in parentheses. Significant variables also in bold. Significance denoted as: * $p \leq 0.05$ (one-tailed test); ** $p \leq 0.01$ (one-tailed test).

that their ecological resilience scores are one-half to one standard deviation higher than metro counties with populations of 250,000 to one million. This indicates that the strain urban populations and development put on the environment may inhibit the development of resilience capacities.

External Assistance and Support

Capacities for resilience, however, can be enhanced with external assistance and funding. The results of the analyses point to public assistance grants as being significantly related to overall disaster resilience and specifically to community capital. The effects, however, are relatively small. The coefficient for the overall disaster resilience index model is 0.0001. This means that increasing public assistance grants by three standard deviation units (2,280 projects funded) boosts disaster resilience index scores by one standard deviation unit (0.25 points)—or, for example, a jump from moderate resilience to high resilience. The coefficient for the community capital model is 0.00003. Approximately a four and one-half standard deviation increase (3,420 projects funded) in public assistance grants is needed to improve community capital by one standard deviation (0.10 points). These increases in grant awards are unrealistic given that 75 percent of the counties analyzed were able to secure 550 grants or less in the 1998–2012 time period. The trends in the data underscore that this may be even more unattainable for small, rural counties. The group of counties in the top 25 percent (those that secured 551—4,647 project grants) is predominantly larger and more urbanized. Forty-two percent of this group are metro counties with a population of one million or more; 26 percent are metro counties with populations of 250,000 to one million; and 26 percent are urban counties with populations of 20,000 to 250,000. These data trends indicate that attention needs to be given to the underlying causes of lower grant awards, particularly among small, rural counties.

While hazard mitigation grants were not associated with overall disaster resilience, the variable was positive and significant in institutional resilience model. Again, the effect is small. The coefficient for the institutional resilience model is 0.0006, indicating that to improve institutional resilience by one standard deviation (0.17) requires approximately 22 HMGP grants per year or 285 grants total—a feat not achieved by any county in the sample. Nonetheless, it is notable that this variable emerges as significant for the specific component of resilience that it is intended to improve. Institutional resilience predominantly involves mitigation planning and activities—efforts facilitated by HMGP grants. This suggests that FEMA funding of hazard mitigation projects across the Gulf Coast has had success; however, it also cautions that mitigation alone is not enough and should be part of a bigger strategy for developing resilience capacities.

Disaster Intensity

While grant awards are positively associated with resilience, disaster intensity was correlated with lower resilience scores. Hurricane intensity was negatively and significantly related to overall disaster resilience. With a coefficient of -0.0001, the results indicate that a hurricane of sufficient intensity as to create $2.3 billion in property damage is associated with a one standard deviation (0.25 point) decrease in disaster resilience.

Hurricane intensity was also associated with decreases in capacities for preparedness and response. The coefficients for these models were larger than for overall disaster resilience indicating that the property damage associated with severe hurricanes can impede the development of capacities needed for these stages of the disaster. Tornado intensity is also negatively and significantly associated with capacities for preparedness.

State Context

Contrary to expectations, home rule was not significantly associated with disaster resilience in any of the models indicating that this specific institution when taking into account the other variables in the model does not account for differences in resilience capacities. Broader state context, however, did account for this variation as expected. Counties in Alabama were statistically distinct from those in Florida with higher overall resilience scores while Texas counties were statistically lower. Louisiana parishes did not emerge as statistically distinct from Florida counties for overall disaster resilience, and Mississippi counties were associated with the lowest resilience ratings. The results confirmed that state context matters for resilience.

CONCLUDING THOUGHTS ON ADAPTIVE CAPACITIES FOR RESILIENCE

The empirical analyses pointed out factors that we should consider in the evaluation of adaptive capacities for resilience including the county's urban-rural character, state context, disaster experience, and success in securing external grants. The results indicated that low resilience is associated with small, rural counties and those that have experienced very intense disasters in the past while high resilience is coupled with greater numbers of grants. Additionally, state context in Alabama, Florida, and Louisiana was found to be more favorable for the development of county adaptive capacities than in Mississippi and Texas.

These results should be interpreted broadly. We must remember that variables are only abstractions of the dynamics at play in reality. The regression results reveal correlations, not necessarily causation, because the indicators used to create the resilience indices and the variables in the regression models are taken from sources with inconsistent years. Rather, the results highlight factors that should be carefully considered in disaster

management policy-making and future studies of resilience to nurture the development of this resource.

SUMMARY

Adaptive capacity refers to the collective strengths and abilities to prevent, withstand, and manage a disaster event. An index of adaptive capacity for resilience has been developed in this chapter using multiple measures across six categories of resilience: social, community capital, economic, institutional, infrastructure, and ecological. Indices for the individual components of the resilience and the disaster phases were also constructed. These indices were analyzed spatially to determine patterns in adaptive capacity. Counties in Texas and Mississippi on average score moderate to low while the capacity scores in Louisiana and Alabama are moderate to very high. The counties in Florida exhibit varied adaptive capacities. The capacity scores were examined further through a regression analysis to test if a county's urban-rural character, success in securing external grants, disaster experience, and state context influenced its adaptive capacity. The results indicated that low adaptive capacity is associated with small, rural counties and those that have experienced very intense disasters while high capacity is coupled with a greater number of grants. Additionally, state context in Alabama, Florida, and Louisiana was found to be more favorable for the development of county adaptive capacities than in Mississippi and Texas.

DISCUSSION QUESTIONS

1. Are there additional indicators that should be used to measure adaptive capacities? Should some of the measures included in the adaptive capacity index calculation be excluded? If so, why?
2. Find your county or parish and note its adaptive capacity scores, do you agree with these assessments? Why or why not?
3. In addition to state mandates for planning, what else might incentivize the building of local adaptive capacities?
4. Given the finding that rural counties have lower adaptive capacity, what can be done to strengthen their resilience?
5. What do the overall trends in adaptive capacities across the Gulf Coast indicate for the future?

NOTES

1. Susan L. Cutter, Christopher G. Burton, and Christopher T. Emrich, "Disaster Resilience Indicators for Benchmarking Baseline Conditions," *Journal of Homeland Security and Emergency Management*, 7 (2010): 1–22.

2. Hazard Reduction and Recovery Center, *Advancing the Resilience of Coastal Localities: Developing, Implementing and Sustaining the Use of Coastal Resilience Indicators: A Final Report,* Walter G. Peacock, et al. (College Station: Texas A&M University, 2010).

3. See Table 9 for a list of indicators used to construct the CDRI in *Advancing the Resilience,* 33–4.

4. Ibid.

5. Ibid, 21; Cutter, Burton, and Emrich, "Disaster Resilience," 6.

6. Susan L. Cutter, et al., "A Place-Based Model for Understanding Community Resilience to Natural Disasters," *Global Environmental Change,* 18 (2008): 598–606.

7. *Advancing the Resilience.*

8. Cutter, Burton, and Emrich, "Disaster Resilience."

9. Barry Flanagan, et al., "A Social Vulnerability Index for Disaster Management," *Journal of Homeland Security and Emergency Management,* 8 (2011): 1–22; Susan L. Cutter, Bryan J. Boruff, and W. Lynn Shirley, "Social Vulnerability to Environmental Hazards," *Social Science Quarterly,* 84 (2003): 242–61.

10. This indicator is calculated differently than Cutter, Burton, and Emrich, "Disaster Resilience." Cutter, Burton, and Emrich focus on educational equity, measured as the percent of the population with college education to the percent of the population with no high school diploma. They position this indicator negatively affects resilience. While inequalities of any kind can impede the development of resilience, measuring educational equity in this manner can penalize counties with high educational attainment. Therefore, this study focuses on educational attainment rather than equity.

11. Data at the time of the construction of this index were not available from the US Census on the county level for the population over 65 years of age.

12. Cutter, Burton, and Emrich, "Disaster Resilience" also include in their index the indicator innovation, measured as the percent of the population employed in creative class occupations. The creative class thesis put forth by Richard Florida contends that those employed in occupations that require critical thinking, including engineers, scientists, researchers, educators, and artists, promote economic growth and innovation within their cities. This thesis, however, has been largely criticized. Studies have shown that the innovation and economic growth purported to be associated with the creative class has not materialized (e.g., Michele Hoyman and Christopher Faricy, "It Takes a Village: A Test of the Creative Class, Social Capital, and Human Capital Theories," Urban Affairs Review, 44 (2009): 311–33; Andy C. Pratt, "Creative Cities: The Cultural Industries and the Creative Class," Geografiska Annaler, 90 (2008): 107–17; Stephen Rausch and Cynthia Negrey, "Does the Creative Engine Run? A Consideration of the Effect of Creative Class on Economic Strength and Growth," *Journal of Urban Affairs,* 28 (2006): 473–89.) Therefore, this indicator was excluded from the resilience index.

13. Timothy Beatley, *Planning for Coastal Resilience: Best Practices for Calamitous Times,* (Washington, DC: Island Press 2009).

14. Jerome H. Kahan, Andrew C. Allen, and Justin K. George, "An Operational Framework for Resilience," *Journal of Homeland Security and Emergency Management* 6 (2009): 1–48; Philip Buckle, "Assessing Social Resilience," in *Disaster Resilience: An Integrated Approach,* ed. Douglas Paton and David Johnston (Springfield, IL: Charles C Thomas Publisher Ltd., 2006) 88–103.

15. Francis L. Edwards, "All Hazards, Whole Community: Creating Resiliency," in *Disaster Resilience: Interdisciplinary Perspectives*, ed. Naim Kapucu, Christopher V. Hawkins, and Fernando I. Rivera (New York: Routledge, 2013), 21–48.

16. Adam Rose, "Defining and Measuring Economic Resilience to Disasters," *Disaster Prevention and Management* 13 (2004): 307–14.

17. Dennis S. Mileti, *Disasters by Design: A Reassessment of Natural Hazards in the United States* (Washington, DC: Joseph Henry Press, 1999).

18. Beatley, *Planning*; Buckle, "Assessing."

19. Thomas A. Birkland, "Federal Disaster Policy: Learning, Priorities, and Prospects for Resilience," in *Designing Resilience: Preparing for Extreme Events*, ed. by Louise K. Comfort, Arjen Boin, and Chris C. Demchak (Pittsburgh: University of Pittsburgh Press, 2010), 106–28; C.E. Gregg and B.F. Houghton, "Natural Hazards," in *Disaster Resilience: An Integrated Approach*, ed. Douglas Paton and David Johnston (Springfield, IL: Charles C Thomas Publisher, Ltd. 2006), 19–37.

20. Cutter, Burton, and Emrich, "Disaster Resilience" also include the percent of housing units covered by FEMA's National Flood Insurance Program. This indicator does not vary for the sample included in this analysis because all counties studied participate in NFIP. Therefore it is not included in the calculation of the institutional resilience index.

21. David R. Godschalk et al., *Natural Hazard Mitigation: Recasting Disaster Policy and Planning* (Washington, DC: Island Press, 1999).

22. "Community Rating Fact Sheet," last accessed June 30, 2013, *http://www.fema.gov/library/viewRecord.do?id=2635.*

23. FEMA, Citizen Corps, *A Guide for Local Officials (Washington*, DC: FEMA, 2011), accessed June 30, 2013, *http://www.ready.gov/guides.*

24. "StormReady Guidelines," last accessed June 30, 2013, *http://www.storm ready.noaa.gov/guideline_chart.htm.*

25. David Johnston, Julia Becker, and Jim Cousins, "Lifestyles and Urban Resilience," in *Disaster Resilience: An Integrated Approach*, ed. Douglas Paton and David Johnston (Springfield, IL: Charles C Thomas Publisher Ltd., 2006), 40–64.

26. Coastal Recovery Commission of Alabama, *Roadmap for Resilience: Toward a Healthier Environment, Society and Economy for Coastal Alabama*, 2011, accessed June 30, 2013, *http://crcalabama.org/wp-content/uploads/2011/02/CRC-Report-02-2011.pdf.*

27. Robert O. Schneider, "Hazard Mitigation: A Priority for Sustainable Communities," in *Disaster Resilience: An Integrated Approach*, ed. Douglas Paton and David Johnston (Springfield, IL: Charles C Thomas Publisher Ltd., 2006), 66–86.

28. For a discussion of the reliability of the ecological measure, see Appendix I.

29. Schneider, "Hazard Mitigation."

30. "Severe Repetitive Loss Program," last accessed June 30, 2013, *http://www.fema.gov/severe-repetitive-loss-program.*

31. This is the method used by Cutter, Burton, and Emrich, "Disaster Resilience." See Appendix J for more details on this method.

32. There is missing data for the indicator floodplain population development across seven counties. For these cases, the average of the ecological resilience index was based on the mean of the other two indicators in this category.

33. See Table 9 for a list of indicators used to construct the CDRI. *Advancing the Resilience*, 33–4.

34. The resilience scores are reported in Appendix K.

35. The component index resilience scores are reported in Appendix L.

36. Birkland, "Federal Disaster."

37. The resilience scores for each disaster phase are reported in Appendix M.
38. Linda Labao and David S. Kraybill, "The Emerging Roles of County Governments in Metropolitan and Nonmetropolitan Areas: Findings from a National Survey," *Economic Development Quarterly*, 19 (2005): 245–59.
39. Bonnie Erikson, "Social Networks: The Value of Variety," *Contexts*, 2 (2003): 25–31.
40. National Center for the Study of Counties, *Emergency Management in County Government*, Wes Clark (Athens: Carl Vinson Institute of Government University of Georgia, 2006).
41. American City and County, *Homeland Security Outlook: Local Governments Reveal Purchasing Plans for 2006*, (2006), accessed June 30, 2013, *http://americancityandcounty.com/site-files/americancityandcounty.com/files/archive/americancityandcounty.com/mag/homelandsecurity06.pdf*.
42. David McEntire and Gregg Dawson, "The Intergovernmental Context," in *Emergency Management: Principles and Practices for Local Government, Second Edition*, ed. William L. Waugh Jr. and Kathleen Tierney (Washington, DC: International City/County Management Association, 2007), 65.
43. Beatley, *Planning*.
44. Subject #10, personal interview by Ashley D. Ross, Biloxi, Mississippi, February 20, 2011.
45. Subject #30, personal interview by Ashley D. Ross, Gulf Shores, Alabama, March 19, 2011.
46. The amount of time and paperwork involved in the recovery process was commonly cited by county emergency managers during personal interviews conducted March 15—June 21, 2012.
47. National Association of Counties, *County Authority: A State by State Report*, Matthew Sellers (Washington, DC: NACO, 2010), 6.
48. Alabama Policy Institute, "Home Rule in Alabama," last accessed June 30, 2013, *http://www.alabamapolicy.org/research/home-rule-in-alabama/*.
49. *County Authority*, 12.
50. "SB 129," last accessed June 30, 2013, *http://www.legislature.state.al.us/SearchableInstruments/2005RS/Bills/SB129.htm*.
51. "Home Rule," last accessed June 30, 2013, *http://www.encyclopediaofalabama.org/face/Article.jsp?id=h-1153*.
52. "Understanding Florida's Home Rule Power," last accessed June 30, 2013: *http://www.floridaleagueofcities.com/Resources.aspx?CNID=645*.
53. This includes Charlotte County, Hillsborough County, Lee County, Leon County, Miami-Dade County, Pinellas County, Sarasota County, and Wakulla County, according to Florida Association of Counties, "Charter County Information," last accessed June 30, 2013, *http://www.fl-counties.com/about-floridas-counties/charter-county-information*.
54. Frank P. Sherwood, *County Governments in Florida* (New York: iUniverse, 2008).
55. National Association of Counties, *Dillion's Rule or Not?*, Adam Coester (Washington, DC: NACO, 2004), 3.
56. "Parish Government Structure," last accessed June 30, 2013, *http://www.lpgov.org/PageDisplay.asp?p1=3010*.
57. "Home Rule," last accessed June 30, 2013, *http://www.macbanetwork.org/book/2004/home_rule.pdf*. Note that italics were added for emphasis.
58. Christopher Flores III et al., "Local Government Structure and Function in Texas and the United States," paper preapred for the Policy Research Project: Fiscal Capacity of Texas Cities, September 15, 1997, accessed June 30, 2013, *http://uts.cc.utexas.edu/~rhwilson/fiscalprp/structure.html*.
59. "Home Rule Charters," last accessed June 30, 2013, *http://www.tshaonline.org/handbook/online/articles/mvhek*.

60. Bruce B. Clary, "The Evolution and Structure of Natural Hazard Policies," *Public Administration Review,* 45 (1985) 20–8.
61. Robert J. Louden, "Who's in Charge Here? Some Observations on the Relationship Between Disasters and the American Criminal Justice System," in *Disciplines, Disasters, and Emergency Management,* ed. David A. McEntire (Springfield, IL: Charles C Thomas, Ltd., 2007), 224.
62. Birkland, "Federal Disaster;" Godschalk et al., *Natural Hazards.*
63. "General State Planning Legislation," last accessed June 30, 2013, *http://ofb .ibhs.org/content/data/file/statutes2009.pdf.*
64. Samuel Brody, "Are We Learning to Make Better Plans? A Longitudinal Analysis of Plan Quality Associated with Natural Hazards," *Journal of Planning Education and Research,* 23 (2003): 191–201.
65. "Survey of State Land-Use and Natural Hazards Planning Laws, 2009," last accessed June 30, 2013, *http://ofb.ibhs.org/page;jsessionid=549644DA1 BD1147F56D5BD822A8AE566?execution=e1s1&pageId= state_land_use.*
66. U.S. Department of Agriculture, Economic Research Service, *2003 Rural-Urban Continuum Codes* [Downloadable Data File] (Washington, DC: USDA, 2004), accessed April 5, 2012, *http://www.ers.usda.gov/data-products /rural-urban-continuum-codes.aspx#.Udj8CKzlf2w.*
67. The U.S. Department of Agriculture defines metropolitan as "one urbanized area of 50,000 or more population plus adjacent territory and have a high degree of social and economic integration."
68. "Categories of Work," last accessed June 30, 2013, *http://www.fema.gov/ public-assistance-local-state-tribal-and-non-profit/categories-work#catC*
69. Ibid.
70. FEMA Library, *FEMA Public Assistance Funded Projects Summary* [Downloadable Data File] (Washington, DC: FEMA, 2012), accessed June 30, 2013, *http://www.fema.gov/library/viewRecord.do?id=6299.*
71. FEMA Library, *FEMA Hazard Mitigation Program Summary* [Downloadable Data File] (Washington, DC: FEMA, 2012), accessed June 30, 2013, *http:// www.fema.gov/library/viewRecord.do?id=6293.*
72. Flooding is not included in the model because the data collected to measure maximum intensity of flood events was highly correlated to a statistically significant degree with the public assistance grants and hazard mitigation grant program variables. Additionally, a variable to capture the BP *Deepwater Horizon* oil spill is not included because the indicators used to create the adaptive capacity for disaster resilience index are largely from the year 2010 and before. Since the oil spill occurred April 2010, the effects of this event are not captured in the resilience scores.
73. Hazards & Vulnerability Research Institute, *The Spatial Hazard Events and Losses Database for the United States, Version 10.0* [Online Database] (Columbia, SC: University of South Carolina, 2012), accessed September 5, 2012, *http://www.sheldus.org.*
74. NOAA, "Fujita Tornado Damage Scale," last accessed June 30, 2013, *http:// www.spc.noaa.gov/faq/tornado/f-scale.html.*
75. National Oceanic and Atmospheric Administration, *Storm Prediction Center Severe Weather GIS* (SVRGIS) [Online Database] (Norman, OK: Storm Prediction Center, 2012), accessed October 5, 2012, *http://www.spc.noaa .gov/gis/svrgis/.*
76. "Parish Government Structure."
77. "Charter County Information," last accessed June 30, 2013, *http://www.fl -counties.com/about-floridas-counties/charter-county-information.*
78. Analyses were conducted coding the Alabama counties as home rule; the results were substantively the same.

79. The state dummy variables also capture other state-level dynamics not discussed in this chapter. For example, state culture may be reflected. On this, see: Christopher L. Dyer and James R. McGoodwin, "Tell Them We're Hurting: Hurricane Andrew, the Culture of Response, and the Fishing Peoples of South Florida and Louisiana," in *The Angry Earth: Disasters in an Anthropological Perspective,* ed. Anthony Oliver-Smith and Susanna M. Hoffmann (New York: Routledge, 1999), 213–31.

80. The variables are interval level because the raw index scores (not the standardized z-scores prepared for the maps) are used.

81. Descriptive statistics for variables in the model are available in Appendix N.

6 Exploring the Adaptive Process of Resilience across the Gulf Coast

"Disaster recovery is the least understood aspect of emergency management among both scholars and practitioners," noted hazards scholar Gavin Smith in *Planning for Post-Disaster Recovery*.[1] Some of our lack of understanding is due to the inherent qualities of the recovery process. It is not linear, does not occur within specific bounds of time or physicality, and is overall a messy process. Resilience promises, however, that despite the complications posed by this process, we can create positive changes in a community following a disaster event. To accomplish these changes on a local level requires commitment to the adaptive process of resilience. This process is exemplified by four attributes: improvisation, coordination, engagement of the community, and endurance. This chapter traces these qualities through a case study of one community's recovery from the BP *Deepwater Horizon* oil spill. Also explored is the aspect of coordination, specifically how local administrative and political elites facilitate coordination to develop disaster resilience.

THE ADAPTIVE PROCESS

The adaptive process takes place after a disaster has occurred. The initial response to a disaster largely relies on pre-developed plans and arrangements for emergency response to the event. A community's adaptive capacities—its social, economic, institutional, infrastructure, and ecological strengths—determine how well it is able to respond to a disaster. Often disasters degrade, at least temporarily, a community's capacity. Therefore, the adaptive process takes place once the initial shock of the event dissipates and community capacity is somewhat restored. In this space, there is the opportunity for coordination to meet short-term demands brought on by the event by connecting resources with needs through collaborative networks, not command-and-control. It also invites citizen and private partners to participate in long-term recovery planning and efforts, seeking to create a new and possibly improved environment.

There are four attributes that characterize the adaptive process. The first is *improvisation*. The adaptive process of resilience begins when local solutions are initiated to meet local needs post-disaster. Impromptu action to restore functioning and rebuild the community tends to be more flexible and needs-driven. The second is *coordination.* Connecting resources to meet response and recovery needs post-disaster is an imperative part of the adaptive process. Coordination is needed to meet basic needs following a disaster event, and collaboration among stakeholders is imperative in the recovery process for positive, sustainable solutions to be implemented.

The third attribute of the adaptive process is *engagement of the community.* Involvement of the community and key stakeholder groups in decision-making related to recovery projects is needed to create outcomes that are sustainable and that adapt to—ideally, improve upon—the post-disaster environment. Engagement of broad community groups should help produce better solutions as a diverse set of interests is represented. The fourth is *endurance.* Recovery solutions created in the post-disaster context are often put together piecemeal over extended periods of time. To ensure that the outcomes created continue beyond the disaster event, the lessons learned must take on some quality of endurance. Formalizing programs and plans into policy is one way that endurance can be achieved. In other circumstances, a lesson learned may be so profound that it becomes part of the community's collective memory, and thus part of social norms and behavior in the post-disaster environment.

Not all of these attributes may be evident; certainly there is not "one size fits all" in terms of how the adaptive process unfolds. It works on multiple levels, horizontally across citizen groups and vertically connecting municipal governments to state and federal agencies. It also is a dynamic process unfolding over time and to varying degrees. This means that it is a process that can be difficult to trace. Nonetheless, it is important that we study how it manifests within communities so that we may better understand how resilience develops. The following case study looks at an example of the adaptive process that occurred in Baldwin County, Alabama following the BP *Deepwater Horizon* explosion and oil spill.

A Case Study: The Coastal Resiliency Coalition of Baldwin County, Alabama

On April 20, 2010 the BP-operated Macondo 252 oil well exploded off the coast of Louisiana, spewing crude oil into the Gulf of Mexico.[2] The well's drilling rig, *Deepwater Horizon,* caught fire later the same day killing 11 of its 126 person crew. Two days later the rig sunk, and oil continued to gush into the Gulf for a total of 87 days until the well was successfully capped on July 15. By that time, nearly five million barrels or over 200 million gallons of crude oil had been released into the Gulf; this was nearly 20 times the volume associated with the Exxon *Valdez* tanker accident of 1989. The BP oil spill contaminated 250 square miles of the ocean affecting the states of Texas, Louisiana, Mississippi, Alabama, and Florida including 53 counties and parishes. The spill also captured national and international media attention as the long struggle to cap the well threatened the ecological and economic health of the region.

In the days following the BP *Deepwater Horizon* explosion concerned elected officials and business leaders from Baldwin County, Alabama met together at a local realty office to brainstorm ideas of how to manage this unprecedented event; of particular importance for this group were the economic and health impacts of the spill. This meeting included "the mayors of Gulf Shores, Orange Beach and Foley, as well as representatives of the Alabama Gulf Coast Chamber of Commerce, South Baldwin Chamber of Commerce, Gulf Shores/Orange Beach Tourism, Faulkner State Community College and the Baldwin County Economic Development Alliance."[3] From this gathering emerged the Coastal Resiliency Coalition (CRC); the meeting place became known as the "War Room" as this organization led a fight for the survival of local businesses and economies.

The primary focus of the CRC was initially to help businesses withstand the economic shock of the oil spill and ultimately to restore economic well-being and growth to the tri-city area including Gulf Shores, Foley, and Orange Beach. Businesses in Baldwin County rely directly or indirectly on tourism;[4] the county generates a quarter of the state's tourism revenue.[5] This revenue dropped significantly following the oil spill. Baldwin County reported a 9 percent drop in tourist/travel related employment in 2010 compared to 2009—the equivalent of 2,532 jobs. In addition, overall tourism earnings decreased by 8 percent totaling over $76 million in the same year.[6] The oil spill coincided with the economic downturn that negatively affected the entire nation. From the perspective of a Gulf Shores city council member, already vulnerable businesses that had "scrimped and saved and hung on" during the recession were ready for the summer tourist season only to "open their doors for business to find no customers because of this oil spill."[7]

To address this economic loss, the CRC met in the War Room twice a week, and in between meetings, focus groups were held with local stakeholder groups including restaurateurs, small business owners, and realtors. According to the same city council member, these meetings exposed that local businesses "don't communicate with each other, even restaurants don't communicate with other restaurants about what problems they may be having in common. From a city's point of view, you don't usually hear from the business community unless you're doing something they don't like. Then they ban together. They go to a meeting. But they don't ban together and become proactive."[8] The CRC provided a forum for local businesses to join together and make plans to address the economic impact of the oil spill. It also connected businesses to important resources that facilitated economic recovery.

In the aftermath of the oil spill, multiple business and employment assistance groups set up local offices in the Baldwin County area. These included the Small Business Association, the Alabama Career Center, and the University of South Alabama's Small Business Development Center.[9] The CRC in conjunction with the South Baldwin Chamber of Commerce brought these groups together to form the Baldwin Business Support Center (BSC). The BSC was focused on helping small business owners file claims with BP and learn strategies for expanding their product line, training employees, and finding new markets in an effort to recover from economic loss associated with the oil spill.[10]

The BSC operated "on faith" initially with limited support from various revenue streams;[11] more substantial funding was secured in 2011 with a $50,000 grant from BP and $200,000 award from the Community Foundation of South Alabama.[12] A year into operations, BSC began to intently focus on promoting business sustainability by offering assistance with the development of business plans and providing programs to teach techniques for running a "lean enterprise."[13]

These programs continued to expand in the following years with a focus on three "C's—counseling, connecting and competing—all with the goal of making the coastal business community more resilient before the next crisis comes," according to director Rick Miller.[14] The BSC counsels business owners to develop business and marketing plans in efforts to improve their operations.[15] The center also works to connect local businesses with banks for financing as well as state and federal governments for assistance programs, and it offers workshops on financial modeling and budgeting that help local businesses increase their competitiveness and profit margin. The BSC continues its operations today supported through a partnership between Alabama Gulf Coast Area Chamber of Commerce, South Baldwin Chamber of Commerce, Faulkner State Community College, and Baldwin County Economic Development Agency.[16]

Beyond its efforts with the BSC, the CRC worked with local groups in the region to rebrand the Gulf Coast. Developing marketing strategies and taking an active role in communications were critical activities of the CRC as a flurry of media attention was focused on the Gulf Coast and on Alabama beaches in particular. One CRC activist and Gulf Shores city council member reflected: "The spill was in late April; the press kept on saying that oil would be on Alabama beaches that weekend. But it wasn't. There was not anything here until after Memorial Day. But the media damaged and cost us business in May."[17] Oil did wash ashore in Baldwin County in June, and the beaches were spotted with tar balls. This raised serious health concerns that the CRC monitored carefully. Those active in the coalition, however, became frustrated with the proliferation of mixed messages circulated by national media; in particular, tensions were high over those that focused on environmental and health testing conducted by outside experts reporting directly to research entities or media outlets without first communicating with local leaders.[18] Instead of relying on these sources, the CRC took cues from local leadership that sought out the expertise and guidance of state health officials.[19]

One big health concern was the safety of Gulf seafood. These concerns were quickly answered with scientific testing. In late August of 2010 state marine scientists reported that Gulf fish and shrimp were safe to eat.[20] Two months later the Federal Department of Agriculture and the National Oceanic and Atmospheric Administration released a statement that all Gulf seafood samples tested within safety thresholds.[21] Despite these reports, negative perceptions of Gulf seafood lingered. In an effort to recast the Alabama coast, the CRC in conjunction with Gulf Shores and Orange Beach Tourism hosted "Supper on the Sand" on April 17, 2011, a date marking the one year anniversary of the oil spill.[22] The event took place at Gulf State National Park Beachside Pavilion to highlight the clean beaches and safe waters. It was a celebration of recovery from the spill and featured Gulf seafood, which was praised by attendee celebrity chef Guy Fieri. As tourism increased the following summer, the CRC breathed a sigh of relief but knew there was still work to be done.

Much of the continuing efforts of the CRC have involved addressing mental health issues of the community related to the oil spill. In the months following the spill, local fishermen and businessmen were under acute stress; this was linked to the suicide of one local boat captain.[23] The CRC recognized that this was an issue as critical as, and tangential to, economic recovery. The coalition teamed up with the Alabama Department of Mental Health's Project Rebound, an organization established after Hurricane Ivan, to offer crisis counseling to communities following a disaster.[24] The CRC kept track of call-ins to Project Rebound[25] and brought together mental health officials and experts in the region to help supplement counseling efforts.[26] This included extending counseling services to local schools to address stress experienced by children of families that were experiencing financial and emotional issues following the oil spill.[27] The coalition also remained focused on helping those economically displaced by the spill to find jobs. "The best way you can relieve somebody's stress is to get them a good-paying job. And that gives them confidence in the future," remarked Bob Higgins the CRC chairman in 2011, a year after the spill.

In 2012 the CRC gained status as a 501(C) (3) nonprofit organization.[28] Its efforts to help local businesses survive and rebound from the oil spill have largely been realized. Tourist revenue set record highs in 2012 generating $40 million more in taxable lodging revenue than 2011.[29] Retail sales were also 8 percent higher in 2012 than 2011. Additionally, Baldwin County has experienced recent population growth according to the latest census.[30] It is also the focus of new development projects to restore part of a 1.6 mile section of the shoreline and to rebuild and expand the convention center at the Gulf State National Park.[31] These projects were announced by Alabama's governor in May 2013 and will be funded with BP oil spill fines distributed through the Restore Act passed by Congress in 2012.[32] In all, the economic future of Baldwin County looks bright. But if it were to encounter challenges, another economic shock or downturn, the CRC will mobilize again. Donna Watts, president of the South Baldwin Chamber, characterized the coalition's role as: "It's like a family having a crisis plan. If the house catches on fire, where are we going to meet? Everybody knows that when the crisis happens, the CRC or the War Room is where we go to help each other and to communicate thoroughly and find resources."[33]

The Four Attributes of the Adaptive Process as Related to the Coastal Resiliency Coalition

The establishment and ongoing operations of the Coastal Resiliency Coalition (CRC) is an example of the adaptive process of resilience at work. The CRC emerged in the aftermath of the BP *Deepwater Horizon* oil spill. The spill was an unforeseen and unprecedented disaster. The establishment of the CRC in the early days of the spill was the product of improvised action on part of local business and elected leadership. No local plans existed on how to deal with a disaster event of this type and scale; existing emergency response frameworks were better suited for hurricane events. Therefore, the simple act of calling an impromptu meeting to identify local issues and brainstorm local solutions was the first step in building a resilient response and recovery to the spill.

The CRC also exhibited a high degree of coordination and collaboration. It had the primary goal of connecting local businesses with the resources needed to help them survive the spill. The coalition coordinated the establishment of the Baldwin Business Support Center which effectively linked existing state and local employment and business assistance agencies and programs in a central location. It also collaborated with mental health agencies to expand local services to schools and parts of the community in need and coordinated with local chambers of commerce, businesses, and municipal governments to promote economic diversity and new marketing strategies for the region. The strength of the coalition has been its ability to facilitate collaboration by uniting resources and services with common goals to address the needs of the local community.

The coalition engaged the community in multiple ways in its efforts to address local economic well-being. Leaders of the coalition were assigned to meet with stakeholder groups including restaurateurs, realtors, and hotel owners to determine what the community needed. Additionally, the coalition invited the input and expertise of local academic institutions and brought together multiple local and statewide business associations. It also relied on its active members to represent citizen needs. Given that leaders of the group included elected city council members, chamber and economic development organization presidents, much of its community engagement took place outside coalition meetings.[34]

Finally, the CRC has exhibited endurance. It gained status as a nonprofit organization, and the Business Support Center continues its operations today. While the coalition has tapered off its activity, meeting less and no longer issuing a newsletter, its presence in the community is still felt.[35] It continues to promote economic growth and small business sustainability. Moreover, there is an understanding among community members that the

CRC can be mobilized again to coordinate local efforts in the event of a future crisis.[36] Its lasting legacy, therefore, is more a method of collaboration among concerned local citizens and leaders than an organizational structure. Its membership may change; its War Room may even move to another physical location, but its mission to connect resources to meet local needs will endure.

THE ADAPTIVE PROCESS AND COORDINATION

While the four attributes of improvisation, coordination, engagement of the community, and endurance are indicative of the adaptive process of resilience, it is not necessary for all to manifest to identify a community as "resilient." Some of these attributes may be present while others are not. For example, improvised action may not be marked in a community that has extensively developed recovery plans. Such a community may follow prescribed courses of action following a disaster, but this does not detract from their resilience. Some contend that this is actually more resilient.[37] While improvisation need not be present in all decision-making there is a general consensus that all adaptive processes leading to resilient outcomes will be accompanied by some degree of coordinated collective action.

Coordinating Collective Action

Collective action is at the heart of the adaptive process, but on its own it is not enough to produce resilient outcomes. Some type of central coordination is needed that local administrative and political elites can facilitate. Hazards scholars Douglas Paton and Li-ju Jang elaborate on this:

> As people enter the response phase, resilience will reflect the ability of people to work together to generate solutions to emergent problems and implement them using their collective expertise and resources. As the response phase progresses, resilience will increasingly involve interaction between communities and societal-level institutions (e.g., emergency response) and will be influenced by the degree to which emergency response agencies empower community action (e.g., mobilizing and coordinating community volunteers to assist in recovery efforts).[38]

Coordination can be understood as *actions taken to organize or facilitate connections among various groups and/or resources so that they may work together to achieve specific outcomes or goals.* Coordination is critical in the adaptive process because it connects collaborative decision-making and collective action that occur on multiple levels within a community. In the words of Paton and Jang it "empowers community action." Certainly coordination of the community can be taken up by various leaders (e.g., church clergy, president of a neighborhood association). Past disasters have shown that nonprofits and emergent groups often take ownership of recovery in different areas.[39] While this leadership can be incredibly important for recovery, local administrative and political elites are best positioned to organize community efforts on a broad scale. This is largely due to the authority and responsibility vested in these positions that make them legally responsible for governance. During any emergency, citizens look to top executives for leadership.[40]

Public administration scholars Scott Somers and James Svara caution, however, that "to be meaningful, leadership must be more than symbolic; it must ensure effective coordination of response and recovery efforts."[41] This implies that emergency managers and local elected officials are well positioned to lead response and recovery efforts in communities where they have established good relationships. Hazards scholar Gavin Smith addresses this as "integration" or the strength and endurance of relationships. He proposes that integration is developed on two levels: 1.) *horizontal* to refer to relationships among "local government officials, quasi-governmental organizations, business owners, local financial institutions, the media, community and emergent groups, and area residents;"[42] and 2.) *vertical* to refer to connections with groups that provide external assistance, including state and federal government as well as corporations, national lending institutions and insurance companies.[43] A community with weak horizontal integration lacks stakeholder involvement to create innovative solutions and instead may be engrossed in group conflict.[44] Weak vertical integration may limit a community's ability to fully capitalize on external assistance and direct how external funding will be allocated.[45] Therefore, the coordination local administrative and political elites facilitate is critical for the adaptive process as it strengthens horizontal and vertical integration of the community. Examples of specific types of activities these officials coordinate as well as the stakeholder groups involved are summarized in Table 6.1 and touched upon in the following discussion.

Role of Emergency Managers in Coordination

From the 1950s to 1970s emergency managers were civil defense directors and their focus was on command-and-control or authority-driven management based on hierarchical designations of responsibility.[46] Since then the field has become typified by collaborative management that emphasizes integrating a wide range of organizations to "build the strongest possible team and to use it effectively to create a disaster-resilient community."[47] In this regard, emergency managers are responsible for the coordination of multiple groups across the four stages of disasters. They lead the design and implementation of policies and programs to reduce risk to hazards and prepare communities for effective response and recovery to emergency and disaster events. As one county emergency manager interviewed for this study put it, "My job is to be a conductor. I have to have general knowledge in all areas and motivate our team to get the job done."[48]

Table 6.1 Coordination Activities by Emergency Managers and Local Elected Officials

Activity	Stakeholders Typically Involved	Coordinators	Disaster Phase(s)
Assess vulnerabilities Evaluate community risk to hazard events so that issues may be identified and properly addressed.	Emergency management staff State and/or federal emergency management officials Planners and developers Experts: demographers, ecologists, economists, engineers	Emergency managers	Mitigation and recovery
Generate public awareness for disaster preparedness Educate the public on preparations needed for effective disaster preparedness.	Local media First and emergency responders School districts and universities officials Local service providers (health and utility) Local businesses and business groups Nonprofit and volunteer groups Public: individual citizens and groups	Emergency managers and to a lesser degree local elected officials	Mitigation
Planning Establish plans to reduce vulnerabilities and prepare community for hazard events. Includes land-use planning to reduce and/or prevent development in high-risk areas. Also includes recovery planning – both pre- and post-event – to establish frameworks for goals and procedures for reconstruction and the distribution of assistance.	Emergency management staff State and federal emergency management officials State transportation officials Local government officials and employees Neighboring local governments First and emergency responders School district and university officials Local service providers (health and utility) Planners and developers Local businesses and business groups Nonprofit and volunteer groups Military representatives Banking and finance institutions Insurance agency representatives	Emergency managers and local elected government officials	Mitigation, preparedness, and recovery

(Continued)

Table 6.1 (Continued)

Activity	Stakeholders Typically Involved	Coordinators	Disaster Phase(s)
Design standard operating procedures Establish plans and procedures regarding the human and material resources needed in case of an emergency event.	Emergency management staff State and federal emergency management officials State transportation officials Local government officials and employees Neighboring local governments First and emergency responders School district and university officials Local service providers (health and utility) Local businesses Military representatives	Emergency managers	Preparedness
Grant-writing Secure external funding for projects and programs to reduce vulnerabilities and rebuild after disaster events.	Emergency management staff State and/or federal agency representatives Local government officials and employees Local planners Nonprofit and volunteer groups	Emergency managers and local elected government officials	Mitigation and recovery
Developing communication regarding emergencies and disasters Dissemination of information regarding hazards in general or in reference to specific events.	Local, state, and national media State and federal emergency management officials First and emergency responders School districts and universities officials Local service providers (health and utility) Local businesses Nonprofit and volunteer groups Public: individual citizens and groups	Emergency managers and local elected government officials	All stages but particularly important in response stage
Collaboration with public-private partners Establish relationships with public and private groups to effectively match resources with needs.	Emergency management staff First and emergency responders School district and university officials Local service providers (health and utility) Local businesses and business groups Military representatives	Emergency managers and local elected government officials	All stages but critical in response and recovery

In the mitigation stage of disasters, policies to reduce vulnerabilities well before a disaster event occurs are developed. This requires assessment of local vulnerabilities by emergency management officials in collaboration with local government officials, planners, engineers, and environmentalists. Mitigation projects include a range of activities from the improvement of infrastructure to the buying of at-risk properties. Local emergency management officials lead the coordination of many of these efforts by securing funding then also guiding implementation of these works with local government authorities.

While mitigation is important, most emergency management activity focuses on disaster response. A study by disaster scholar Thomas Drabek found that emergency managers have better perceptions of disaster response with the use of more coordination strategies.[49] Coordination for response begins in the preparedness stage where plans and public awareness for emergencies and disasters are generated. Emergency managers organize and lead public awareness campaigns for disaster preparations. Key partners in this effort include local media, local government, as well as civic, business, and faith-based organizations. Citizen groups specially trained in emergency and disaster response, including CERTs, are also helpful in educating their members as are more informal groups such as neighborhood watches.[50] Emergency managers also work on establishing mutual aid agreements with neighboring local governments, school districts, and regional district councils. These agreements are a critical way to expand limited resources as they set up the sharing of personnel and equipment in the case of need.[51]

During preparedness, emergency managers also coordinate planning that incorporates key stakeholder groups in formulating responses to multiple contingencies. Planning not only outlines procedures for response in various areas (e.g., evacuation, search and rescue), it should also establish jurisdictional responsibilities in order to avoid confusion and conflict among groups with overlapping authority.[52] Planning to accomplish both requires extensive coordination. For example, emergency managers work with multiple entities to plan the details of response operations for evacuation and reentry during a disaster event. The depth of organization required for such preparedness plans is substantial. Planning for evacuation in St. Bernard Parish, Louisiana—a jurisdiction with a population just under 36,000[53]—brought in over a dozen groups including the parish fire and police departments, transit system, ambulance services, hospital system, and pet shelter.[54] Also involved were representatives from the local National Guard and the Governor's Office of Homeland Security and Emergency Preparedness. The plan involved congregating and registering evacuees in one area of the parish then busing them to a predesignated shelter in another part of the state whose facilities were reserved for and ready to meet the needs of the parish evacuees.

When a disaster strikes, the emergency managers take on the critical task of coordinating response efforts between first responders and local groups as well as with external agencies including governments and nonprofits.

This typically requires emergency managers to coordinate improvised efforts with nonprofit organizations as most plans prove to be working frameworks at best during actual disaster events. Initial response coordination is needed with multiple groups—local public service (i.e. electric, medical) providers, government and military representatives, nonprofits and Red Cross volunteers—to direct the evacuation of citizens, search and rescue efforts, and provide basic necessities such as food, water, ice, and shelter to first responders and citizens that have remained in the disaster-stricken area.

Once immediate needs are met during disaster response, coordination shifts into a role of matching resources with needs in the short-term and long-term recovery process. This involves organizing nonprofit and volunteer group efforts to assist in clean-up and rebuilding as well as the integration of stakeholders and citizens into recovery planning and decision-making. Additionally, emergency managers are central to the process of applying for and managing government and private sector grants for recovery and mitigation projects.

Role of Local Elected Officials in Coordination

Local elected officials approach disaster management much differently than emergency managers. They are connected to their constituents electorally, and, therefore, have responsibility and incentives to the represent the public's needs in local decision-making. These needs, however, must be prioritized in the resource-constrained environment of local governance. Pre-event mitigation and preparedness often take lower precedence than more immediate concerns including unemployment, crime, education, and public services.[55] Moreover, policies to regulate development of the private sector such as zoning and building codes can be contentious among elected officials as they perceive it as damaging to the economic interests of the public.[56] Therefore, much of the involvement of local elected elites, particularly municipal council members,[57] takes place during disaster recovery where they can shape the development of the community and meet their constituents' needs in tangible ways.

In the aftermath of disasters, mayors and city council members are very concerned with the restoration of the economy and future economic growth. The establishment of the Coastal Resiliency Commission in Gulf Shores, Alabama was motivated by these concerns, and mayors and city council members were key actors in the establishment and operations of this organization. As this case illustrates, local elected officials can effectively coordinate recovery programs that connect various groups across multiple sectors with citizens. Coordinating groups is often achieved by local elected officials through citywide or precinct meetings. These forums provide a space where local officials can share information and engage stakeholder groups. For instance, one council member in Gulfport, Mississippi interviewed for this study described the way he coordinated with his constituents during the BP oil spill:

I have my town hall meetings within my ward. I've got three different community centers in my ward, and I use the central community center of my ward . . . to keep my citizens abreast of what's going on. And also access WJZD . . . that's the radio station here in Gulfport [for public service announcements].[58]

Organizing community meetings contributes to the strengthening of horizontal integration. Horizontal ties are also developed with neighboring municipalities by local elected officials that lead efforts to establish mutual aid agreements. Local officials also establish vertical relationships as they are involved with securing funding from government and external agencies.[59]

Evaluation of Coordination Activities

Coordination is essential in translating local collective action to resilient outcomes. Emergency managers and municipal elected officials have key roles in this coordination. To better understand these roles the types and quality of coordination efforts local administrative and political elites are involved in are systematically analyzed using original survey data. This information was collected in 2011 and 2012 in the states of Alabama, Florida, Louisiana, Mississippi, and Texas. More than 50 emergency managers from counties and parishes across the Gulf Coast are represented in these responses, and responses from over 200 municipal elected officials including mayors and council members across 122 municipalities are included in the dataset.[60]

The involvement of county emergency managers in various disaster management tasks is illustrated in Figure 6.1. Depicted are the responses to the survey question, *How routinely would you say you do the following?* a.) Grant writing, paperwork, and record-keeping; b.) Design standard operating procedures and other guidelines for various disaster scenarios; c.) Develop communication with citizens, first responders, public and private entities; d.) Work on collaboration with public and private partners; e.) Examine county vulnerabilities to assess risk; f.) Generate public awareness for disaster preparedness; g.) Work on zoning ordinances and other policies that steer development away from areas at high risk for flooding and wind damage; and h.) Engage the public or community organizations in disaster planning. Possible responses ranged from "almost never" (coded 1) to "often" (coded 3). The average rate of frequency is marked by a triangle with average frequency reported to the side. The length of the bars for each activity indicates the range (min to max values) of responses.

The data shows that the most frequent activities are grant writing/record-keeping/paperwork and collaboration with public and private partners (e.g., first responders, citizens, and public/private entities). Emergency managers surveyed are involved in these on almost a daily basis. This frequency of this involvement underscores the tension inherent to the job of emergency managers. On one hand they are coordinators; on the other hand, they

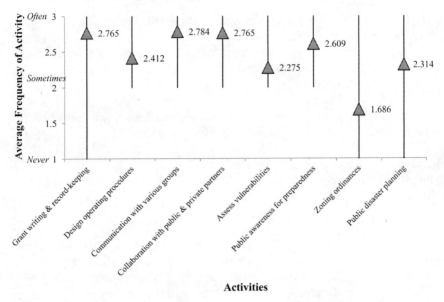

Activities

Figure 6.1   Average Frequency of Activities by County Emergency Managers

Source: Author's original surveys of county emergency managers.

Notes: The frequency of activities is denoted as: 1 = almost never, 2 = sometimes, and 3 = often. The lines represent the range of responses, and the triangles the average frequency for each category. The averages were calculated for 51 observations.

are bureaucrats. Coordination and collaboration with public and private partners develops horizontal integration and builds resilience from the bottom-up. Grant writing, record-keeping, and paperwork largely fulfill requirements mandated by federal and state agencies to be in compliance with emergency management operations. While many of these tasks are necessary (and beneficial as in the case of grant funding), they often compete for the organizational resources available, thereby, detracting from the collaboration that emergency managers can engender.

Developing communication with various groups is the second most frequent activity reported by survey participants. Following this, generating public awareness for preparedness, designing standard operating procedures, engaging the public in disaster planning, and assessing vulnerabilities are most frequent. The least frequent task is developing zoning ordinances. As the bars indicate, some respondents reported "almost never" taking part in the development of zoning ordinances. Some participants also responded "almost never" for grant writing and engaging the public in planning.

The involvement of municipal officials in various coordination activities is shown in Figure 6.2. The data shown reflect responses to the question that asks about their involvement with recent disasters while in office: *What action(s) were you involved with during response and recovery efforts?* The findings show that less than half the respondents reported any

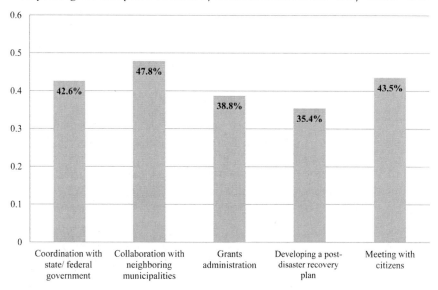

Figure 6.2   Municipal Elected Officials' Rate of Involvement in Disaster Management Activities

Source: Author's original surveys of municipal elected officials.

Notes: The percentage of municipal elected officials reporting involvement in each activity is shown; total observations was 209.

activity underscoring the low priority assigned to disaster management by local elected officials. However, those active most frequently engaged in collaboration with neighboring municipalities. This is followed by meeting with citizens, coordination with state and federal government, and grants administration. The least cited response was developing a post-disaster recovery plan. These responses indicate that municipal elected officials across the Gulf Coast are working to build horizontal integration among neighboring municipalities and citizen groups. Moreover, they are interested in developing good ties with those that can provide assistance and in overseeing the distribution of funding for recovery. They are not, however, as interested in planning. Nonetheless, they do play an active role in the adaptive process through their coordination efforts. The quality of this coordination is explored in the next section.

Analysis of Coordination Ratings

Coordination evaluations are taken from the survey question that asked participants to rate coordination and collaboration in past disaster response with citizen groups as well as with nonprofit and volunteer groups. County emergency managers were also asked to rate coordination with public-private partners, neighboring county emergency managers, local government officials, as well as state and federal emergency management officials. In addition to citizens and nonprofits, municipal elected officials were asked to evaluate coordination with neighboring municipalities and county emergency management as well as state and federal government. Possible responses included "poor" (coded 1), "adequate" (coded 2), "good" (coded 3), and "excellent" (coded 4). Among county emergency managers, ratings of coordination with neighboring county emergency managers were the highest (average 3.8); the lowest ratings were for the federal emergency management (average 2.8). Among municipal elected officials the highest ratings were given to nonprofit groups (average 3.4) and the lowest to federal government (2.6). To determine the conditions that may facilitate good coordination of administrative and political elites with various groups four propositions are explored and tested.

Urban-Rural Character

The first is the urban-rural character of the county or municipality. Urban and rural localities typically face different demands for emergency management. While urban municipalities and counties have larger populations to manage and provide for during disaster events, rural localities have more dispersed populations which can make the delivery of services equally challenging.[61] Given these constraints, rural local government officials have been found to have less activity in the development of the economy (e.g., collaborative planning with other local governments, workforce development) and the provision of public services (e.g., 911 emergency, housing assistance, health clinics).[62] Therefore, we can expect:

Proposition 6.1: Local emergency managers and elected officials in urban settings are more likely to positively evaluate coordination in disaster response and recovery.

To measure the urban-rural character of counties, a variable ranging from one to six is constructed using the Rural-Urban Continuum or Beale Codes from the U.S. Department of Agriculture.[63] One refers to rural counties with populations less than 2,500; six refers to metropolitan counties with population exceeding one million. The urban quality of municipalities is measured by population size. This data was obtained from the U.S. Census Bureau.[64]

Disaster Severity

The second factor considered in assessing coordination ratings is disaster severity. Severe disasters can completely wipe out communities, and recovery from such devastating events requires the entire community to work together. Local administrative and political elites that recognize this may approach the management of disasters differently and pursue coordination and collaboration with internal and external groups more intently. In a national study of county emergency managers, public administration scholars Michael McGuire and Chris Silva found that problem severity—issues so great that manipulating internal structures and resources is not enough—is positively associated with the level of collaboration pursued.[65] Similarly, we can expect:

Proposition 6.2: The more severe the disaster experienced, the more likely county emergency managers and municipal elected officials will give positive coordination evaluations.

To measure disaster severity, two variables are used. The first is maximum property damage caused by hurricane events from 2002–2011 in millions of dollars. This data was obtained from SHELDUS.[66] The second is the severity of the impact of the *Deepwater Horizon* oil spill in terms of economic loss. This variable ranges from zero, indicating no impact, to five, indicating the most severe loss, and is based on the economic claim zones assigned to each jurisdiction by BP.[67] These variables are measured on the county level only.

Leadership

Another factor that may affect coordination is leadership. Because coordination requires leadership skills and relationships built over time, it is important to assess how both affect ratings of coordination. We can expect those individuals that have experience and/or leadership qualities to more effectively coordinate with various groups during response and recovery and, therefore, have higher ratings of that collaboration.

Proposition 6.3: County emergency managers and municipal elected officials with leadership qualities and experience are more likely to have more positive evaluation of coordination during disaster response and recovery.

To measure leadership quality and experience two variables are used on the county level. The first is the emergency managers' response to the open-ended question: *What would you say is the primary role of emergency managers when dealing with disasters?* The responses were grouped into two categories—those that indicate coordination and all other responses. Emergency managers that view their role as a coordinator should have higher ratings of collaboration during disasters. The second variable included is years of experience and was also taken from survey responses. The number of years of experience is important because it should indicate the time the emergency manager has had to develop working relationships with those internal and external to the community.

To measure leadership quality and experience on the municipal level variables were included that indicate if the municipal elected official reported holding a leadership position in business groups, local government, or faith-based groups. These indicate a willingness on the part of the respondent to lead in various settings. It also represents the experience the individual has which can positively contribute to coordination during disasters.

Resources for Emergency Management

The final factor explored is resources. Local administrative and political elites in jurisdictions with greater fiscal and human resources devoted to emergency management have a greater base of capacity by which to build effective coordination. Studies have shown that organizational capacity is positively associated with higher preparedness[68] and disaster mitigation.[69] Moreover, these resources indicate a commitment by local government to support emergency management—a commitment that should manifest in the way local administrative and political elites collaborate with other groups. Accordingly, we can expect:

Proposition 6.4: County emergency managers and municipal elected officials in jurisdictions with greater local resources for emergency management should more positively evaluate coordination during disaster response and recovery.

Emergency management resources are measured by two variables. The first is as the percentage of local government expenditures for first responder services. This data was obtained from U.S. Census Bureau.[70] The second variable is the number of emergency management staff reported in the survey of county emergency managers.

Method

The dependent variable, coordination rating, was collapsed into two categories for analysis good/excellent and adequate/poor. It is appropriate to combine these categories because respondents may assign different meanings to the term. Grouping them in this manner reflects positive or negative evaluations and leaves little room for error. Given the binary nature of the dependent variable, logit analyses were conducted. Because state context may influence disaster response and recovery, the observations were clustered by state, and state dummy variables were included in the model. A separate regression analysis was conducted for each dependent variable—county coordination ratings across seven groups and municipal coordination ratings across six groups. The number of observations varied for municipal regression analyses due to missing (nonresponse) data.

Findings regarding Coordination Ratings

The results of the regression analyses exploring the factors related to coordination ratings are presented in Table 6.2 for county emergency managers' perceptions and Table 6.3 for municipal elected officials' perceptions.[71] Given that coefficients of logit analyses can be difficult to interpret, the findings are discussed in terms of significance and predicted probabilities.[72] The factors related to coordination ratings are discussed in terms of the propositions posed above.

The urban-rural quality of a jurisdiction has different effects on the perceptions held by county emergency managers and municipal elected officials. For emergency managers this only affects evaluations of coordination with citizens; for municipal officials it influences their perceptions of local and state government. Predicted probabilities indicate that an urban emergency manager has a 99 percent likelihood of rating coordination with citizens

Table 6.2 Factors Related to County Emergency Manager Ratings of Coordination

		How Would You Rate Coordination with the Following Groups during Past Disasters?					
		Citizens	Non-Profits	Private Partners	Local Govt.	State EM	Federal EM
Urban-Rural	Urban index	1.618*	0.681	0.011	0.926	0.662	0.117
		(0.629)	(0.764)	(0.337)	(0.798)	(0.733)	(0.090)
Disaster Experience	Hurricane max damage	0.001	0.005	0.001**	0.0166**	-0.001	0.001**
		(0.002)	(0.005)	(3.75e-04)	(0.002)	(0.001)	(1.50e-04)
	BP oil spill economic loss	-0.593	-1.502	-0.616	1.788	-1.858*	-0.697
		(0.729)	(2.224)	(0.639)	(1.057)	(0.870)	(0.445)
Resources	EM office expenditures	-3.085	1.168	-6.886	-4.998	8.380	5.485*
		(2.251)	(7.196)	(5.994)	(5.849)	(4.355)	(2.387)
	EM number of staff	-3.135	-2.354	-0.271	-3.174	-0.119	0.600*
		(1.877)	(2.395)	(0.212)	(2.505)	(1.094)	(0.306)
Leadership	Coordinator role	0.932	-0.228	-0.321	4.062**	-0.585	0.493*
		(0.561)	(1.201)	(0.946)	(0.300)	(1.369)	(0.229)
	Years of experience	0.007	0.0500**	0.0599**	0.125	-0.037	0.005
		(0.036)	(0.008)	(0.021)	(0.114)	(0.025)	(0.028)
State	Alabama	18.04**	14.21**	17.31**	12.71**	-29.13**	-17.65**
		(1.570)	(2.645)	(1.482)	(2.008)	(1.125)	(1.231)

(Continued)

Table 6.2 (Continued)

	How Would You Rate Coordination with the Following Groups during Past Disasters?					
	Citizens	Non-Profits	Private Partners	Local Govt.	State EM	Federal EM
Louisiana	-2.061	-2.193	**3.641****	**-9.123****	**2.134****	1.517
	(1.402)	(3.136)	(1.206)	(2.970)	(0.760)	(0.904)
Mississippi	**13.17****	7.732	**16.55****	3.039	**12.94****	**14.22****
	(2.070)	(8.495)	(1.593)	(4.118)	(3.691)	(1.253)
Texas	-4.186	-5.638	0.825	3.048	-4.718	**-1.127***
	(2.750)	(6.768)	(1.618)	(3.033)	(3.127)	(0.485)
Constant	-5.415	-8.060	**-2.508***	1.033	**-4.816***	1.854
	(4.647)	(8.178)	(1.274)	(7.249)	(1.948)	(1.792)
N	54	54	54	54	54	54
Pseudo R²	0.35	0.26	0.27	0.49	0.37	0.27

Notes: Logit analyses conducted with observations clustered by state. Coefficients reported with robust standard errors in parentheses. Significance denoted as: ** p < 0.01 and * p < 0.05 (one-tailed tests). Significant variables are also shown in bold. Dependent variable, coordination rating, coded: 1 = good/ excellent and 0 = adequate/poor.

Table 6.3 Factors Related to Municipal Elected Official Ratings of Coordination

		How Would You Rate Coordination with the Following Groups during Past Disasters?					
		Citizens	Non-Profits	Neigh. Munis.	County EM	State Govt.	Federal Govt.
Urban-Rural	Population size	2.52e-04 (4.14e-04)	-3.65e-04 (2.82e-04)	-4.45e-04* (1.95e-04)	-8.38e-04** (2.25e-04)	-6.86e-04** (1.56e-04)	-2.92e-04 (2.19e-04)
Disaster Experience	Hurricane max damage	1.70e-04 (7.42e-04)	0.001 (0.001)	0.001 (0.001)	0.001** (1.62e-04)	-0.001** (3.23e-04)	-0.001* (2.34e-04)
	BP oil spill economic loss	0.101 (0.871)	-0.131 (0.619)	0.979** (0.379)	1.163** (0.382)	0.587** (0.147)	0.313* (0.146)
Resources	EM expenditures	-0.934* (0.377)	12.90** (1.253)	-0.323** (0.064)	15.39** (0.983)	16.01** (1.016)	0.550 (0.920)
	EM number of staff	-0.364 (0.376)	-0.280 (0.303)	-0.294 (0.447)	-0.113 (0.124)	-0.043 (0.382)	-0.211 (0.293)
Leadership	Business leader	-0.612 (0.404)	-1.103** (0.308)	-0.429 (0.219)	-0.796* (0.368)	-0.057 (0.371)	-0.660 (0.526)
	Local govt. leader	0.435 (0.474)	1.705** (0.274)	1.089** (0.356)	0.553* (0.224)	-0.036 (0.653)	0.108 (0.750)
	Faith-based leader	-0.612 (0.782)	0.201 (0.445)	0.499 (0.429)	-0.309 (0.996)	-0.578 (0.461)	0.108 (0.298)
State	Alabama	2.080** (0.646)	1.934** (0.364)	16.61** (1.186)	0.127 (0.134)	1.483** (0.283)	-0.052 (0.484)

(*Continued*)

Table 6.3 (Continued)

	How Would You Rate Coordination with the Following Groups during Past Disasters?					
	Citizens	Non-Profits	Neigh. Munis.	County EM	State Govt.	Federal Govt.
Louisiana	0.578	0.608	15.03**	−0.770**	−1.049**	−0.245
	(1.139)	(1.009)	(1.125)	(0.117)	(0.084)	(0.177)
Mississippi	1.714**	0.846*	0.830	14.65**	1.349**	1.029**
	(0.380)	(0.419)	(0.713)	(1.139)	(0.198)	(0.094)
Texas	1.150	0.643	1.525**	1.668**	0.671*	0.657*
	(1.492)	(0.966)	(0.299)	(0.547)	(0.332)	(0.303)
Constant	−1.950*	−0.648	0.674	−0.0184	−0.977	−0.284
	−0.858	−0.728	−1.115	−1.214	−0.982	−1.098
N	164	161	164	164	159	154
Pseudo R^2	0.08	0.09	0.16	0.17	0.12	0.05

Notes: Logit analyses conducted with observations clustered by state. Coefficients reported with robust standard errors in parentheses. Significance denoted as: ** $p < 0.01$ and * $p < 0.05$ (one-tailed tests). Significant variables are also shown in bold. Dependent variable, coordination rating, coded: 1 = good/excellent and 0 = adequate/poor.

positively while an emergency manager in the most rural setting has a 37 percent likelihood of the same. Urbanized settings among municipal elected officials, however, are significantly related to lower coordination ratings of neighboring municipalities, county emergency managers, and state government. Predicted probabilities indicate the effect of population size is relatively small for ratings of local government—only a decrease of 1 to 6 percent—but much larger for ratings of state government. A municipal official in a city with the smallest population in the sample has an 84 percent likelihood of rating the state positively while an official in the largest city has a 53 percent likelihood of the same.

Another influence on coordination perceptions is the severity of past disasters. For both county emergency managers and municipal elected officials, experiencing severe damages from hurricane events is associated with more positive ratings of one another. Emergency managers in counties that have experienced severe hurricanes also rate collaboration with private partners and federal emergency management as positive. Municipal officials, on the other hand, in similar counties rate coordination with state and federal government negatively. Their ratings improve among those who experienced the worst of the BP oil spill. Municipal officials in counties with the highest economic loss due to the oil spill have positive ratings of neighboring municipalities, county emergency management, and state government. Emergency managers, however, perceive things differently and have negative evaluations of state government in this scenario. These differences may be attributed to the distinct vantage points administrators and politicians have in disaster recovery. For example, states in the Gulf Coast, Louisiana in particular, circumvented federal emergency management protocol with their response to the BP oil spill.[73] Municipal elected officials may have seen this positively while emergency managers might have viewed it as problematic.

Resources also emerged as significant for explaining coordination ratings, especially those evaluations by municipal elected officials. In counties where local government spending on emergency services is higher local politicians were more likely to positively rate coordination with nonprofits, county emergency management, and state government. In counties where spending was very low, municipal elected officials were more likely to positively evaluate coordination with citizens and neighboring municipalities. Much of the coordination between municipalities involves the establishment of mutual aid agreements. Therefore, this finding may indicate that collaboration with neighboring municipalities and citizens serves to supplement limited local resources.

For county emergency managers, resources only affected coordination ratings of federal emergency management officials. Emergency managers in counties with high local government spending on first response services and with a greater number of emergency management staff are more likely to positively evaluate working with the federal government. This simply may be the product of having the time for and access to communication with federal officials. The majority of county emergency managers interviewed did not perceive collaboration with federal agencies positively; most saw it as "a pain in the ass to put it lightly." The individual that offered this characterization summed up the issue as many others had: "The problem is poor information and rotation of teams. It creates inconsistency."[74]

Leadership qualities also accounted for differences in coordination ratings. County emergency managers are more likely to positively evaluate collaboration with local and federal governments if they perceive their role as a coordinator. Moreover, those with more years of experience are more likely to positive rate coordination with citizens, nonprofits, and private partners. Examination of the predicted probabilities shows that while the effect of emergency manager leadership is small for local government, citizen, and nonprofit ratings, it increases the likelihood of positive ratings with federal government by 10 percent and by 6 percent for private partner collaboration. Given that these two groups are often perceived as difficult to work with, this finding is important.

Leadership experience among municipal elected officials has a mixed effect. Having a local government leadership role in the past is associated with positive ratings of coordination with nonprofits, neighboring municipalities, and county emergency managers. Clearly this experience translates to good coordination. Leadership experience in business groups, however, is negatively associated with good coordination for nonprofits and county emergency managers. This may reflect a prioritization of economic development that conflicts with these groups during disaster recovery.

CONCLUDING THOUGHTS ON THE ADAPTIVE PROCESS

The analyses of this chapter explored the role local administrative and political elites play in the adaptive process. The analyses have shown that coordination among groups in the aftermath of a disaster is facilitated by local leadership. County emergency managers with more years of experience and municipal elected officials with past local government experience are particularly positioned to lead these efforts. In addition to leadership, local resources for emergency management are important. Although some horizontal coordination appears to emerge as a substitute for limited resources, vertical ties to state and federal government are stronger in counties that have greater local resources for emergency management. Disaster experience also facilitates coordination among groups. Severe hurricane damage and economic loss due to the BP oil spill have been shown to be factors that trigger local collaboration.

These findings highlight the factors that contribute to good coordination among groups across the Gulf Coast and, thereby, deepen our understanding of recovery and the adaptive process. However, it is important to bear in mind that good coordination is not the equivalent of resilient outcomes. Although coordination is an essential component of the adaptive process, resilience requires that good coordination is accompanied by, as hazards scholar Dennis Miletti emphasizes,[75] measures to mitigate against future risk and improve the pre-disaster environment. More research on how such measures, including pre-event recovery planning,[76] evolve on the local level is needed.

SUMMARY

This chapter examined the adaptive process of resilience that is theorized to occur during the response and recovery stages of a disaster. The four attributes of the adaptive process—improvisation, coordination, engagement of the community, and endurance—were linked to the Coastal Resiliency Coalition's response to the BP *Deepwater Horizon* oil spill. This group emerged in an impromptu fashion to bring together the local community in collectively supporting the recovery of businesses affected by the spill. In addition to this case study, the attribute of coordination was also explored through survey responses of county emergency managers and municipal elected officials regarding their coordination activities and ratings of coordination during the adaptive process. The findings of these analyses indicate that county emergency managers frequently engage in collaborative efforts with public and private groups. Municipal elected officials also frequently meet with citizens in efforts to coordinate local action but tend to neglect disaster planning. Positive ratings of coordination by emergency managers and elected officials are associated with severe disaster damages, greater county emergency management resources, and local leadership.

DISCUSSION QUESTIONS

1. What other cases exemplify the adaptive process like the Coastal Resiliency Coalition does?
2. What might be the importance of creating a central meeting location (similar to the Coastal Resiliency Coalition's War Room) for disaster recovery?
3. In addition to fiscal resources, the number of emergency management staff is significant in the regression analysis of coordination ratings with the federal government by emergency managers. Why might this be the case?
4. Given the resource constraints most local governments manage, how might emergency management resources be leveraged to improve coordination during disaster recovery?

5. What kinds of policies and programs could incentivize pre-disaster recovery planning on the local level?

NOTES

1. Gavin Smith, *Planning for Post-Disaster Recovery: A Review of the United States Disaster Assistance Framework* (Fairfax, VA: The Public Entity Risk Institute, 2011), 5.
2. Description of the oil spill is according to John R. Harrald, "The System Is Tested: Response to the BP Deepwater Horizon Oil Spill," in *Emergency Management: The American Experience 1900–2010* 2nd *Edition,* ed. Claire B. Rubin (Fairfax, VA: Public Entity Risk Institute, 2007), 213–15.
3. Guy Busby, "Coastal Resiliency Coalition continues mission two years after spill," *Press-Register* (May 7, 2012), accessed June 30, 2013, *http://blog .al.com/press-register-business/2012/05/coastal_resiliency_coalition_c.html).*
4. Subject #30, personal interview by Ashley D. Ross, Gulf Shores, Alabama, March 18, 2011.
5. "Economic Impact Report, 2010," last accessed June 30, 2013, *http://images .alabama-staging.luckie.com/publications/main-content/2010TourismReport .pdf.*
6. Ibid.
7. Subject #30.
8. Ibid.
9. Ibid.
10. "Baldwin Business Support Center gets $50,000 boost from BP grant," last accessed June 30, 2013. *http://blog.al.com/live/2011/09/baldwin_business_ support_cente.html.*
11. Subject #30.
12. "Baldwin Business."
13. Subject #30.
14. "Baldwin Business."
15. Ibid.
16. "Baldwin Business Support Center gets $50,000 boost from BP grant," *Press-Register* (September 28, 2011), accessed June 30, 2013, *http://blog.al.com/ live/2011/09/baldwin_business_support_cente.html.*
17. Subject #30.
18. Meeting of the Coastal Resiliency Coalition, personal observation by Ashley D. Ross, Gulf Shores, Alabama, April 3, 2011.
19. Subject #30.
20. Casandra Andrews, "Marine scientist: Gulf fish 'absolutely safe' to eat now," *Press-Register* (August 20, 2010), accessed June 30, 2013, *http://blog.al.com/ live/2010/08/marine_scientist_gulf_fish_abs.html.*
21. "NOAA and FDA Announce Chemical Test for Dispersant in Gulf Seafood; All Samples Test Within Safety Threshold," last accessed June 30, 2013, *http:// www.noaanews.noaa.gov/stories2010/20101029_seafood.html.*
22. David Ferrara, "Supper on the Sand: Guy Fieri hosts as hundreds celebrate oil spill recovery," *Press-Register* (April 18, 2011), accessed June 30, 2013, *http:// blog.al.com/entertainment-press-register/2011/04/supper_on_the_sand_guy_ fieri_h.html.*
23. Rich Phillips, "Family: Oil disaster devastated captain who committed suicide," CNN (June 25, 2010), accessed June 30, 2013, *http://www.cnn.com/ 2010/US/06/25/gulf.oil.disaster.suicide/index.html.*

24. "Project Rebound," last accessed June 30, 2013, *https://www.mb.alabama .gov/ProjectRebound/*.
25. David Ferrara, "Coastal Resiliency Coalition looks for new ways to shape south Baldwin County," *Press-Register* (April 25, 2011), accessed June 30, 2013, *http://blog.al.com/live/2011/04/coastal_resiliency_coalition_l.html*.
26. Subject #30.
27. Ibid.
28. Ferrara, "Coastal Resiliency Coalition looks."
29. Hal Scheurich, "2012 Baldwin CO. tourism numbers released," Fox 10 (November 2, 2012), accessed June 30, 2013, *http://www.fox10tv.com/dpp/ news/local_news/baldwin_county/2012-baldwin-county-tourism-numbers-released*.
30. John Sharp, "2012 Census data shows Baldwin County continues its growth; international migration into Mobile and Jefferson counties," *Press-Register* (March 20, 2013), accessed June 30, 2013, *http://blog.al.com/ live/2013/03/2012_census_data_shows_baldwin.html*.
31. Beth Clayton, "Governor announces coastal restoration projects," *Alabama Political Reporter* (May 3, 2013), accessed June 30, 2013, *http://www.alreporter .com/al-politics/political-news/state-news/4567-governor-announces -coastal-restoration-projects.html*.
32. Bruce Alpert, "Congress passes Restore Act, flood insurance extension in massive transportation bill," *Times-Picayune* (June 29, 2012), accessed June 30, 2013, *http://www.nola.com/politics/index.ssf/2012/06/congress_passes_restore_act_fl .html*.
33. Busby, "Coastal Resilience Coalition continues."
34. Subject #30.
35. Busby, "Coastal Resilience Coalition continues."
36. Ibid.
37. Smith, *Planning*.
38. Douglas Paton and Li-ju Jang, "Disaster Resilience: Exploring All Hazards and Cross-Cultural Perspectives," in *Community Disaster Recovery and Resiliency: Exploring Global Opportunities and Challenges*, ed. DeMond S. Miller and Jason D. Rivera (Boca Raton, FL: Auerback Publications, 2011), 83.
39. Smith, *Planning*, 266.
40. Scott Somers and James H. Svara, "Assessing and Managing Environmental Risk: Connecting Local Government Management with Emergency Management," *Public Administration Review*, 69 (2009): 183.
41. Ibid, 184.
42. Smith, *Planning*, 23.
43. Ibid, 24.
44. Ibid, 23–24.
45. Ibid, 24.
46. Francis L. Edwards and Daniel C. Goodrich, "Organizing for Emergency Management," in *Emergency Management: Principles and Practices for Local Government, Second Edition*, ed. William L. Waugh Jr. and Kathleen Tierney (Washington, DC: International City/County Management Association, 2007) 39–53; William L. Waugh Jr. and Gregory Streib, "Collaboration and Leadership for Effective Emergency Management," *Public Administration Review*, 66 (2006): 131–40.
47. Ann Paton, "Collaborative Public Management," in *Emergency Management: Principles and Practices for Local Government, Second Edition*, ed. William L. Waugh Jr. and Kathleen Tierney (Washington, DC: International City/County Management Association, 2007), 72.
48. Subject #54, personal interview by Ashley D. Ross, Robertsdale, Alabama, June 21, 2012.

49. Thomas E. Drabek, *Strategies for Coordinating Disaster Responses* (Boulder: University of Colorado, Natural Research and Applications Information Center, 2003), 144.

50. Edwards and Goodrich, "Organizing," 51.

51. Ibid, "Organizing," 53.

52. Kathleen J. Tierney, "Emergency Medical Preparedness and Response in Disasters: The Need for Interorganizational Coordination," *Public Administration Review*, 45 (1985): 77–84.

53. U.S. Census, "Profile of General Population and Housing Characteristics: 2010," accessed June 30, 2013, *http://factfinder2.census.gov*.

54. Meeting of the St. Bernard Parish Department of Homeland Security and Emergency Preparedness, personal observation by Ashley D. Ross, Chalmette, Louisiana, June 7, 2012.

55. Susan L. Cutter et al., *Community and Regional Resilience: Perspectives from Hazards, Disasters, and Emergency Management,* , Community and Regional Resilience Initiative (CARRI) Research Report 1 (Columbia: Hazards and Vulnerability Research Institute, University of South Carolina, 2008), 7, last accessed June 5, 2011, *http://www.resilientus.org/library/FINAL_CUTTER_9–25–08_1223482309.pdf*; Dennis S. Mileti, *Disasters by Design: A Reassessment of Natural Hazards in the United States* (Washington, DC: Joseph Henry Press, 1999), 219. This is also the case for local governments in general; for example, see analysis of city manager attitudes regarding emergency management in Sandra Sutphen and Virginia Boot, "Issue Salience and Preparedness as Perceived by City Managers," in *Cities and Disasters: North American Studies in Emergency Management*, ed. Richard T. Sylves and William L. Waugh Jr. (Springfield, IL: Charles C Thomas, Ltd., 1990), 133–53.

56. William L. Waugh Jr., "Emergency Management and State and Local Government Capacity," in *Cities and Disasters: North American Studies in Emergency Management,* ed. Richard T. Sylves and William L. Waugh Jr. (Springfield, IL: Charles C Thomas, Ltd., 1990), 228–29.

57. Mayors as executives of their cities are involved in disaster response. Council members typically are not part of initial response but are involved in recovery.

58. Subject #8, personal interview by Ashley D. Ross, Gulfport, Mississippi, February 8, 2011.

59. Subject #13, personal interview by Ashley D. Ross, Gulfport, Mississippi, February 21, 2011.

60. The number of observations is lower than the total number of participants in the surveys due to missing (nonresponse) data.

61. William L. Waugh Jr., "Management Capacity and Rural Community Resilience," in *Disaster Resiliency: Interdisciplinary Perspectives,* ed. Naim Kapucu, Christopher V. Hawkins, and Fernando I. Rivera (New York: Routledge, 2013), 297.

62. Linda Labao and David S. Kraybill, "The Emerging Roles of County Governments in Metropolitan and Nonmetropolitan Areas: Findings from a National Survey," *Economic Development Quarterly,* 19 (2005): 245–59.

63. U.S. Department of Agriculture, Economic Research Service, *2003 Rural-Urban Continuum Codes* [Downloadable Data File] (Washington, DC: USDA, 2004), accessed April 5, 2012, *http://www.ers.usda.gov/data-products/rural-urban-continuum-codes.aspx#.Udj8CKzlf2w*.

64. U.S. Census, "Profile of General Population."

65. Michael McGuire and Chris Silva, "The Effect of Problem Severity, Managerial and Organizational Capacity, and Agency Structure on Intergovernmental Collaboration: Evidence from Local Emergency Management," *Public Administration Review,* 70 (2010): 280.

66. Hazards & Vulnerability Research Institute, *The Spatial Hazard Events and Losses Database for the United States, Version 10.0 [Online Database]* (Columbia: University of South Carolina, 2013), accessed September 5, 2012, *http://www.sheldus.org*.

67. See Appendix E for source of data and description of coding.

68. Brian J. Gerber, David B. Cohen, and Kendra B. Stewart. "U.S. Cities and Homeland Security: Examining the Role of Financial Conditions and Administrative Capacity in Municipal Preparedness Efforts." *Public Finance and Management*, 7 (2007): 152–88.

69. Samuel D. Brody, Jung Eun Kang, and Sarah Bernhardt, "Identifying factors influencing flood mitigation at the local level in Texas and Florida: the role of organizational capacity," *Natural Hazards, 52* (2010): 167–84.

70. U.S. Census, "USA Counties: 2002," accessed June 30, 2013, *http://censtats.census.gov/usa/usa.shtml*.

71. Descriptive statistics for variables in both models are available in Appendix O. Note that there are tables for the municipal regressions because the observations varied due to missing (nonresponse) data.

72. In the calculation of predicted probabilities, all variables were held at their means.

73. Harrald, "The System."

74. Subject #49, personal interview by Ashley D. Ross, Port St. Jo, Florida, June 14, 2012.

75. Mileti, *Disasters*.

76. Smith, *Planning*.

7 Intersecting Perceptions with Realities to Assess Resilience across the Gulf Coast

Resilience as a resource relies on individuals to nurture it on the local level. Given that human action is largely influenced by perception, how individuals perceive their community's resilience may shape its development. This chapter examines the intersection of perceptions and realities of local disaster resilience in two ways. First, resilience "realities" based on approximations of adaptive capacity are overlapped with perceptions of the adaptive process to identify the county characteristics associated with high, moderate, and low resilience. Second, perceptions of county resilience held by county emergency managers are compared to "realities" of resilience to determine which conditions are related to accurate assessments of resilience. This is important because it may point to what hazards scholars call cognition or the recognition of risk related to hazards. Where cognition is lacking, appropriate action may not be taken to properly respond to hazardous events. This can accelerate a situation into a disaster and detract from a community's resilience.

IDENTIFYING PROFILES OF RESILIENCE ACROSS THE GULF COAST

Resilience has two components—adaptive capacity and the adaptive process—that are theoretically mutually reinforcing. Adaptive capacities are the strengths a community possesses and develops prior to a disaster event. Ideally they prevent a disaster from occurring, but if a severe hazard temporarily overwhelms local capabilities they should reemerge to enable the adaptive process. This process involves collaboration to pursue recovery in a manner that improvises solutions to local problems, coordinates collective action, engages the community, and works to formalize solutions to endure beyond the short-term. This recovery process should produce outcomes that feedback into adaptive capacities to buffer against future hazards.

To assess resilience in its entirety approximations of both adaptive capacity and the adaptive process are needed. While adaptive capacity is amenable to objective measurement because it entails tangible policies and outcomes, the adaptive process is more difficult to estimate because it involves action that may vary across communities. Assessments of the process of adaption, therefore, have been based on perception in this study. Aligning these perceptions with adaptive capacity "realities" creates groups of cases with high, moderate, and low resilience whose profiles can be explored.

Plotting Resilience

To plot how perceptions of the adaptive process of resilience intersect with realities of adaptive capacities for resilience, the capacity index presented in Chapter 5 is used. This index is the aggregation of multiple indicators from secondary sources across the components of social, economic, institutional, infrastructure, and ecological resilience. Community capital is also included. The adaptive capacity index is standardized to rank each county in relation to one another as having very high (coded 5), high (coded 4), moderate (coded 3), low (coded 2), or very low (coded 1) capacity for resilience. Generally speaking counties ranked higher on this index have populations with low social vulnerability to hazards, greater connections among citizens, economic diversity and robustness, policies to mitigate against hazards, sound infrastructure, and protected environmental features that buffer against hazards.

The adaptive process is measured as ratings of coordination and collaboration during past disaster response and recovery. These ratings are taken from county emergency manager survey responses and are averaged to represent the overall quality of the adaptive process. The survey asked participants to rate coordination with the following groups: 1) citizens and citizen groups; 2) private partners; 3.) nonprofit partners including faith-based and volunteer groups; 4) local elected officials including municipal and county government; 5) neighboring county emergency managers; 6) state emergency management officials; and 7) federal emergency management officials. Possible responses included "poor" (coded 1), "adequate" (coded 2), "good" (coded 3), and "excellent (coded 4).

While ratings of past coordination and collaboration during disaster response and recovery were also given by municipal elected officials, the regression analyses in Chapter 6 indicated that there are differences between local administrative and political elites' evaluations of the adaptive process. Given that the primary role of emergency managers, unlike that of local politicians, is to prepare for and coordinate effective response to disaster events, their ratings were chosen to represent the adaptive process. While this is only one vantage point, these assessments involve consideration of multiple stakeholder groups which should be indicative of broad community efforts to engage in the adaptive process. The average coordination ratings across the groups were: 3.18 for citizens, 3.35 for private partners, 3.49 for nonprofit partners, 3.51 for local government, 3.78 for neighboring county emergency managers, 3.47 for state emergency management, and 2.80 for federal emergency management.

For each county, the measures of adaptive capacities and the adaptive process are paired and plotted. Adaptive capacity is broken into two categories: 1) high which includes rankings of high and very high (numerical equivalent of 4 and 5); and 2) moderate to low which incorporate rankings of moderate, low, and very low (numerical equivalent of 1, 2, and 3). The adaptive process is also grouped into high and low categories. High includes ratings that are on average the equivalent of "good" or "excellent" (numerically expressed as 3 or 4), and low includes average ratings that range from "poor" (numerical equivalent of 1) to above "average" (2.99). This means that some cases with coordination rankings higher than "average" but not quite the equivalent of "good" are considered low coordination. These standards ensure comparability and set up groupings where the highest categories represent the most developed attributes of resilience.

Four groups emerge from pairings of adaptive capacity and the adaptive process as shown in Figure 7.1. Group 1 includes those cases that are ranked high on capacity and have high average ratings of the adaptive process. There are 18 counties that fall into this group. Group 2 also includes cases that have high ratings of coordination but moderate to very low capacity.[1] There are 29 counties that exhibit this combination of qualities. Group 3 is characterized by high capacity but low ratings of coordination.[2] There are only two cases in this category. Finally, Group 4 includes those cases that have low ratings of coordination and moderate to low adaptive capacities.[3] There are six counties in this category. This group faces the most challenges in developing resilient outcomes as they lack capacity for and good coordination conducive to resilience.

Factors that Affect Resilience

Which attributes do the most resilient cases exhibit? Exploring the groups created by intersecting resilience perceptions and realities can identify factors associated with local resilience. Four factors are examined in this analysis: state context, urban-rural character, disaster severity, and fiscal and human resources.

State Context
State context conditions the environment in which resilience develops on the local level as states set up institutions and rules that affect disaster management. While there are many dynamics at play within states, one political institution that may affect local government is home rule. States that allow counties to self-govern including Florida, Mississippi, and Louisiana may exhibit different patterns of resilience than those that do not, namely Texas.

Home rule is included in the model as a dummy variable, coded as 1 for those counties with home rule and 0 for those without home rule. Data was obtained from the National Association of Counties and supplemented with information from the Police Jury Association of Louisiana[4] and the Florida Association of Counties.[5] Because Alabama allows only a very limited form

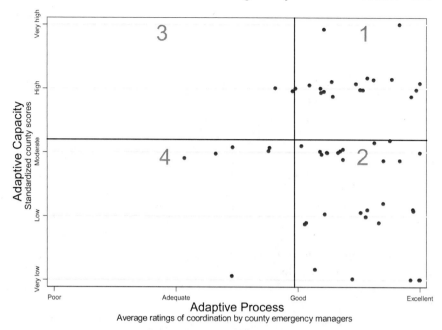

Figure 7.1   Plotting Resilience across the Gulf Coast[1]

Sources: The sources for the adaptive capacity measure are outlined in Appendix G. The data used to construct the adaptive process measure were taken from the author's original surveys of county emergency managers.

[1]Each point represents a county in terms of its adaptive capacity and adaptive process. The points were "jittered" to offset overlapping cases for visual presentation. Similarly, the vertical and horizontal reference lines are moved slightly to accommodate the offset points. Adaptive capacity is measured as the standardized county score for resilience aggregated across six areas: social, community capital, economic, institutional, infrastructure, and ecological. The adaptive process is measured through survey data of county emergency managers as the average of ratings of coordination during past disasters with the following groups: citizens, private partners, nonprofits, local government officials, neighboring county emergency managers, state emergency management, and federal emergency management.

of home rule, the counties from this state are not considered home rule in the analysis.[6]

Urban-Rural Character

The urban-rural character of localities should also influence disaster management on the local level. Urban counties have a greater demand for emergency services, but rural counties also face the challenge of delivering services to a dispersed population.[7] Six categories to represent the urban-rural character of counties were created using the Rural-Urban Continuum or Beale Codes from the U.S. Department of Agriculture.[8] The first includes metropolitan counties[9] with a population of one million or more. The second category includes metropolitan counties with a population of 250,000 to one million; the third group is comprised of metropolitan counties with a population less than 250,000. The fourth group includes nonmetropolitan but urban counties with populations of 20,000 or more while the fifth category includes urban counties with a population of 2,500 to 19,999. The final category includes completely rural counties with population less than 2,500.

Disaster Severity

Disaster severity should influence local disaster resilience as it degrades the capacity of those that have suffered substantial damage; on the other hand, disasters offer the opportunity for improving on pre-event conditions. Disaster severity is considered across three types of events—hurricanes, tornadoes, and the BP *Deepwater Horizon* oil spill. Hurricane severity is measured as average hurricane maximum property damage caused by hurricane events from 2002–2011 in millions of dollars. This data was obtained from SHELDUS.[10] Tornado severity is measured as average maximum Fujita-scale (F-scale) value recorded for tornado events during the time period 2002–2011. This information was obtained from NOAA's National Weather Service Storm Prediction Center.[11] The BP oil spill variable was constructed from economic loss zones and ranges from zero—no economic impact—to five—the most economic impact. See Appendix E for details regarding this measure. Higher values on all the disaster indicators indicate more severe disaster events.

Resources for Emergency Management

A greater pool of resources in terms of staff, expertise, and funding should enable counties to invest more in disaster management and cultivate their resilience. Resources are measured in multiple ways. The first is external grants secured from the Federal Emergency Management Agency. This includes the average number of Public Assistance grants for all categories of work awarded during the time period 1998–2012.[12] Also considered are the average number of Hazard Mitigation Grant Program projects awarded to each county from 1989 to 2011.[13] The second set of indicators reflects human resources, namely the average number of emergency management staff by county. These data were taken from surveys of county emergency managers. The third set of indicators in the resource category represents the qualifications of the county emergency manager. This includes average years of experience and percentage of those managers with college degrees. Information on emergency manager qualifications was gathered from responses to the emergency manager survey.

Method

The county-level data for state context, urban-rural character, disaster severity, and resources were aggregated for each resilience group. This involved averaging some indicators and taking cross-tabulations of others. Table 7.1 presents this information across the resilience groups. The profiles that

Table 7.1 Patterns across Resilience Groups

		Group 1 High High	Group 2 Mod. to low High	Group 3 High Low	Group 4 Mod. to Low Low
Adaptive Capacities	Adaptive Process				
State Context Percent of counties by state	Alabama	5.6%	0.0%	0.0%	0.0%
	Florida	27.8%	34.5%	50.0%	33.3%
	Louisiana	55.6%	17.2%	50.0%	16.7%
	Mississippi	0.0%	10.3%	0.0%	0.0%
	Texas	11.1%	37.9%	0.0%	50.0%
Urban/Rural Character Percent of counties by urban/rural classification	Metro: ≥1 million pop	27.8%	24.1%	0.0%	0.0%
	Metro: 250,000–1 million pop	16.7%	24.1%	0.0%	33.3%
	Metro: <250,000 pop	5.6%	20.7%	100%	16.7%
	Urban: 20,000 pop	27.8%	13.8%	0.0%	0.0%
	Urban: 2,500–19,999 pop	22.2%	10.3%	0.0%	50.0%
	Rural: <2,500 pop	0.0%	6.9%	0.0%	0.0%
Disaster Severity Hurricane	Average maximum property damage in millions of dollars	$365.6	$461.7	$791.7	$315.2
Tornado	Average F-scale (scale ranges 0–5)	1.3	1.1	0	0.5
Oil spill	Average economic loss claim zones (scale ranges 0–5)	2.1	1.4	2.5	1.25

(Continued)

Table 7.1 (Continued)

		Group 1	Group 2	Group 3	Group 4
		High	Mod. to low	High	Mod. to Low
		High	High	Low	Low
	Adaptive Capacities				
	Adaptive Process				
Fiscal and Human Resources	*Grants* Average number of PA Grants awarded 1998–2012	884.8	715.1	238.3	693.3
	Average number of HMGP funding awarded 1989–2011	24.4	27.0	16.0	18.0
	EM office Average number of staff in emergency management office	4.6	4.4	2	3.8
	Percent of emergency management offices with 3 to 5 employees	44.4%	51.2%	0%	66.7%
	Percent of emergency management offices with 6 employees or more	27.8%	20.7%	0%	16.7%
	EM Average years of experience	14.9	21.7	16.5	18.5
	qualifications Percentage with college degrees	66.7%	39.3%	50.0%	50.0%
	Number of cases	18	29	2	6

Sources: Urban-rural data were adapted from the USDA's Beale codes. Disaster data were taken from SHELDUS, NOAA, and BP. Resource data were taken from FEMA and original surveys of county emergency managers collected by the author.

emerge are discussed in the following section beginning with the most resilient category represented by Group 1 then moving to the least resilient class represented by Group 4. Finally Groups 2 and 3 data are considered as indicative of a profile for moderate resilience.

Most Resilient Profile

The most resilient counties are represented by Group 1's characteristics. Over 50 percent of the cases in this group are from Louisiana, and nearly one-third is from the state of Florida. Both of these states permit home rule for county and parish governments, and both have considerably reorganized and invested in their state emergency management institutions and infrastructure following severe storms—Hurricane Andrew (1992) and Hurricane Katrina (2005).

The majority of counties in the most resilient category are metropolitan areas, and none are rural with populations under 2,500. The counties in this group have experienced somewhat severe disaster damages. They have the highest tornado damage of all the groups with an average F-scale of 1.3 and the second-highest hurricane property damage of $365.6 million. They also have the second to highest average BP economic loss claim zone—2.1. This indicates that the majority of the areas in these counties are in BP economic loss Zone C which is the third tier of economic loss behind Zone A and B.

Regarding fiscal and human resources, Group 1 has secured the most Public Assistance grants of the four groups and the second-most Hazard Mitigation grants from the Federal Emergency Management Agency (FEMA). This group also has the highest average emergency management office staff with an average of 4.6 employees and the highest percentage (27.8 percent) of emergency management office staff numbering six employees or more. Emergency managers in this group have the least amount of average experience (14.9 years) but comprise the highest percentage of college graduates (66.7 percent).

Least Resilient Profile

The least resilient counties are represented by Group 4. They have moderate to low adaptive capacities and low ratings of the adaptive process. There are only six counties that fall into this category; however, three of these cases are from Texas and two are from Florida. While these numbers seem marginal, they represent approximately one-in-five of Texas counties and one-in-ten Florida counties. Beyond state context, these cases largely reflect experiences of smaller counties and parishes with 50 percent of the cases in this group being urban areas with populations of 2,500 to 19,999.

This group has had little disaster experience. In terms of property damage they have been impacted by hurricanes the least of all the groups, averaging

$315.2 million, and tornado damage has been small with an average of 0.5 on the F-scale. They have also been least affected economically by the BP oil spill. Their average claim zone score is 1.25 indicating that most of the counties in this group are in Zone D—the lowest category of economic loss.

Counties in this group have secured fewer FEMA Public Assistance and Hazard Mitigation grants than Groups 1 and 2. Similarly, the number of employees in county emergency management offices ranks third behind Groups 1 and 2 with an average of 3.8. Sixty-seven percent of the counties in this group have emergency management office staff ranging from three to five, and only about 17 percent have staff of six or more. The average of county emergency manager experience is 18.5 years which is the second highest of the four groups. Additionally, 50 percent of county emergency managers in this category have a college education.

Moderate Resilience Profile

While Group 1 represents the most resilient cases and Group 4 the least resilient cases given their adaptive capacity and process pairings, Groups 2 and 3 are indicative of moderate development of resilience. Group 2 cases have high ratings of the adaptive process but moderate to low capacity while Group 3 is the opposite—low ratings of the adaptive process but high capacity. This middle ground is important because a majority (56 percent) of the cases fall into these categories.

The cases in Groups 2 and 3 are counties and parishes from all of the Gulf Coast states, except Alabama.[14] Sixty-nine percent of Texas counties, 61 percent of Florida counties, and all of the Mississippi counties studied are found to have moderate resilience. By contrast only 35 percent of the Louisiana parishes included in the sample are in this middle ground. There is also a mix of urban-rural counties in these two groups. Approximately 50 percent of the cases in Groups 2 and 3 are metropolitan counties with populations ranging from 250,000 to over one million. Another quarter is metropolitan areas with populations less than 250,000. There are urban counties with smaller populations as well, and the two counties in the study that are rural with populations less than 2,500 belong to Group 2.

These groups are mixed with regards to their disaster experience as well. They have the highest hurricane property damage with $461.7 million for Group 2 and $791.7 million for Group 3. However, Group 3 has not experienced recent tornadoes, and Group 2's experience has been moderate in comparison to the other groups with an average F-scale of 1.1. BP oil spill damages have been greatest for Group 3 (average of 2.5 claim zone) while Group 2 has been largely unaffected (average of 1.4 claim zone).

Group 2 has had success at securing Public Assistance and Hazard Mitigation grants from FEMA. It ranks second in average PA grants and first for

HMGP grants of the four groups. It also has the second to highest average number of county emergency management office staff with 4.4 employees, and its emergency managers have the highest average experience—21.7 years. However, it has the lowest percentage of county emergency managers with higher education; less than 40 percent have a college degree. Group 3, on the other hand, has the fewest number of grants and emergency management staff. Its county emergency managers also have less average years of experience than Groups 2 and 4.

Resilience Patterns

The patterns that emerge among the resilience groups indicate that state and institutional context matter. Highly resilient cases belong to states with home rule institutions. Further examination reveals that 55 percent of the most resilient cases (those in Group 1) are counties that have adopted home rule while only 35 percent of those cases in the moderate category (Groups 2 and 3), and none of the counties in the least resilient group (Group 4) have home rule charters. Additionally, the majority of the cases in the most resilient group are parishes from Louisiana while the majority in the least resilient group is counties from Texas. Clearly, state dynamics affect how resilience develops locally.

The urban-rural character of counties also matters; however, the patterns that emerge for this factor are much more mixed. Each profile of resilience includes counties of varying sizes. The only pattern that is evident is that the most resilient cases do not include small, rural counties, which indicates that there are particular challenges for building resilience in rural settings.

Disaster experiences also emerged as having distinct patterns among the groups. The most resilient cases have suffered some disaster damages but not the most severe. The most severe disasters have hit the moderately resilient group while the least resilient group has little experience with disasters. This indicates that disasters can offer the opportunity to build resilience but that they also disadvantage communities by straining their capacities.

Resources are also clearly connected to resilience. The counties that exhibit the most resilience have secured the greatest number of PA grants as well as a considerable amount of HMGP grants from FEMA. Additionally, the most resilient cases have emergency management offices with the greatest number of staff and have the highest percentage of emergency managers with college degrees. The moderate to least resilient cases have medium-sized to small emergency management staff and emergency managers who have considerable years of experience but not the highest rate of college graduation.

In all, these patterns point to state and rural context as important for the development of local resilience. Also, the severity of the disasters a county has experienced as well as the resources it can muster are linked to its degree of resilience. The next section looks at another factor that may influence local resilience—emergency managers' perceptions of their county's level of resilience.

EXPLORING PERCEPTIONS OF RESILIENCE
ACROSS THE GULF COAST

To further assess how perceptions of resilience align with resilience "realities," county emergency manager assessments of their community's resilience are explored. Given the central role that county emergency managers have in directing planning and preparations pre-disaster and response and recovery post-disaster, we would expect their assessments of resilience to be fairly accurate. Inaccurate assessments of resilience, particularly those that overestimate, may point to inabilities to recognize risk. This recognition of risk is termed cognition and is critical because it "transforms emergency management . . . into a dynamic process, one that is based on the human capacity to learn, innovate, and adapt to changing conditions . . ."[15] The alignment of emergency managers' perceptions resilience with realities of resilience, therefore, is important for understanding local disaster resilience.

Cognition and Perceptions of Resilience

"Cognition" is a term that public administration scholar Louise Comfort uses to indicate the recognition of hazards risk. She contends that cognition is essential for emergency management because it is the insight that triggers the emergency response process in a manner that is dynamic and adaptable.[16] If risk is not recognized and "no action—or inadequate action—is taken the situation can rapidly escalate into a threatening, imminent disaster."[17] On the other hand, cognition creates action that "transforms emergency management from a static, rule-bound set of procedures into a dynamic process, one that is based on the human capacity to learn, innovate, and adapt to changing conditions . . ."[18] In other words, cognition or recognition of risk is critical for the adaptive process of resilience—impromptu, collaborative action that engages the community to adapt to the post-disaster environment.

Therefore, examination of the alignment of perceptions and realities of resilience can help us better understand the attributes of those communities that have greater potential for effectively engaging in the adaptive process. Perceptions that overestimate a county's resilience may be indicative of a broader lack of cognition which would impede the development of resilient actions. On the other hand, perceptions that are aligned with resilience realities, or those that underestimate them (perhaps erring on the side of caution), should signal the presence of cognition. This cognition, Comfort contends, should transform emergency management into a process that produces resilient outcomes.

Alignment of Perceptions with Realities

To evaluate how perceptions of resilience align with realities of resilience, the measure of adaptive capacities used in the first section of this chapter and presented in Chapter 5 is adopted as the indictor of resilience "realities." Because this index is created from objective secondary sources, it captures concrete evidence of the degree to which capacities for resilience have been developed in a county. Recall that the adaptive capacity index is measured on a scale of very high (coded 5), high (coded 4), moderate (coded 3), low (coded 2), and very low (coded 1).

Perceived community resilience by county emergency managers is measured as responses to the survey question: *If your county experienced a severe disaster this year, how easy would you say it would be to bounce back from the damages incurred?* Possible responses included: "very easy" (coded 5), "easy" (coded 4), "average-not difficult or easy" (coded 3), "somewhat difficult" (coded 2), and "very difficult" (coded 1). This question captures emergency managers' assessment of their county's capabilities to respond to and recover from a severe disaster event. We can assume that this assessment includes some calculation of risk as emergency managers weigh their county's vulnerabilities against its strengths in the event of a severe hazard. Those perceptions that overestimate resilience measured in objective terms may indicate a lack of cognition.

The distribution of resilience perceptions held by county emergency managers is presented in Figure 7.2. The figure shows the percentage of responses by resilience group; percentages are depicted by bubble size (the bigger the bubble, the higher the percentage). Group 1—the most resilient category with high adaptive capacity and high ratings of the adaptive process—has the greatest variation in responses ranging from 11 percent of county emergency managers in this group saying it would be "very easy" to bounce back from a severe disaster to 17 percent saying it would be "very difficult." Group 4—the least resilient group with low capacity and low ratings of the adaptive process—also exhibits considerable variation in responses, but the majority (50 percent) of county emergency managers in this category evaluated their resilience as "average." The responses of the moderate resilience groups—Groups 2 and 3—are concentrated on "somewhat easy" and "somewhat difficult."

The alignment of these perceptions of resilience with resilience realities was calculated as the difference between the numerical value of the county's adaptive capacity and of the survey response regarding hypothetical resilience.[19] No difference between the two values was considered "aligned" as perception matched reality. If perception of resilience exceeded resilience reality, the case was considered an "overestimation." If reality exceeded perception, the case was labeled an "underestimation" of resilience. Since overestimations of resilience could signal a lack of cognition, aligned and underestimated perceptions are grouped to create a variable for empirical analysis that is coded 1 for overestimations and 0 for aligned or underestimated perceptions. While adaptive capacity data are available for all 75 counties in the sample, only 55 counties are represented in the survey data measuring perceptions. Therefore, this analysis focuses on those cases.

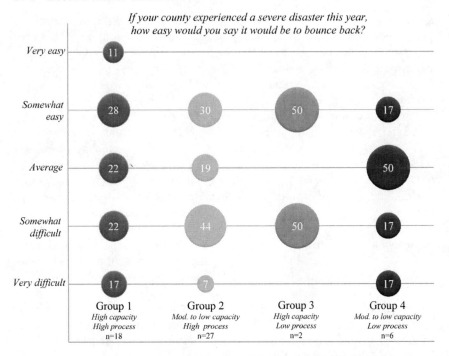

If your county experienced a severe disaster this year, how easy would you say it would be to bounce back?

Percentage of Responses by Resilience Group

Figure 7.2   Perceptions of County Resilience

Source: Author's original survey of county emergency managers.

Notes: The size of the bubbles corresponds to the percentage of responses given for each category; the percentage is also noted by the number inside the bubble. Note that the number of cases for Group 2 is reduced to 27 due to missing (nonresponse) data.

Map of Alignment across the Gulf Coast

The alignment of resilience perceptions with resilience realities is presented spatially in Figure 7.3.[20] Counties shaded in black overestimated their resilience, meaning that they gave a survey response that rated their jurisdiction's resilience as higher than the ranking of their adaptive capacity. Counties shaded in dark gray have aligned perceptions and realities; county emergency managers in these cases gave survey responses that matched their level of adaptive capacity. Cases shaded in light gray indicate underestimation of resilience meaning that ratings of resilience were lower than the ranking of capacity. Counties and parishes shaded in the patterned hash marks are those that did not respond to the survey question about rating resilience.

Seventeen counties, 31.5 percent of the cases in the sample, overestimated their resilience while 22 counties, 40.7 percent, underestimated it. Fifteen counties, 27.8 percent of the cases, had perceptions that aligned with their

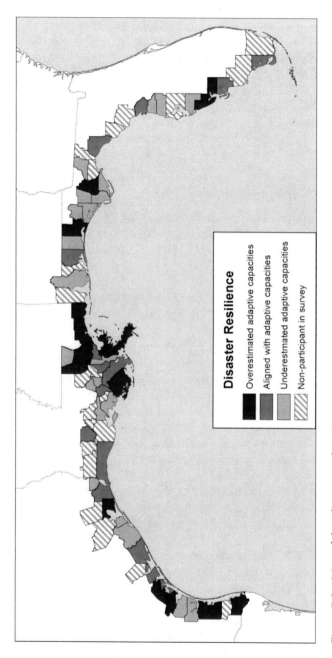

Figure 7.3   Map of the Alignment of Resilience Perceptions and Realities

level of resilience. In reference to the resilience groups—only 11 percent of the most resilient cases (Group 1—those with high adaptive capacities and high rating of the adaptive process) overestimated their resilience. Overestimation of resilience was much higher with the moderate resilience group (Groups 2 and 3—those with mixed capacities and ratings of the adaptive process) and the least resilient group (Group 4—those with low capacity and low ratings of the adaptive process). Forty-five percent of those moderate resilience and 33 percent of those with the least resilience misjudged their county's capacities. Clearly there is wide variation in the alignment of resilience perceptions and realities. The following section examines the factors that may be related to overestimations of resilience through a regression analysis.

Analysis of Overestimations of Resilience

Overestimations of resilience may be connected to multiple county- and individual-level factors. These include county characteristics, disaster experience, and fiscal and human resources for emergency management. Each are discussed in turn.

County Characteristics

County characteristics should influence assessments of resilience as they condition the environment in which the county emergency manager operates. Emergency managers in counties that have developed their capacities for and have coordination conducive to resilience should be able to accurately assess disaster resilience. There is a level of awareness regarding hazards in environments that already have a baseline of high resilience. For example, those interviewed for this study from counties with high resilience expressed an understanding that severe disasters are difficult for *any* community to manage,[21] that hazard type matters—resilience in one area may not translate to another[22]—and that recovery can take years to accomplish.[23] Another factor that should affect resilience perceptions is the urban-rural character of the county. Emergency managers in rural settings may have more difficulty than those in urban settings at judging their resilience since the population is dispersed. Accordingly, we may expect:

  Proposition 7.1: Emergency managers in counties with high disaster resilience are less likely to overestimate their county's resilience.

  Proposition 7.2: Emergency managers in rural counties are more likely to overestimate their county's resilience.

Disaster resilience is measured on a scale of high (coded 3), moderate (coded 2), or low (coded 1) using the previously identified groups. Counties with high resilience are those that have high levels of adaptive capacity and high ratings of the adaptive process; this includes Group 1 cases. Counties with moderate resilience have either high capacity and low quality adaptive process or vise versa. Counties that are considered moderate are those included in Groups 2 and 3. Finally, low resilience is designated for those counties with low adaptive capacity and low ratings of the adaptive process. This includes cases in Group 4.

The urban-rural character of each county is measured in the same manner as the first analysis in this chapter. This data is taken from the U.S. Department of Agriculture and ranks counties on a one-to -six scale with higher values indicating smaller, more rural counties.[24]

Disaster Experience

In addition to county characteristics, disaster experience should influence perceptions of resilience. An emergency manager in a county that has experienced severe disasters should have a firmer grasp on the capabilities of the county and therefore more accurately assess resilience. However, this may be time sensitive as institutional and individual memory tends to fade as severe events are further in the past. Given this, we may expect:

Proposition 7.3: As the severity of past disasters increases, the likelihood of overestimating resilience decreases.

Proposition 7.4: As the years increase since the last severe disaster event occurred, the likelihood of overestimation of resilience also increases.

Disaster severity is examined across three types of disasters—hurricanes, tornadoes, and the BP *Deepwater Horizon* oil spill. Again, the same data used in the first analysis of this chapter are employed here. Hurricane severity is measured as hurricane maximum property damage;[25] tornado severity is measured as the maximum Fujita-scale (F-scale) value;[26] and the impact of the BP oil spill is measured as the average economic loss zone assigned to each county.[27]

Years since the last severe disaster event is measured as responses to the survey event: *What was the worst disaster your county has experienced in the past ten years?* This variable records the number of years since the event mentioned ranging from zero to ten. Some respondents indicated that there has not been a severe disaster in the past decade; these responses are coded as eleven.

Resources for Emergency Management

Finally, resources for emergency management should affect perceptions of resilience. Counties that have greater fiscal and human resources invested in their emergency management should enable county emergency managers to more fully develop local disaster capabilities. County emergency manager qualifications may also affect the accuracy of their perceptions of resilience. Those with more years of experience and higher education should have the awareness and skill set needed to accurately assess their county's resilience. Therefore, we can expect:

Proposition 7.5: Emergency managers in counties with greater fiscal and human resources are more likely to accurately assess their county's resilience.

Proposition 7.6: Emergency managers with more years of experience and education are more likely to accurately assess their county's resilience.

Fiscal and human resources are measured in the same manner as the first analysis of this chapter. The funding secured from FEMA, including the total number of PA[28] and HMGP[29] grants is included in the model. The number of emergency management office staff as well as the emergency manager's years of experience and highest level of education is also considered. These data were taken from the survey of county emergency managers.

Method

Because the variable of interest—overestimation of resilience perception—is binary (coded one for overestimations and zero for alignment or underestimations), a logit regression was run. Given that the state context should influence the development of local resilience, the observations were clustered by state.[30] There are missing data due to nonresponse on some of the variables included in the model.

Findings

The regression results are shown in Table 7.2.[31] County level of disaster resilience as well as disaster experience is significantly associated with overestimations of resilience. Additionally, county emergency manager level of education is statistically significant. Because the coefficients of logit analyses are difficult to interpret, these results are discussed in terms of predicted probabilities.[32]

Emergency managers in counties that have higher levels of disaster resilience are less likely to inaccurately assess resilience. Predicted probabilities indicate that emergency managers in counties with the least resilience have a 60 percent likelihood of overestimating their resilience. This decreases to 32 percent likelihood with moderately resilient counties and drops even further with the most resilient counties to a 13 percent likelihood of overestimation. This indicates that levels of county disaster resilience and accurate assessments of resilience are closely associated.

Hurricane and tornado maximum intensity are also significantly related to overestimations of resilience, but this relationship is not as expected. Emergency managers in counties that have experienced severe damage from hurricanes and tornadoes are more likely to overestimate resilience than those that have experienced less damage. The predicted probability of overestimating resilience in a county with the most hurricane damage is 59 percent while in a county with the least amount of damage is 17 percent. Similarly, the likelihood of overestimation in a county with the most tornado damage is 49 percent while in a county with the least damage is 18 percent. This underscores that experience with a severe disaster is not the equivalent of resilience. Experience does not make a community resilient to disasters; rather, it opens opportunities to develop resilience which may or may not be fully realized.

Table 7.2 Factors Related to Overestimations of Resilience

Overestimation of resilience measured as . . .
1 = Perceptions of resilience overestimated county adaptive capacity
0 = Perceptions of resilience aligned with/underestimated county adaptive capacity

County Context	Level of disaster resilience	**−1.154****
		(0.359)
	Rural county index	0.074
		(0.319)
Disaster Experience	Hurricane max damage	**0.001***
		(0.001)
	Tornado max damage	**1.004***
		(0.409)
	BP oil spill economic loss	0.123
		(0.086)
	Year since last severe disaster	**0.219****
		(0.035)
Fiscal and Human Resources	PA grants	1.97e-05
		(5.70e-04)
	HMGP grants	−0.006
		(0.016)
	EM office number of staff	−1.096
		(0.765)
	EM years of experience	0.041
		(0.060)
	EM college education	**0.719****
		(0.202)
	Constant	−1.534
		(3.405)
	N	51
	Pseudo R^2	0.20

Notes: Logit regression analysis with observations clustered by state; coefficients reported with robust standard errors in parentheses. Significance denoted as: ** $p < 0.01$ and * $p < 0.05$ (one-tail tests). Significant variables are also shown in bold.

Unlike disaster severity, the variable years since the last severe disaster is correlated with overestimations of resilience in the manner expected. An emergency manager that experienced a severe disaster in the past year has an 8 percent likelihood of overestimating county resilience. This likelihood increases to 22 percent in counties that experienced a severe disaster five years ago and to 46 percent in counties that experienced a severe disaster ten years ago. The likelihood of overestimation is greatest, however, with emergency managers in counties that have not experienced a severe disaster in the past decade. These individuals have a 51 percent likelihood of overestimation. This highlights that institutional and individual memories do fade with time which makes the formalization of lessons learned during disaster response and recovery even more important.

Finally, emergency manager level of education is significantly associated with overestimations of resilience. Contrary to the expectation that higher education would be coupled with accurate assessments of resilience, emergency managers with college educations are actually more likely to overestimate resilience. An emergency manager with a college education has a 35 percent likelihood of overestimating resilience while an individual with a high school degree, vocational/technical degree, or some college has a 21 percent likelihood of overestimation. This underscores that higher education alone is not sufficient for sound disaster management.[33]

In sum, emergency managers in counties with high levels of disaster resilience are less likely to overestimate resilience while those in counties that have experienced considerable hurricane and tornado damages are more likely to overestimate their resilience. The age of the disaster event also influences the accuracy of resilience assessments. As the years increase since the last severe disaster the likelihood of overestimating resilience also increases.

Concluding Thoughts on the Intersection of Resilience Perceptions and Realities

The analyses in this chapter have examined the intersection of resilience perceptions and realities. In doing so, we have seen that disaster events clearly open opportunities to develop local resilience. In the first analysis both the most resilient and moderate resilient groups have experience with past disasters while the least resilient group had very little experience with disasters. However, the findings of the second analysis cautions that experiencing a disaster does not directly translate into building local resilience as inaccurate assessments of resilience were correlated with the severity of disaster damages. Also, the influence of experience with past disasters shifts over time as misperceptions of resilience are more likely as the disaster event ages. These findings underscore that experiencing a disaster event can open opportunities for resilience; however, these must be actively pursued and nurtured for local disaster resilience to develop.

SUMMARY

This chapter examined how perceptions and realities of resilience intersect. Perceptions of the adaptive process were plotted against an index of adaptive capacities to create four resilience groups. Examination of these groups' characteristics shows that the most resilient cases are counties from

Louisiana and Florida. The most resilient counties have experienced severe disasters but not the most hurricane damage; however, they have managed to secure the most FEMA grants. They also have high levels of human capital within their emergency management offices with the highest number of staff and highest percentage of college-educated emergency management directors of all four groups. On the other hand, the least resilient cases are predominantly smaller, urban counties with populations less than 20,000. Collectively they have little disaster experience and fewer fiscal and human resources.

Perceptions of county-level resilience were compared to resilience realities in the second analysis to examine the factors related to overestimations of resilience which may signal lack of cognition or recognition of risk. The results of a logit regression analysis indicated that emergency managers in counties with low levels of disaster resilience but high hurricane and tornado damages are more likely to overestimate their resilience. Additionally, as the years since the last severe disaster increase the likelihood of overestimation also increases. Finally, emergency managers with college educations were also more likely to overestimate resilience.

DISCUSSION QUESTIONS

1. Consider the cases with moderate levels of resilience. What policies can these counties pursue to improve disaster resilience?
2. Why is the scenario of Group 3—high adaptive capacity but low ratings of the adaptive process—so rare in the sample? What does this indicate about local disaster resilience?
3. In addition to perceptions of coordination, how else can the quality of the adaptive process be measured?
4. Consider if your county has adopted a home rule charter. In your opinion, does this facilitate or hinder local emergency management?
5. What can communities do to make lessons learned during severe disasters endure?

NOTES

1. Cases in this category scored a three or lower on the adaptive capacity scale and ranked average coordination as three or higher.
2. Cases in this group scored a four or higher on the adaptive capacity scale and ranked average coordination as less than three.
3. Cases in this category scored a three or lower on the adaptive capacity scale and ranked average coordination as less than three.
4. "Parish Government Structure," last accessed June 30, 2013, *http://www.lpgov.org/PageDisplay.asp?p1=3010*.
5. "Charter County Information," last accessed June 30, 2013, *http://www.fl-counties.com/about-floridas-counties/charter-county-information*.

6. Analyses were conducted coding the Alabama counties as home rule; the results were substantively the same.

7. William L. Waugh Jr., "Management Capacity and Rural Community Resilience," in *Disaster Resiliency: Interdisciplinary Perspectives,* ed. Naim Kapucu, Christopher V. Hawkins, and Fernando I. Rivera (New York: Routledge, 2013), 297.

8. U.S. Department of Agriculture, Economic Research Service, *2003 Rural-Urban Continuum Codes* [Downloadable Data File] (Washington, DC: USDA, 2004), accessed April 5, 2012, *http://www.ers.usda.gov/data-products/rural-urban-continuum-codes.aspx#.Udj8CKzlf2w.*

9. U.S. Department of Agriculture defines metropolitan as: "one urbanized area of 50,000 or more population plus adjacent territory and have a high degree of social and economic integration."

10. Hazards & Vulnerability Research Institute, *The Spatial Hazard Events and Losses Database for the United States, Version 10.0* [Online Database] (Columbia: University of South Carolina, 2013), accessed September 5, 2012, *http://www.sheldus.org.*

11. National Oceanic and Atmospheric Administration, *Storm Prediction Center Severe Weather GIS (SVRGIS)* [Online Database] (Norman, OK: Storm Prediction Center, 2012), accessed October 5, 2012, *http://www.spc.noaa.gov/gis/svrgis/.*

12. Federal Emergency Management Agency Library, *FEMA Public Assistance Funded Projects Summary* [Downloadable Data File] (Washington, DC: FEMA, 2012), accessed June 30, 2013, *http://www.fema.gov/library/viewRecord.do?id=6299.*

13. Federal Emergency Management Agency Library, *FEMA Hazard Mitigation Program Summary* [Downloadable Data File] (Washington, DC: FEMA, 2012), accessed June 30, 2013, *http://www.fema.gov/library/viewRecord.do?id=6293.*

14. There are, however, only two counties from Alabama in the study, and only one responded to the survey of county emergency managers.

15. Louise K. Comfort, "Crisis Management in Hindsight: Cognition, Communication, Coordination, and Control," *Public Administration Review,* 67 (2007): 189.

16. Ibid.

17. Louise K. Comfort et al., "Designing Adaptive Systems for Disaster Mitigation," in *Designing Resilience: Preparing for Extreme Events,* ed. Louise K. Comfort, Arjen Boin, and Chris C. Demchak (Pittsburgh: University of Pittsburgh Press, 2010), 33.

18. Comfort, "Crisis Management," 189.

19. For example, consider this scenario: A county emergency manager responded to the survey that bouncing back from a severe disaster would be "very easy." The county's adaptive capacity is ranked as "high." A survey response of "very easy" is coded 5; "high" adaptive capacity is coded 4. Capacity minus perception = $4 - 5 = -1$. This is considered "overestimation." Alignment would be achieved if the county emergency manager had said that bouncing back would be "easy" (coded 4).

20. Scores for alignment of resilience perceptions with county adaptive capacities are available in Appendix P. The alignment of perceptions with the components of adaptive capacity is discussed in Appendix Q.

21. Subject #52, personal interview by Ashley D. Ross, Port Richey, Florida, June 20, 2012.

22. Subject #42, personal interview by Ashley D. Ross, New Orleans, Louisiana, June 7, 2012.

23. Subject #47, personal interview by Ashley D. Ross, Tallahassee, Florida, June 13, 2012.
24. USDA, *2003 Rural-Urban*.
25. Hazards & Vulnerability Research Institute, *SHELDUS*.
26. NOAA, *SVRGIS*.
27. See Appendix E for data source and description of variable coding.
28. FEMA, *Public Assistance*.
29. FEMA, *Hazard Mitigation*.
30. State dummy variables were not included in the analysis because of the small number of observations. Including state dummies in the regression analysis would also result in the loss of some information as observations from Alabama and Mississippi would be dropped due to collinearity. The results of the model including state dummy variables, however, was substantively similar to the results presented in Table 7.2.
31. Descriptive statistics are available in Appendix R.
32. All variables are held at their means to calculate predicted probabilities.
33. This was a common observation among county emergency managers during interviews, March 15–June 21, 2012. Many noted the need for applied experience to accompany higher education courses on emergency management.

8   Concluding Thoughts on Local Disaster Resilience

In theory, disaster resilience is inherently local. The studies in this book have shown that it is a local phenomenon in practice as well. Meanings of community resilience and the level of adaptive capacity closely couple with county characteristics. The adaptive process has been shown to be largely driven by local collective action to meet community needs, and local administrative and political elites play critical roles in coordinating these efforts. The specific findings related to these aspects of resilience contribute to our understanding of the development of resilience along the Gulf Coast. Insights from these analyses can also be used to inform future studies and possibly create strategies to encourage the development of local disaster resilience.

Key Findings and Questions for Future Studies

While the analyses in this study stretched the data to its max (given the number of variables regressed on the number of observations), the findings tell a cohesive story about resilience in multiple forms. The results of the analyses indicate that resilience as shared meanings, adaptive capacities, a process of adaptation, and the intersection of perceptions and realities is largely accounted for by the urban-rural characteristics of counties, the disaster experiences a county has had, and the resources devoted to emergency management. These findings, summarized in Table 8.1, contribute to our understanding of local disaster resilience.

Urban-Rural Character of Counties
First, the results of the analyses point to the urban-rural character of counties as being important for the individual components of resilience. Small, rural counties were statistically correlated with resilience meanings of self-sufficiency and community responsibility in Chapter 4. These meanings emphasize individual survival and compliance with local disaster response rather than collaboration. Additionally, small, rural counties are found to be associated with lower adaptive capacities in the regression analysis ran in Chapter 5. With regards to the adaptive process, the analyses in Chapter 6 found that larger, more urbanized counties were associated with positive

Table 8.1 Key Findings for Understanding Local Disaster Resilience

Urban-Rural	*Meaning of resilience:*	• Smaller, rural counties—more likely to perceive resilience as self-sufficiency and community responsibility. (Chapter 4)
	Adaptive capacity:	• Smaller, rural counties are associated with lower adaptive capacity. (Chapter 5)
	Adaptive process:	• Larger, more urbanized counties—emergency managers more likely to have positive coordination with citizens but municipal elected officials more likely to have to negative coordination with local, county, and state government. (Chapter 6)
	Overall resilience:	• Most resilient group comprised of counties with various population sizes across metropolitan and urban context but no very small, rural counties. (Chapter 7)
Disaster Experience	*Meaning of resilience:*	• Hurricane damage severe—more likely to perceive resilience as preparedness. (Chapter 4) • BP oil spill severe—more likely to perceive resilience as recovery. (Chapter 4)
	Adaptive capacity:	• Hurricane damage severe associated with lower adaptive capacity. (Chapter 5)
	Adaptive process:	• Hurricane damage severe—emergency managers more likely to have positive ratings of coordination with private partners, local government, and federal government; municipal elected officials more likely to have positive ratings with county emergency management. (Chapter 6) • BP oil spill severe—municipal elected officials more likely to have positive ratings of coordination with all levels of government. (Chapter 6)
	Overall resilience:	• Hurricane damage severe but not the worst of all groups-most resilient. (Chapter 7) • Hurricane severity—overestimated perceptions of resilience. (Chapter 7)

(Continued)

Table 8.1 (Continued)

	Adaptive capacity:	• FEMA Public Assistance grants associated with higher adaptive capacity. (Chapter 5)
Resources	*Adaptive process:*	• Higher local government expenditures on emergency management—emergency managers more likely to have positive ratings of coordination with the federal government; municipal elected officials more likely to have positive ratings of coordination with non-profits, county emergency management, and state government but negative ratings of coordination with citizens and neighboring municipalities. (Chapter 6)
		• Years of county emergency manager experience—emergency managers more likely to have positive ratings of coordination with citizens, nonprofits, and private partners. (Chapter 6)
	Overall resilience:	• Grants, number of emergency management staff, and college-educated emergency managers—most resilient. (Chapter 7)

ratings of coordination with citizens by county emergency managers but negative ratings of coordination with local, county, and state government by municipal elected officials. Plotting these ratings with county adaptive capacities in Chapter 7, however, revealed that the most resilient group—those with high adaptive capacity and high ratings of coordination—is comprised of counties with varied population sizes, with the exception of the smallest, rural counties. These findings highlight that the urban-rural character of counties influences how local administrative and political elites perceive resilience and how the development of resilience unfolds. Rural counties face challenges in developing capacity for resilience.

Future studies should explore this in more depth. What particular aspects of urban and rural counties affect resilience? Dare we ask—is there a population size that is able to most effectively develop local resilience? And what might improve the resilience of rural counties without altering their demographic and geographic characteristics?

Local Disaster Experience

The second key finding of this study focuses on disaster experience. Experience with severe hurricanes, measured in terms of property damage, emerged as a factor associated with lower adaptive capacity in the Chapter 5 regression analysis. But the effect of hurricane experience was not negative for all aspects of resilience. The analysis in Chapter 6 found that emergency managers in counties with severe damage were more likely to positively rate coordination with private partners, local government, and federal government. This is somewhat surprising given that overall ratings of coordination with the federal government were the lowest of all the groups evaluated and that this is where we would expect the bottom-up approach of resilience to considerably conflict with the centralized nature of the federal emergency management framework. Perhaps reforms and lessons learned since Hurricane Katrina have created more positive intergovernmental coordination. Or maybe positive ratings of coordination with federal government have been fostered in these counties through multiple disaster experiences. It is also possible that the emergency management framework is simply working for this type of disaster in the Gulf Region. This does not disregard the frustrations that many local officials have when working with federal agencies, but this may underscore that collaboration with the federal government in response to and recovery from severe hurricane events works to facilitate, rather than impede, local resilience.

Further consideration of hurricane experience in Chapter 7 found that counties with moderately severe (not the most but considerable) hurricane damage belonged to the most resilient group—those with high adaptive capacity and high ratings of the adaptive process. Experience with hurricanes seems to be working as resilience theory would predict. These disasters weaken adaptive capacity but offer the opportunity for collaboration in the post-disaster environment that can strengthen overall resilience. Future studies should focus on tracing this over time and through disaster events. What other factors contribute to resilience as communities manage and recover from hurricane events? Given that these hazards are constant threats in coastal regions, it is a worthy effort to more fully delineate the conditions under which adaptive capacities effectively create a space for the adaptive process to occur and produce resilient outcomes.

In addition to hurricanes, the BP *Deepwater Horizon* oil spill was shown to affect resilience—albeit differently—in the analyses throughout the book. Chapter 4 showed that county emergency managers in areas most impacted by the oil spill were more likely to perceive resilience as recovery while those in counties with severe hurricane damage were most likely to understand it as preparedness. The regression analysis in Chapter 6 found that municipal elected officials in counties most affected by the oil spill were more likely to have positive ratings of all levels of government—neighboring municipalities, county emergency management, state and federal government. No other factor induced such widespread positive ratings among municipal officials. Moreover, the case study in Chapter 6 highlighted that local response lead by municipal politicians was successful at developing community resilience in one county whose economy was adversely affected by the oil spill. Clearly, this type of disaster was different than hurricanes not only in the scope and nature of the oil spill itself but also in the dynamics it created on the local level, many of which created resilient outcomes. More research is needed to fully understand how the *Deepwater Horizon* oil spill engendered high levels of intergovernmental coordination and a focus on recovery. What specifically about this type of disaster fostered resilient actions and outcomes? Can this be translated to response and recovery from other types of disasters?

Local Resources

Local resources for emergency management also consistently influenced resilience. The regression analysis in Chapter 5 found that FEMA Public Assistance grants were associated with higher adaptive capacities. Greater local government expenditures on emergency response services were linked to positive ratings of coordination in Chapter 6. In counties with higher investment in emergency services, emergency managers were more likely to have positive ratings of the federal government and municipal officials were more likely to have positive ratings of coordination with nonprofits, county emergency management, and state government. However, municipal officials were also more likely to positively rate coordination with citizens and neighboring municipalities in counties with fewer resources devoted to emergency services. This may indicate that collaboration substitutes for fiscal resources in some cases, but future studies should examine this further. Additional analyses are also needed to fully appreciate how county emergency manager experience contributes to positive coordination with citizens, nonprofits, and private partners. Identifying the conditions that effectively encourage group collaboration, particularly in resource-constrained environments, can enrich our understanding and application of local disaster resilience. However, the fieldwork conducted for this book project indicate that this is not enough to fully develop resilience.

Concerted efforts are needed to more adequately fund local emergency management. The county emergency managers that participated in this study overwhelming pointed to the need for greater local resources. Resources are needed to add an additional staff member to the emergency management office, fund mitigation projects, buy emergency response equipment, build emergency operations centers with modern technology, and generally equip emergency managers to do their job. Limiting resources to this area of government ultimately undermines local resilience. One emergency manager interviewed for this study put it plainly: "Resources matter for resilience. We can be more proactive with more funding."[1] Future studies should focus on this issue and answer: What conditions facilitate investment in local emergency management? What types of strategies encourage a shared value for funding the development of local resilience?

Concluding Thoughts

This study has endeavored to enrich our knowledge of community disaster resilience by applying theory and concept to one specific region—counties and municipalities along the Gulf Coast. While this is a limited sample, the findings of the analyses in this book should transfer to other localities across the United States. Rural counties regardless of their location face common issues. Similarly, limited resources is a condition that most local governments across the nation manage, and experiences with natural disasters despite the type of event (e.g., hurricane, flood, tornado) typically create comparable local dynamics. In addition to informing studies of local disaster resilience in other areas of the nation, much of the information contained in this book can help to further our investigation of resilience among multiple stakeholder groups across the Gulf Coast.

This book has focused on the perspectives of local administrative and political elites not because the vantages of other stakeholder groups are less important but because these are a sound starting point for more fully understanding community disaster resilience. Hopefully the insights from this study and the data generated can be used to analyze in more depth disaster resilience among Gulf Coast communities. This study has only touched upon one aspect of resilience. Our continued study of local dynamics surrounding disaster resilience is needed to effectively nurture the development of this valuable resource.

NOTE

1. Subject #43, personal interview by Ashley D. Ross, Niceville, Florida, June 11, 2012.

Appendix A
List of Counties and Municipalities in the Study Sample

Original surveys were conducted of county emergency managers and municipal elected officials—mayors and city council members—in jurisdictions within 25 miles of the Gulf Coast, in the states of Alabama, Florida, Louisiana, Mississippi, and Texas.

COUNTIES SAMPLED

Alabama: Baldwin County
Florida: Bay County
Calhoun County
Charlotte County
Citrus County
Franklin County
Gulf County
Hernando County
Lee County
Leon County
Liberty County
Manatee County
Monroe County
Okaloosa County
Pasco County
Santa Rosa County
Sarasota County
Taylor County
Walton County
Washington County
Louisiana: Acadia Parish
Ascension Parish
Assumption Parish
Cameron Parish
Iberia Parish

Jefferson Parish
Lafourche Parish
Orleans Parish
Plaquemines Parish
St. Bernard Parish
St. Charles Parish
St. James Parish
St. Mary Parish
St. Tammany Parish
Tangipahoa Parish
Terrebonne Parish
Washington Parish
Mississippi: Hancock County
Harrison County
Jackson County
Texas: Aransas County
Brazoria County
Calhoun County
Cameron County
Chambers County
Galveston County
Harris County
Jefferson County
Kenedy County
Kleberg County
Liberty County
Matagorda County
Nueces County
Orange County
Refugio County
San Patricio County

MUNICIPALITIES SAMPLED

Alabama: Bay Minette
Dauphin Island
Fairhope
Foley
Gulf Shores
Orange Beach
Robertsdale
Silverhill
Spanish Fort
Florida: Belleair Beach

Bradenton
Bronson
Cape Coral
Cinco Bayou
Clearwater
Destin
Dunedin
El Portal
Fort Walton Beach
Gulf Breeze
Horseshoe Beach
Islamorada
Kenneth City
Key Colony Beach
Key West
Largo
Marathon
Marco Island
Mary Esther
Medley
Mexico Beach
Miami Beach
Milton
Niceville
North Bay Village
Oldsmar
Parker
Pensacola
Pinecrest
Ponce de Leon
Punta Gorda
Springfield
St. Marks
Sunny Isles Beach
Surfside
Sweetwater
Tallahassee
Tampa
Temple Terrace
Wausau
Louisiana: Abita Springs
Albany
Berwick
Gretna
Harahan

Lockport
Loreauville
Maurice
Morgan City
New Orleans
Slidell
Vinton
Westwego
Mississippi: Bay St. Louis
Biloxi
Gulfport
Ocean Springs
Pascagoula
Pass Christian
Waveland
Texas: Alvin
Ames
Anahuac
Bayou Vista
Bayside
Baytown
Bayview
Beaumont
Bishop
Brazoria
Bridge City
Clear Lake Shores
Clute
Corpus Christi
Devers
Dickinson
Driscoll
Edna
El Lago
Galveston
Groves
Houston
Ingleside
Jacinto City
Kemah
La Porte
Laguna Vista
Lake Jackson
Manvel
Mont Belvieu

Nederland
Odem
Old River-Winfree
Oyster Creek
Palacios
Pasadena
Pearland
Point Comfort
Port Aransas
Port Lavaca
Port Neches
Portland
Rockport
San Perlita
Seabrook
South Padre Island
Surfside Beach
Taylor Lake Village
Texas City
Webster
West Orange
Woodsboro

Appendix B
County Survey Questionnaire

COMMUNITY DISASTER RESILIENCE—*Perceptions of community resilience in general and in relation to past disasters.*

1. This research project is focused on the issue of community resilience. What does the term community resilience mean to you? Open answer
2. Resilience in the context of disasters is often thought of as the ability of a community to "bounce back" from disasters. If your county experienced a severe disaster this year, how easy would you say it would be to bounce back from the damages incurred? Response Options: very easy, somewhat easy, average—not difficult or easy, somewhat difficult, or very difficult
3. Let's talk about the disasters your county has experienced. Think about the worst disaster your county has ever experienced . . .
   3A. What was this disaster? Open answer
   3B. How would you rate the severity of this disaster in terms of physical, economic, and psychological damages? Would you say it was . . .
   Response Options: very severe or unprecedented, somewhat severe, severe, or not very severe
   3C. How easy was it for your county to "bounce back" from this disaster?
   Response Options: very easy, somewhat easy, average—not difficult or easy, somewhat difficult, or very difficult
4. Now think about the worst disaster your county experienced in the past ten years . . .
   4A. What was this disaster? Open answer
   If the same disaster is cited as in 3a, skip to question 6.
   4B. How would you rate the severity of this disaster in terms of physical, economic, and psychological damages? Would you say it was . . .
   Response Options: very severe or unprecedented, somewhat severe, severe, or not very severe

4C. How easy was it for your county to "bounce back" from this disaster?
Response Options: very easy, somewhat easy, average—not difficult or easy, somewhat difficult, or very difficult

5. What has changed between these two disaster events—the worst disaster ever and the worst in the past ten years—that you would say influenced the resilience of your county? Open answer

EMERGENCY MANAGEMENT—*Discussion of role, routine activities and resources available as related to county emergency management.*

6. What would you say is the primary role of emergency managers when dealing with disasters? Open answer

7. How routinely would you say you do the following . . .

7A. Grant Writing, paperwork and record keeping –
Response Options: very often, often—almost daily, often—weekly, sometimes—monthly or quarterly, once in a while—yearly, or never

7B. Design standard operating procedures and other guidelines for various disaster scenarios –
Response Options: very often, often—almost daily, often—weekly, sometimes—monthly or quarterly, once in a while—yearly, or never

7C. Develop communication with citizens, first responders, public and private entities—Response Options: very often, often—almost daily, often—weekly, sometimes—monthly or quarterly, once in a while—yearly, or never

7D. Work on collaboration with public and private partners –
Response Options: very often, often—almost daily, often—weekly, sometimes—monthly or quarterly, once in a while—yearly, or never

7E. Examine county vulnerabilities to assess risk –
Response Options: very often, often—almost daily, often—weekly, sometimes—monthly or quarterly, once in a while—yearly, or never

7F. Generate public awareness for disaster preparedness –
Response Options: very often, often—almost daily, often—weekly, sometimes—monthly or quarterly, once in a while—yearly, or never

7G. Work on zoning ordinances and other policies that steer development away from areas at high risk for flooding and wind damage –
Response Options: very often, often—almost daily, often—weekly, sometimes—monthly or quarterly, once in a while—yearly, or never

7H. Engage the public or community organizations in disaster planning –

Response Options: very often, often—almost daily, often—weekly, sometimes—monthly or quarterly, once in a while—yearly, or never

8. Overall, how would you rate the disaster responses capabilities of the municipalities within your county? By capabilities we mean financial resources, training and expertise of first responders, and available technology, to name a few.

8A. Would you say the capabilities of your county's municipalities are . . .
Response Options: excellent, good, adequate, or need improvement

8B. How would you characterize the differences in capabilities among municipalities? Would you say that there are . . .
Response Options: large differences, some differences but not big, or very little differences

8C. To what degree would you say municipal capability affects your county's overall resilience to disasters?
Response Options: a lot, some, or a little

9. A large part of emergency management is coordination between public entities. To give us a better idea of the coordination efforts you undertake, please tell us approximately how many . . .

9A. Municipalities are within your county? Open answer

9B. Independent law agencies? Open answer

9C. EMS service districts? Open answer

9D. Fire departments? Open answer

9E. Public utility providers? Open answer

10. Still thinking of coordination, do you have mutual aid agreements with neighboring counties?
Response Options: yes, no

PLANNING—*Assessment of county disaster plans.*

11A. Does your county have a formalized disaster plan?
Response Options: yes, no

11B. How many municipalities in your county have adopted it (or do they all have their own plans)? Open answer

11C. In general, would you say that the plan is followed?
Response Options: yes, no

COMMUNICATION—Communication is a key component of disaster management. How often would you say that you communicate with the following . . .

12A. Average citizens and citizen groups –
Response Options: almost daily, weekly, monthly, quarterly, yearly, or rarely

12B. Private partners, for example grocery stores and other key industries –
Response Options: almost daily, weekly, monthly, quarterly, yearly, or rarely

12C. Nonprofit partners, for example faith-based or volunteer groups –
Response Options: almost daily, weekly, monthly, quarterly, yearly, or rarely

12D. Municipal elected officials, for example mayors and council members –
Response Options: almost daily, weekly, monthly, quarterly, yearly, or rarely

12E. County elected officials, for example county commissioners –
Response Options: almost daily, weekly, monthly, quarterly, yearly, or rarely

12F. Neighboring county emergency management directors –
Response Options: almost daily, weekly, monthly, quarterly, yearly, or rarely

12G. State emergency management officials –
Response Options: almost daily, weekly, monthly, quarterly, yearly, or rarely

12H. Federal emergency management officials –
Response Options: almost daily, weekly, monthly, quarterly, yearly, or rarely

COORDINATION—*Based on past disaster response and recovery experiences, how would you rate coordination and collaboration with the following . . .*

13A. Average citizens and citizen groups –
Response Options: almost daily, weekly, monthly, quarterly, yearly, or rarely

13B. Private partners, for example grocery stores and other key industries –
Response Options: almost daily, weekly, monthly, quarterly, yearly, or rarely

13C. Nonprofit partners, for example faith-based or volunteer groups –
Response Options: almost daily, weekly, monthly, quarterly, yearly, or rarely

13D. Municipal elected officials, for example mayors and council members –
Response Options: almost daily, weekly, monthly, quarterly, yearly, or rarely

13E. County elected officials, for example county commissioners –
Response Options: almost daily, weekly, monthly, quarterly, yearly, or rarely

13F. Neighboring county emergency management directors –
Response Options: almost daily, weekly, monthly, quarterly, yearly, or rarely

13G. State emergency management officials –
Response Options: almost daily, weekly, monthly, quarterly, yearly, or rarely

13H. Federal emergency management officials –
Response Options: almost daily, weekly, monthly, quarterly, yearly, or rarely

BACKGROUND—*Personal and professional background.*

14. Is your position appointed?
Response Options: yes, no

15. Is emergency management your full-time job or are you responsible for other county tasks or work another job?
Response Options: full-time, part-time

16. How many years of experience do you have in the field of emergency management? Open answer

17. What is the highest level of education you have completed?
Response Options: some high school, completed high school, some college, completed technical or vocational school, completed college, some graduate school, or completed graduate school

18. Approximately how many individuals work in your Emergency Management office? Open answer

Appendix C
Municipal Survey Questionnaire

PAST DISASTERS—*In this section you will be asked questions regarding your municipality's disaster history. We consider "natural" disasters to be those caused by nature, for example hurricanes and flooding, while "environmental "disasters refer to those catastrophic events that are manmade and have a negative environmental impact, for example chemical or oil spills.*

1. Thinking about the worst disaster experienced in the past ten years, how would you rate the severity of this disaster in terms of physical, economic, and/or psychological damages?
Response Options: not very severe, somewhat severe, severe, or very severe/unprecedented

2. Thinking about the worst disaster your municipality experienced in the past ten years, how easy was it for your community to "bounce back" both economically and socially?
Response Options: very difficult, somewhat difficult, average (not difficult or easy), easy, very easy

3. Has your municipality experienced an environmental or natural disaster while you have held your elected position?
Response Options: yes, no

   3A. If you answered "yes" to Q3—What action(s) were you involved with during response and recovery efforts? (select all that apply)
   Response Options: coordination with state/federal government, collaboration with neighboring municipalities, applying for disaster relief funding, developing a post-disaster recovery plan, grants administration, expert consultation, town hall meetings with citizens, meetings with business groups, meetings with neighborhood associations, other (please specify)

   3B. If you answered "no" to Q3—Is your local government still undertaking recovery and rebuilding efforts from a past disaster?
   Response Options: yes, no

   3C. If you answered "yes" to Q3B—What action(s) have you been involved with in recovery efforts?

Response Questions: coordination with state/federal government, collaboration with neighboring municipalities, applying for disaster relief funding, developing a post-disaster recovery plan, grants administration, expert consultation, town hall meetings with citizens, meetings with business groups, meetings with neighborhood associations, other (please specify)

MUNICIPAL CHARACTERISTICS—*In the next section you will be asked questions regarding your municipality's population, economy, and resources.*

4. To what degree do you regularly observe neighbors helping neighbors in your municipality?
   Response Options: rarely, some of the time, often, all of the time
5. How much of your community would you consider to be financially vulnerable? Consider "vulnerability" to represent the following scenario—families where if one or more heads of the household were to lose their job meeting monthly expenses would be very difficult or impossible within a short amount of time (one to two months).
   Response Options: 0% (none) to 100% (all) in increments of 5%
6. Which of the following are critical parts of your municipality's economy? (select all that apply)
   Response Options: tourism, service/restaurant, industry/machinery, military, agriculture, banking/business, fishing, oil/gas, other (please specify)

DISASTER MANAGEMENT—*In this section you will be asked questions regarding how your municipality manages disasters. We consider disaster "response" to refer to the first actions governments and emergency agencies take to ensure the safety and soundness of the municipality. Disaster "recovery" refers to the long process that may take years to rebuild and rebound from the damages and trauma incurred by past disasters.*

7. How would you rate the training and expertise of your municipality's disaster first responders (i.e. police, emergency medical teams, firemen)?
   Response Options: poor, adequate, good, excellent
8. How would you rate your municipality's fiscal and human resources as related to disaster response?
   Response Options: not sufficient, somewhat sufficient, sufficient, very sufficient
9. Does your municipality have a formalized disaster plan for disaster response?
   Response Options: yes, no
10. What methods does your municipal government rely on to communicate with citizens during disasters? (select all that apply)

Response Options: local TV stations, local newspaper, local radio stations, city website, internet social media (Facebook and/or Twitter), other (please specify)

11. During past disaster response and recovery, how would you characterize the collaboration and coordination of your local government with the following: (federal government offices and officials, state government offices and officials, county emergency officials, neighboring municipalities, volunteer and faith-based groups, municipal citizens)
    Response Options: poor, adequate, good, excellent, don't know

12. How would you characterize working with the following entities to secure disaster funding for recovery projects? (federal government, state government, nonprofit groups and foundations, corporations (such as British Petroleum)
    Response Options: poor, adequate, good, excellent, don't know

13. During past disasters, how would you characterize the autonomy of your local government to make decisions in response to the disaster?
    Response Options: poor, adequate, good, excellent

14. In your state, which level of government has the most responsibility and decision-making power with regards to disasters?
    Response Options: municipal, county, other regional administration, state, federal

15. Which critical lessons has your municipal government learned from past disasters? (select all that apply)
    Response Options: pre-disaster risk analysis and assessment is important, communication must be improved between local government and responding agencies, communication must be improved between local government and citizens, municipal government autonomy must be preserved for good disaster response, coordination with other local governments is important, collaboration with state agencies is fundamental for response and recovery, collaboration with federal agencies is fundamental for response and recovery, coordination with medical facilities including those in neighboring municipalities is critical, involving volunteer and faith-based groups in response and recovery is important, citizen involvement is important for response and recovery, advising citizens to make more intensive preparations to be adequately ready for disasters, providing citizens with incentives for disaster preparation is important, transportation and evacuation routes must be thoroughly planned and properly executed, proper records of municipal response and spending must be kept, recovery planning is important, control of information must be maintained to get out the right message to citizens and those outside of the municipality, mental health concerns cannot be overlooked following a disaster, other (please specify)

YOUR BACKGROUND—*You will be asked a few questions regarding your personal and professional background.*

16. In which of the following organizations have you been appointed or elected to a service or leadership position in the past? (select all that apply)
    Response Options: city council, school board, parent-teacher organization, youth organizations, historical society, neighborhood association, city clean-up/beautifying organization, volunteer/nonprofit organization, church/faith-based boards or organizations, business/professional organization, civic club, other (please specify), none of the above

17. What is the highest level of education you have completed?
    Response Options: some high school, completed high school, some college, completed technical or vocational school, completed college, completed graduate school

18. Please tell us who has completed this survey. Select your government/job position.
    Response Options: mayor, council member, city manager, city emergency manager, county emergency manager, emergency responder, city secretary, county secretary, other (please specify)

Appendix D
Descriptions of Community Resilience Given by County Emergency Mangers

The following lists the responses given by county and parish emergency managers across the Gulf Coast to the survey question—*What does community resilience mean to you?*:

- "Being able to respond to a disaster even though you have been hit multiple times; ability to survive storm, not just to return to rebuild."
- "Being prepared and educating the community for all disasters."
- "Bouncing back to the way things were before."
- "Community is resilience means preparations for emergencies and disasters."
- "Community resilience is a quick recovery to all disasters."
- "Community resilience is about people helping people."
- "Community resilience is about taking care of yourself and area."
- "Community resilience is based on community understanding of how to prepare and to recover from disasters, and in general knowing what to expect."
- "Community resilience is how well a community's government and other decision makers can continue to function after a disaster."
- "Community response to commands given by Emergency Management."
- "Community's ability to rapidly recover from a disaster."
- "Folks and businesses are prepared for disasters and work together as a team during all phases of emergency management."
- "How community can come back from a disaster."
- "How prepared to weather storm and come back to regain normal operations."
- "How quick you can recover, and how well prepared you are to recover."
- "How resilient a community is to disasters of any kind."
- "How well prepared and how quick we can bounce back."
- "It takes the whole community to prepare, respond, and recover from a disaster."
- "Our people's eagerness and willingness to rebuild and repair and to get back to the way things were before."

- "Preparing county residents and business owners by giving them the training and resources to become disaster prepared so they can be self-sufficient and self-reliant until government help can arrive."
- "Resilience is about self-sufficiency—how prepared each individual family is to deal with a disaster."
- "Resilience is return to pre-disaster conditions."
- "Resilience is survivability, the ability of an area to withstand the onslaught of winds and water with little damage."
- "Resilience is the ability to rebound after a disaster."
- "The ability for a community to conduct the necessary mitigation and preparation activities to minimize the impact of an incident in order to improve and expedite the response and recovery time for a community to return to "normal" activities."
- "The ability for a community to prepare, respond and recover from a disaster."
- "The ability to bounce back and/or resist disasters. It's about how prepared are you and how quickly can you recover."
- "The ability to resume normal economic and social activity."
- "The community's ability to come back together; self-reliance."
- "The level, ability and speed with which the community can bounce back after a major disaster. This is based on physical buildings, roads and human ability—inner strength and belief based on self-empowerment."
- "The people are aware and prepared, and community organizations support policies that make community capable of being to withstand effects of hazard events."
- "To be able to lessen any destruction during an emergency in order to increase the pace of regaining normalcy."
- "To be as prepared as we can be to be able to avoid or manage any disaster event."
- "To have plans and procedures in place to bring community back to normal. It's also about not repeating past mistakes."

Appendix E
Description of BP Oil Spill Economic Loss Claim Measure

To measure the impact of the BP *Deepwater Horizon* oil spill multiple measures were considered, including the amount of claims (in number or dollar amount) paid to individuals and/or local governments. Other possibilities included measures of ecological degradation such as damage to wetland and beaches. These measures, however, were not available on a comparable scale across all the counties in the sample. Therefore, the BP economic loss zones were adopted to serve as a proxy for the impact of the oil spill on counties

The economic loss zones assigned to each county were devised by BP to calculate the appropriate amount to compensate individuals and business owners for financial losses related to the oil spill. There are four zones: Zone A, B, C, and D. Zone A has been assigned to areas that have been most impacted by the spill. These areas are predominately located in the state of Louisiana, although there are very small regions of Alabama, Florida, and Mississippi that are also classified Zone A. Zones B and C indicate areas that are moderately affected, and Zone D is assigned to areas that were least affected, which are predominantly inland counties and parishes in the states of Alabama, Mississippi, Louisiana, and Florida.

These zone designations are used to determine the eligibility of claims and calculate the compensation paid to claimants. The details of these claims based on the economic loss zone designations are available on the BP court-ordered settlement program website: http://www.deepwaterho rizonsettlements.com. For example, Exhibit 15 outlines the risk transfer premium paid to claimants. Each zone is assigned a multiplying factor to be combined with losses. Zone A has the highest multiplying factors (e.g., 2.5 for tourist businesses) while Zone D has the lowest (e.g., 1.25 for tourist businesses).

In addition to claims details, BP released as part of their court-ordered settlement program maps of the economic loss zones, available at: http://www.deepwaterhorizonsettlements.com/Documents/Economic%20SA/Ex1A_Map_of_Economic_Loss_Zones.pdf. Exhibit 1A spatially maps the economic loss zones. However, the zones do not correspond to political jurisdictions, and most counties and parishes have multiple zones in their boundaries. Therefore, a coding scheme was devised to aggregate the economic loss zones by county and parish. The values assigned to the various scenarios included in the coding scheme are intended to rank the severity of the impact of the oil spill in each jurisdiction based on the criteria that Zone A losses are always greater than Zone B, Zone B losses are always greater than Zone C, and Zone C losses are always greater than Zone D. This created a hierarchy of rankings based on the possible combinations of zone classifications in each jurisdiction, as detailed below.

Table E.1   Coding for BP Oil Spill Impact

	Score	Criteria
ZONE A	5.00	County/parish area is completely covered by Zone A.
	4.75	County/parish area is nearly completely (95%) covered by Zone A.
	4.50	County/parish area is predominantly covered (over 50%) by Zone A with areas also covered by Zone B and/or Zone C and/or Zone D.
	4.25	County/parish area is predominantly covered (over 50%) by Zone A with areas also covered by Zone C and/or Zone D.
	4.00	County/parish area is predominantly covered (over 50%) by Zone A with areas also covered by Zone D.
ZONE B	3.75	County/parish area is predominantly covered (over 50%) by Zone B with areas also covered by Zone A and/or Zone C and/or Zone D.
	3.50	County/parish area is completely covered by Zone B.
	3.25	County/parish area is predominantly covered (over 50%) by Zone B with areas also covered by Zone C and/or Zone D.
	3.00	County/parish area is predominantly covered (over 50%) by Zone B with areas also covered by Zone D.
ZONE C	2.75	County/parish area is predominantly covered (over 50%) by Zone C with areas also covered by Zone A and/or Zone B and/or Zone D.
	2.50	County/parish area is predominantly covered (over 50%) by Zone C with areas also covered by Zone B and/ or Zone D.
	2.25	County/parish area is completely covered by Zone C.
	2.00	County/parish area is predominantly covered (over 50%) by Zone C with areas also covered by Zone D.

ZONE D	1.75	County/parish area is predominantly covered (over 50%) by Zone D with areas also covered by Zone A and/or Zone B and/or Zone C.
	1.50	County/parish area is predominantly covered (over 50%) by Zone D with areas also covered by Zone B and/or Zone C.
	1.25	County/parish area is predominantly covered (over 50%) by Zone D with areas also covered by Zone C.
	1.00	County/parish area is completely covered by Zone D.
NONE	0.00	County/parish is not in a BP oil spill claim zone.

Appendix F
Descriptive Statistics for Chapter 4 Regression

Table F.1 Descriptive Statistics for Chapter 4 Regression

Factors that Explain Differences in Perceptions of Community Resilience				
	Mean	Standard Deviation	Minimum Value	Maximum Value
Dependent Variables				
Bounce back resilience meaning	0.26	0.44	0	1
Preparedness resilience meaning	0.17	0.38	0	1
Continuity resilience meaning	0.15	0.26	0	1
Recovery resilience meaning	0.13	0.34	0	1
Self-sufficiency resilience meaning	0.09	0.29	0	1
Community responsibility resilience meaning	0.09	0.29	0	1
Independent Variables				
Urban-rural	2.93	1.49	1	6
BP oil spill economic loss zones	1.74	1.28	0	4.75
Hurricane max property damage	417.31	427.34	0	1333.33

Appendix G
Adaptive Capacity Data Descriptions, Labels, and Sources

Table G.1 Adaptive Capacity Data Descriptions, Labels, and Sources

Social Resilience

Variable and Description	Label	Source
Education	ed	American Communities Survey 2010 5 Year
Percent of the population with a bachelor's degree or higher		http://factfinder2.census.gov/faces/nav/jsf/pages/index.xhtml
Nonelderly population	age	U.S. Census 2009 Population Estimates, USA Counties Database
Percent nonelderly population (elderly = 65 and over)		http://censtats.census.gov/usa/usa.shtml
Transportation access	transp	American Communities Survey 2011 5 Year
Percent of households with a vehicle		http://factfinder2.census.gov/faces/nav/jsf/pages/index.xhtml
Communication capacity	comm	American Communities Survey 2011 5 Year
Percent housing units with a telephone		http://factfinder2.census.gov/faces/nav/jsf/pages/index.xhtml
Language competency	lang	Language spoken at home ACS 3 yr 2010
Percent of population over 5 yrs old who speak English "very well"		http://factfinder2.census.gov/faces/tableservices/jsf/pages/productview.xhtml?pid=ACS_10_3YR_S1601&prodType=table

(Continued)

Table G.1 (Continued)

Variable and Description	Label	Source
Nonspecial needs population	spec	Census 2000 SF3
Percent population without a physical disability		http://factfinder2.census.gov/faces/nav/jsf/pages/index.xhtml
Health insured population	hth_cov	U.S. Census Small Area Health Insurance Estimates 2007, via USA Counties
Percent population with health insurance (under 65 years)		http://censtats.census.gov/cgi-bin/usac/usacomp.pl

Community Capital

Variable and Description	Label	Source
Place attachment	migrat	American Communities Survey 2009 3 Year
Net international migration per 1,000 population		http://factfinder2.census.gov/faces/nav/jsf/pages/index.xhtml
Place attachment	born	American Communities Survey 2010 5 Year estimates
Percent population born in state that still resides in that state		http://factfinder2.census.gov/faces/tableservices/jsf/pages/productview.xhtml?pid=ACS_10_5YR_B05002&prodType=table
Political engagement	voter	Secretary of State/Department of State for Each State 2008
Percent voter turnout in 2008 presidential election		http://elections.sos.state.tx.us; http://www.sos.louisiana.gov; http://www.sos.ms.gov;
		http://www.sos.alabama.gov/elections; https://doe.dos.state.fl.us

Variable and Description	Label	Source
Religious social capital	relig	Association of Statisticians of American Religious Bodies (ASARB) 2010, TOTRATE
Religious adherents per 1,000		http://www.thearda.com/Archive/Files/Downloads/RCMSCY10_DL2.asp
Civic social capital	civorg	County Business Patterns 2009 Code 8134
Civic organizations per 10,000		http://www.census.gov/econ/cbp/index.html
Advocacy social capital	sociorg	County Business Patterns 2009 Code 8133
Social advocacy organizations per 10,000		http://www.census.gov/econ/cbp/index.html

Economic Resilience

Variable and Description	Label	Source
Housing capital	house	Census 2010 SF1
Percent owner occupied housing		http://factfinder2.census.gov/faces/nav/jsf/pages/index.xhtml
Employment	employ	American Communities Survey 2010 5 Year
100–Percent pop unemployed		http://factfinder2.census.gov/faces/nav/jsf/pages/index.xhtml
Income inequality	GINI	US Census, 2006-2010 American Community Survey
Gini Index by county (1=0.461 to 0.645; 2 = 0.439 to 0.460; 3 = 0.422 to 0.438; 4 = 0.402 to 0.421; 5 = 0.207 to 0.401)		http://www.census.gov/prod/2012pubs/acsbr10-18.pdf
Economic diversity	single	NAICS 2012
Percent of pop not employed in farming, fishing, forestry, or extraction		http://factfinder2.census.gov/faces/nav/jsf/pages/index.xhtml
Female labor force	fem_lab	American Community Survey 2010 5 Year

(*Continued*)

Table G.1 (Continued)

Variable and Description	Label	Source
Percent of labor force (16 years old and over) that is female		http://factfinder2.census.gov/faces/nav/jsf/pages/index.xhtml
Business robustness	bus	SUSB 2009 County totals
Ratio of large to small businesses employees		http://www.census.gov/econ/susb/
Health care access	hth_acc	American Medical Association, 2009 via USA Counties Database
Total physicians per 10,000		http://censtats.census.gov/cgi-bin/usac/usacomp.pl

Institutional Resilience

Variable and Description	Label	Source
Mitigation plan-covered population	plan	FEMA Mitigation Plan Status (April 2012)
Percent population with multi-hazard mitigation plan		http://www.fema.gov/multi-hazard-mitigation-plan-status
Spending on first responder services	serv	US Census 2002, USA Counties
Percent local government expenditures for health and hospitals, fire and police		http://censtats.census.gov/usa/usa.shtml
CRS-covered population	crs	FEMA's CRS Eligible Communities (2012)
Percent population in Community Rating System Communities/ Counties		http://www.fema.gov/library/viewRecord.do?id=3629

Variable and Description	Label	Source
Political fragmentation *Number of municipalities, school districts, and special districts*	polfrag	US Census, 2007 Governments Integrated Directory http://harvester.census.gov/gid/gid_07/options.html
Disaster experience *Number of Presidential disaster declarations, 2002–11*	declar	FEMA Historical Disaster Declarations http://gis.fema.gov/DataFeeds.html
Citizen Corps-covered population *Percent pop covered by county Citizen Corps council*	citcorps	Citizen Corps (November 2012) https://www.citizencorps.gov/cc/CouncilMapIndex.do
Storm Ready-covered population *Percent population in Storm Ready counties or communities*	stready	NOAA's Strom Ready Communities http://www.stormready.noaa.gov/communities.htm

Infrastructure Resilience

Variable and Description	Label	Source
Nonvulnerable housing *Percent of housing not mobile homes*	mobile	American Communities Survey 2010 5 Year http://factfinder2.census.gov/faces/nav/jsf/pages/index.xhtml
Rental shelter capacity *Percent vacant rental units*	vac	Census 2010 SF1 http://factfinder2.census.gov/faces/nav/jsf/pages/index.xhtml
Hospital capacity *Number of hospital beds per 10,000*	bed	County and City Data Book: 2007 (Actual data from 2004) https://www.census.gov/statab/ccdb/ccdbstcounty.html
Evacuation/access capacity *Primary and secondary road miles per square mile*	roads	Census 2010 Tiger/Line Shapefiles http://www.census.gov/cgi-bin/geo/shapefiles2010/main

(Continued)

Table G.1 (Continued)

Variable and Description	Label	Source
Nonvulnerable housing	house_age	American Communities Survey 2010 5 Year
Percent housing units built 1970–94		http://factfinder2.census.gov/faces/nav/jsf/pages/index.xhtml
Hotel shelter capacity	hotels	County Business Patterns 2009
Number of hotels/motels per square mile (excludes casino hotels)		http://www.census.gov/econ/cbp/index.html
School shelter capacity	school	HAZUS Data aggregated by county/ FEMA Hazus 2.0 2011
Number of public schools per square mile		http://www.fema.gov/hazus-software

Ecological Resilience

Variable and Description	Label	Source
Impervious surfaces	imperv	National Land Cover Database 2006 Percent Developed Imperviousness
Percent impervious surface in square miles of land area		http://www.mrlc.gov/nlcd06_data.php
Wetland preservation	wet	NOAA CSC Coastal Change Analysis Program (C-CAP) Land Cover Atlas
Net change (1997 to 2006) in percent wetland area between 1996 to 2006		http://stateofthecoast.noaa.gov/wetlands/welcome.html
Floodplain housing development	srl	Number of Severe Repetitive Loss Properties per County (FEMA 2007)
Number of severe repetitive loss properties		http://www.fema.gov/library/viewRecord.do?id=2711
(0=0; 1=1 to 20; 2=21 to 30;3=31 to 40; 4=41 and over)		

Appendix H
Adaptive Capacity Raw Data by Component

Table H.1 Adaptive Capacity Raw Data by Component

Social Resilience

County/parish	state	ed	age	transp	comm	lang	spec	hth_cov
Baldwin County	AL	0.18	83.00	96.79	96.84	97.80	91.75	81.70
Mobile County	AL	0.13	87.50	92.92	96.75	97.80	90.01	84.80
Bay County	FL	0.14	85.20	94.78	97.05	97.40	91.98	78.70
Calhoun County	FL	0.08	85.10	94.35	97.35	97.00	91.22	77.40
Charlotte County	FL	0.17	65.70	94.81	97.47	96.90	92.36	74.40
Citrus County	FL	0.13	69.10	95.79	95.95	98.20	91.93	76.90
Collier County	FL	0.23	73.20	95.19	97.22	83.60	89.42	68.10
Dixie County	FL	0.04	80.50	95.78	95.63	98.30	85.41	82.20
Escambia County	FL	0.16	85.10	92.35	94.46	97.00	90.07	80.40
Franklin County	FL	0.14	83.20	90.49	95.11	98.50	92.76	72.70
Gulf County	FL	0.10	84.50	94.60	98.03	96.70	89.57	78.30
Hernando County	FL	0.12	73.70	94.98	98.07	96.90	91.91	79.30
Hillsborough County	FL	0.19	88.20	93.16	95.95	89.80	91.27	78.90
Jefferson County	FL	0.10	84.00	93.41	96.20	96.90	92.90	76.60
Lee County	FL	0.18	77.30	95.09	97.44	89.60	92.31	71.80
Leon County	FL	0.25	90.80	93.35	95.04	97.50	88.93	75.80

(Continued)

Table H.1 (Continued)

County/parish	state	ed	age	transp	comm	lang	spec	hth_cov
Levy County	FL	0.09	81.40	93.04	96.5	97.60	89.07	74.10
Liberty County	FL	0.10	89.20	91.92	4.07	98.40	92.77	74.80
Miami-Dade County	FL	0.18	85.60	88.94	95.27	64.50	91.08	69.80
Monroe County	FL	0.23	83.40	92.51	95.17	90.50	92.97	70.20
Okaloosa County	FL	0.19	86.30	95.89	96.28	96.30	92.08	75.30
Pasco County	FL	0.14	79.30	95.09	97.13	95.50	91.58	79.70
Pinellas County	FL	0.21	79.00	91.85	96.54	94.50	92.29	80.70
Santa Rosa County	FL	0.17	87.50	96.71	96.85	97.70	92.80	79.50
Sarasota County	FL	0.23	69.50	94.10	97.20	95.00	92.13	74.60
Taylor County	FL	0.08	85.70	94.80	99.23	99.30	92.04	80.00
Wakulla County	FL	0.12	86.40	97.22	97.68	99.20	88.61	75.30
Walton County	FL	0.18	83.90	95.27	95.06	97.00	91.84	73.40
Washington County	FL	0.09	85.10	95.24	97.07	97.70	91.44	79.50
Acadia Parish	LA	0.07	87.50	92.43	95.87	96.50	93.65	77.60
Ascension Parish	LA	0.14	91.50	95.06	97.43	97.70	94.21	80.00
Assumption Parish	LA	0.06	87.60	90.69	97.03	96.00	92.25	79.40
Calcasieu Parish	LA	0.13	87.30	93.11	97.56	98.20	92.87	76.10
Cameron Parish	LA	0.08	90.90	96.51	96.26	98.40	92.90	67.20
Iberia Parish	LA	0.09	87.80	89.88	97.19	96.70	92.09	77.20
Jefferson Parish	LA	0.17	86.30	92.43	96.08	92.70	91.90	77.10
Jefferson Davis Parish	LA	0.08	86.30	93.48	96.30	97.30	92.54	77.00
Lafayette Parish	LA	0.18	89.40	92.58	97.08	96.30	92.44	75.00

Lafourche Parish	LA	0.10	87.70	91.65	95.32	96.30	92.39	78.60
Livingston Parish	LA	0.10	90.10	96.20	94.78	98.90	93.79	76.70
Orleans Parish	LA	0.19	88.30	81.60	92.48	96.00	88.65	78.30
Plaquemines Parish	LA	0.11	89.00	94.39	91.40	97.90	90.48	74.90
St. Bernard Parish	LA	0.06	90.80	94.91	81.72	95.40	92.78	82.70
St. Charles Parish	LA	0.13	90.10	96.03	97.98	98.30	92.16	81.90
St. James Parish	LA	0.08	87.40	91.01	97.76	98.80	92.69	78.20
St. John the Baptist Parish	LA	0.11	90.50	93.74	94.58	97.80	91.60	76.90
St. Martin Parish	LA	0.08	89.10	91.30	95.25	95.60	93.42	73.30
St. Mary Parish	LA	0.07	86.70	88.55	98.33	96.80	93.99	78.10
St. Tammany Parish	LA	0.20	87.80	96.20	97.69	98.20	93.78	79.90
Tangipahoa Parish	LA	0.12	88.70	93.10	97.81	97.80	91.03	76.70
Terrebonne Parish	LA	0.09	88.50	92.45	93.84	97.40	93.84	78.30
Vermilion Parish	LA	0.08	87.00	93.75	97.59	95.20	92.11	75.10
Washington Parish	LA	0.08	85.70	91.38	97.27	99.50	93.10	77.10
Hancock County	MS	0.15	84.90	96.76	96.50	98.50	91.03	82.50
Harrison County	MS	0.13	87.90	95.08	95.83	96.60	91.96	78.90
Jackson County	MS	0.12	87.50	96.64	95.41	97.50	92.43	81.70
Aransas County	TX	0.18	76.80	94.63	96.54	93.20	93.71	71.00
Brazoria County	TX	0.16	90.60	96.42	96.84	91.40	92.31	74.70
Calhoun County	TX	0.10	85.50	94.38	97.63	89.10	91.46	74.80
Cameron County	TX	0.08	88.90	90.71	96.49	69.70	92.01	66.30
Chambers County	TX	0.10	91.40	97.37	96.50	94.60	92.08	77.20
Galveston County	TX	0.18	89.00	93.96	97.36	93.10	91.85	78.50

(Continued)

Table H.1 (Continued)

County/parish	state	ed	age	transp	comm	lang	spec	hth_cov
Harris County	TX	0.17	91.90	92.96	96.27	79.00	91.38	68.70
Jackson County	TX	0.11	84.60	92.05	98.70	94.20	91.71	75.00
Jefferson County	TX	0.12	87.00	91.23	97.60	92.40	89.37	77.30
Kenedy County	TX	0.08	88.10	92.68	100.00	81.10	95.77	50.50
Kleberg County	TX	0.14	88.40	91.61	93.03	88.50	93.32	74.10
Liberty County	TX	0.06	88.90	95.25	96.34	94.00	89.19	74.30
Matagorda County	TX	0.09	86.60	93.37	97.44	90.00	92.14	72.90
Nueces County	TX	0.13	88.40	91.54	96.04	87.70	92.39	77.20
Orange County	TX	0.08	86.20	94.59	95.81	98.20	91.31	82.10
Refugio County	TX	0.08	81.90	91.24	96.26	90.70	94.48	75.80
San Patricio County	TX	0.10	87.00	92.35	96.10	88.40	93.12	78.20
Willacy County	TX	0.05	88.20	91.92	96.87	80.30	93.08	74.70

Community Capital

County/parish	state	migrat	born	voter	relig	civorg	sociorg
Baldwin County	AL	0.97	53.51	76.60	531.74	1.17	0.39
Mobile County	AL	0.63	72.69	70.60	612.92	1.12	0.32
Bay County	FL	1.66	39.25	73.80	412.43	0.79	0.24
Calhoun County	FL	0.75	62.76	73.30	407.93	0.00	0.00
Charlotte County	FL	0.85	18.52	72.40	400.54	0.83	0.38
Citrus County	FL	0.62	27.19	74.80	305.98	1.21	0.21
Collier County	FL	6.11	21.39	70.50	345.34	0.66	0.44

Dixie County	FL	0.00	64.19	68.50	288.70	0.67	0.00
Escambia County	FL	0.79	43.37	79.70	531.83	0.79	0.46
Franklin County	FL	0.95	58.75	79.40	408.95	7.09	1.77
Gulf County	FL	-0.06	58.27	79.80	430.56	0.00	1.27
Hernando County	FL	1.30	27.04	72.00	272.36	0.58	0.18
Hillsborough County	FL	3.42	39.13	73.60	397.73	0.86	0.31
Jefferson County	FL	1.76	63.52	77.80	610.32	2.14	1.43
Lee County	FL	3.24	24.80	84.80	376.83	0.78	0.27
Leon County	FL	1.64	54.11	85.50	472.72	1.13	1.58
Levy County	FL	0.76	50.88	72.80	476.41	1.02	0.00
Liberty County	FL	0.00	68.09	77.50	426.18	1.25	1.25
Manatee County	FL	2.46	30.55	74.20	377.78	1.07	0.25
Miami-Dade County	FL	8.01	32.02	70.20	397.58	0.41	0.46
Monroe County	FL	3.34	29.00	81.20	333.71	1.64	1.50
Okaloosa County	FL	1.74	30.90	74.20	477.76	1.18	0.39
Pasco County	FL	1.36	29.33	73.70	218.26	0.81	0.15
Pinellas County	FL	1.96	29.56	72.80	360.16	0.67	0.39
Santa Rosa County	FL	1.25	39.11	71.40	443.00	0.20	0.33
Sarasota County	FL	2.13	20.68	80.10	435.08	1.00	0.46
Taylor County	FL	0.04	67.87	72.20	491.27	1.87	0.47
Wakulla County	FL	0.36	64.39	77.80	226.54	0.61	0.00
Walton County	FL	2.05	39.42	73.90	403.99	0.36	0.91
Washington County	FL	-0.08	52.67	70.70	392.31	0.00	0.00
Acadia Parish	LA	0.08	91.83	69.31	616.29	0.83	0.17

(Continued)

Table H.1 (Continued)

County/parish	state	migrat	born	voter	relig	civorg	sociorg
Ascension Parish	LA	0.57	79.44	73.08	485.17	0.19	0.00
Assumption Parish	LA	0.17	92.84	71.12	658.77	0.00	0.00
Calcasieu Parish	LA	0.38	78.54	66.24	703.26	1.01	0.16
Cameron Parish	LA	2.19	81.91	57.77	807.72	0.00	0.00
Iberia Parish	LA	0.42	87.91	70.25	703.45	0.80	0.27
Jefferson Parish	LA	1.81	74.64	65.19	539.50	0.63	0.29
Jefferson Davis Parish	LA	0.03	90.41	66.71	767.01	0.64	0.64
Lafayette Parish	LA	1.04	80.96	70.10	764.64	0.85	0.47
Lafourche Parish	LA	0.69	89.37	67.50	663.02	0.75	0.32
Livingston Parish	LA	0.52	78.36	70.14	493.17	0.32	0.08
Orleans Parish	LA	1.43	73.06	52.67	557.22	1.44	1.27
Plaquemines Parish	LA	0.13	74.24	63.97	567.53	0.00	0.48
St. Bernard Parish	LA	1.03	84.69	47.05	576.59	0.25	0.00
St. Charles Parish	LA	1.29	82.90	74.64	523.87	0.19	0.39
St. James Parish	LA	0.59	95.37	80.95	781.15	0.00	0.00
St. John the Baptist Parish	LA	0.98	83.46	73.46	444.58	0.21	0.00
St. Martin Parish	LA	0.27	90.89	70.19	591.01	0.38	0.38
St. Mary Parish	LA	1.30	83.88	68.06	548.73	0.20	0.00
St. Tammany Parish	LA	0.59	70.62	69.97	503.65	0.43	0.35
Tangipahoa Parish	LA	0.33	82.40	67.79	472.75	0.51	0.25
Terrebonne Parish	LA	0.65	86.25	64.67	658.37	1.01	0.18
Vermilion Parish	LA	0.36	89.97	67.59	623.11	0.53	0.18

Washington Parish	LA	0.04	80.80	69.10	578.21	1.53	0.22
Hancock County	MS	0.80	44.52	20.29	302.81	0.49	0.00
Harrison County	MS	2.03	53.93	26.10	497.41	1.60	0.55
Jackson County	MS	1.78	57.87	26.35	506.61	0.53	0.30
Aransas County	TX	1.04	63.11	59.78	449.09	0.81	0.00
Brazoria County	TX	1.33	64.27	60.98	569.86	0.39	0.10
Calhoun County	TX	2.29	74.70	52.52	557.78	1.46	0.49
Cameron County	TX	2.93	63.62	43.37	497.28	0.73	0.30
Chambers County	TX	0.66	72.57	58.65	299.26	0.00	0.32
Galveston County	TX	1.59	63.45	55.45	541.37	0.94	0.56
Harris County	TX	4.78	53.34	59.79	583.95	0.39	0.24
Jackson County	TX	0.07	82.56	55.73	720.99	0.70	0.70
Jefferson County	TX	1.86	69.34	58.22	776.79	1.11	0.29
Kenedy County	TX	0.00	97.51	57.22	300.48	0.00	0.00
Kleberg County	TX	2.65	79.94	52.24	671.72	1.31	1.31
Liberty County	TX	1.80	73.36	47.50	516.85	0.53	0.00
Matagorda County	TX	2.59	73.26	57.01	606.15	1.62	0.81
Nueces County	TX	0.88	74.09	50.90	604.34	0.93	0.50
Orange County	TX	0.39	72.17	56.39	624.30	0.49	0.12
Refugio County	TX	0.27	86.23	58.86	779.36	0.00	0.00
San Patricio County	TX	0.66	75.57	45.65	623.06	0.29	0.15
Willacy County	TX	0.27	76.03	43.47	621.98	0.00	0.49

(Continued)

Table H.1 (Continued)

Economic Resilience

County/parish	state	house	employ	gini	single	fem_lab	bus	hth_acc
Baldwin County	AL	72.52	93.40	2	98.14	46.47	0.62	25.63
Mobile County	AL	66.95	90.30	1	98.61	48.23	1.06	30.31
Bay County	FL	63.13	92.50	4	99.37	46.54	0.85	23.49
Calhoun County	FL	76.80	92.00	2	94.49	51.38	0.20	5.06
Charlotte County	FL	79.70	88.70	3	99.50	48.35	1.21	27.27
Citrus County	FL	82.30	87.60	3	98.63	49.01	0.79	23.23
Collier County	FL	72.20	92.50	1	97.76	44.87	0.71	41.35
Dixie County	FL	82.22	89.80	4	96.65	46.16	0.19	2.70
Escambia County	FL	64.88	89.70	2	99.48	47.83	1.30	33.06
Franklin County	FL	74.38	89.30	1	89.15	45.92	0.14	10.64
Gulf County	FL	74.75	91.90	4	97.69	41.59	0.31	10.16
Hernando County	FL	80.53	88.00	4	98.96	48.95	1.01	16.64
Hillsborough County	FL	60.93	91.40	1	98.79	47.83	1.62	37.36
Jefferson County	FL	77.33	88.00	3	93.52	49.23	0.48	5.71
Lee County	FL	71.00	90.10	1	99.17	46.90	0.89	27.41
Leon County	FL	54.44	91.60	1	99.51	50.65	0.75	31.91
Levy County	FL	80.19	89.80	2	93.09	46.76	0.30	6.13
Liberty County	FL	75.60	82.20	2	93.52	36.32	0.00	1.25
Manatee County	FL	71.33	91.10	2	98.50	47.33	0.98	26.29
Miami-Dade County	FL	55.79	91.50	1	99.41	47.57	0.86	40.13
Monroe County	FL	56.70	94.90	1	97.77	43.01	0.45	33.62
Okaloosa County	FL	65.07	92.90	3	99.46	45.12	0.93	31.15

Pasco County	FL	77.13	90.40	3	99.27	47.98	0.90	15.52
Pinellas County	FL	67.44	92.20	1	99.75	48.84	1.06	35.47
Santa Rosa County	FL	76.35	90.60	4	98.71	44.71	0.87	21.75
Sarasota County	FL	74.97	90.80	1	99.72	48.54	0.69	45.46
Taylor County	FL	76.50	86.90	2	96.72	45.79	0.81	7.48
Wakulla County	FL	80.73	92.70	5	98.35	50.62	0.73	4.57
Walton County	FL	72.62	91.80	1	98.74	47.21	0.72	16.51
Washington County	FL	77.78	90.10	2	97.96	44.71	0.92	6.69
Acadia Parish	LA	70.66	93.30	2	86.56	45.47	0.28	8.99
Ascension Parish	LA	80.82	94.70	4	98.99	45.06	0.87	10.59
Assumption Parish	LA	81.57	92.40	4	93.03	44.60	0.12	4.37
Calcasieu Parish	LA	69.64	92.30	1	97.55	46.63	0.94	23.03
Cameron Parish	LA	87.77	98.00	4	91.77	44.42	0.47	1.52
Iberia Parish	LA	70.94	92.20	2	86.90	47.06	0.79	16.64
Jefferson Parish	LA	63.69	93.20	2	98.12	46.89	0.90	45.72
Jefferson Davis Parish	LA	75.33	92.50	3	85.44	43.78	0.48	10.29
Lafayette Parish	LA	65.01	94.50	1	90.96	47.11	0.69	39.58
Lafourche Parish	LA	75.84	95.70	1	91.21	43.84	0.54	16.97
Livingston Parish	LA	79.81	94.80	5	98.78	44.82	0.48	4.22
Orleans Parish	LA	47.84	88.00	1	98.58	49.22	0.94	72.71
Plaquemines Parish	LA	74.82	94.10	4	94.65	47.41	0.44	9.07
St. Bernard Parish	LA	68.87	89.40	4	97.23	43.99	0.77	3.20
St. Charles Parish	LA	79.78	93.30	4	98.04	46.76	1.34	8.91
St. James Parish	LA	83.85	93.70	3	97.53	48.20	0.00	11.87

(*Continued*)

Table H.1 (Continued)

County/parish	state	house	employ	gini	single	fem_lab	bus	hth_acc
St. John the Baptist Parish	LA	79.15	91.00	4	98.79	49.78	1.08	11.04
St. Martin Parish	LA	79.63	92.70	2	90.93	46.05	0.28	4.98
St. Mary Parish	LA	70.17	93.20	3	90.26	43.99	0.69	12.00
St. Tammany Parish	LA	79.52	94.30	2	97.50	46.70	0.65	36.98
Tangipahoa Parish	LA	69.89	89.40	1	96.64	47.16	0.68	12.47
Terrebonne Parish	LA	72.25	94.20	2	87.06	44.23	0.81	19.76
Vermilion Parish	LA	76.02	94.80	2	83.78	43.12	0.35	8.37
Washington Parish	LA	74.33	86.50	1	94.92	48.16	0.51	10.51
Hancock County	MS	76.87	90.40	3	98.74	45.10	1.02	14.40
Harrison County	MS	61.84	91.80	2	99.36	45.99	1.38	26.44
Jackson County	MS	71.68	90.30	2	98.41	45.97	0.00	25.43
Aransas County	TX	74.79	93.20	1	97.09	48.92	0.40	12.08
Brazoria County	TX	74.56	94.50	4	97.13	46.29	0.97	25.29
Calhoun County	TX	71.14	92.10	3	95.85	43.13	1.78	11.18
Cameron County	TX	67.22	92.60	1	97.57	46.51	0.97	14.15
Chambers County	TX	85.26	93.80	5	95.87	41.47	0.95	2.86
Galveston County	TX	68.78	93.10	2	98.53	45.86	1.09	49.16
Harris County	TX	56.78	92.70	1	97.30	44.11	1.25	31.87
Jackson County	TX	73.88	94.70	2	85.79	44.46	0.00	4.90
Jefferson County	TX	63.21	91.10	1	98.85	46.53	1.05	24.42
Kenedy County	TX	35.37	100.00	4	43.48	26.27	0.00	0.00
Kleberg County	TX	56.70	90.70	1	90.81	45.34	0.89	9.14
Liberty County	TX	77.14	91.00	4	95.07	43.26	0.78	5.28

Matagorda County	TX	66.56	89.50	1	89.90	45.53	0.00	10.01
Nueces County	TX	60.72	92.10	1	96.86	45.99	0.98	30.83
Orange County	TX	76.72	92.60	3	98.58	44.07	0.71	5.62
Refugio County	TX	73.21	92.80	4	82.98	42.03	0.35	1.38
San Patricio County	TX	68.74	92.50	3	94.38	44.77	0.00	4.98
Willacy County	TX	76.32	92.60	1	92.66	45.96	2.21	2.94

Institutional Resilience

County/parish	state	plan	serv	crs	pol_frag	declar	citcorp	stready
Baldwin County	AL	100	0.34	100.00	33.00	10	0	100
Mobile County	AL	100	0.13	47.20	27.00	9	100	100
Bay County	FL	100	0.32	100.00	21.00	7	0	100
Calhoun County	FL	100	0.11	0.00	5.00	6	0	100
Charlotte County	FL	100	0.14	100.00	18.00	7	0	100
Citrus County	FL	100	0.10	100.00	11.00	5	0	100
Collier County	FL	100	0.14	100.00	40.00	7	0	100
Dixie County	FL	100	0.09	0.00	5.00	8	0	100
Escambia County	FL	100	0.10	100.00	10.00	7	100	100
Franklin County	FL	100	0.12	100.00	10.00	7	0	100
Gulf County	FL	100	0.08	100.00	6.00	8	0	100
Hernando County	FL	100	0.07	100.00	13.00	4	100	100
Hillsborough County	FL	100	0.10	100.00	76.00	3	100	100
Jefferson County	FL	100	0.14	100.00	3.00	7	0	100
Lee County	FL	100	0.35	100.00	10.00	6	0	100
Leon County	FL	100	0.10	66.42	15.00	7	0	100

(*Continued*)

Table H.1 (Continued)

County/parish	state	plan	serv	crs	pol_frag	declar	citcorp	stready
Levy County	FL	100	0.12	100.00	11.00	7	0	100
Liberty County	FL	100	0.05	0.00	3.00	6	0	100
Manatee County	FL	100	0.10	100.00	60.00	6	0	100
Miami-Dade County	FL	100	0.22	100.00	99.00	6	100	100
Monroe County	FL	100	0.25	100.00	15.00	7	0	100
Okaloosa County	FL	100	0.11	100.00	31.00	7	100	100
Pasco County	FL	100	0.11	100.00	53.00	5	100	100
Pinellas County	FL	100	0.13	100.00	48.00	3	100	100
Santa Rosa County	FL	100	0.12	100.00	12.00	7	0	100
Sarasota County	FL	100	0.39	100.00	24.00	7	100	100
Taylor County	FL	100	0.12	100.00	5.00	7	0	100
Wakulla County	FL	100	0.12	100.00	5.00	7	0	100
Walton County	FL	100	0.14	0.00	17.00	6	0	100
Washington County	FL	100	0.19	0.00	8.00	5	0	100
Acadia Parish	LA	100	0.14	12.92	10.00	7	0	100
Ascension Parish	LA	100	0.15	100.00	4.00	6	0	0
Assumption Parish	LA	100	0.05	0.00	2.00	7	0	0
Calcasieu Parish	LA	100	0.16	100.00	13.00	6	100	100
Cameron Parish	LA	100	0.33	0.00	1.00	5	0	100
Iberia Parish	LA	100	0.24	0.00	6.00	7	100	0
Jefferson Parish	LA	100	0.40	100.00	8.00	12	100	100
Jefferson Davis Parish	LA	100	0.10	0.00	7.00	6	100	0

Lafayette Parish	LA	100	0.11	100.00	9.00	6	0	100
Lafourche Parish	LA	0	0.36	100.00	7.00	10	100	0
Livingston Parish	LA	100	0.06	8.12	10.00	8	100	100
Orleans Parish	LA	100	0.13	100.00	6.00	8	100	0
Plaquemines Parish	LA	100	0.12	0.00	2.00	9	100	0
St. Bernard Parish	LA	100	0.11	0.00	3.00	9	100	0
St. Charles Parish	LA	100	0.17	100.00	1.00	10	0	100
St. James Parish	LA	100	0.14	100.00	3.00	7	0	0
St. John the Baptist Parish	LA	100	0.07	100.00	3.00	7	0	0
St. Martin Parish	LA	0	0.17	0.00	5.00	9	100	100
St. Mary Parish	LA	100	0.30	22.51	10.00	7	0	0
St. Tammany Parish	LA	100	0.39	100.00	14.00	7	0	0
Tangipahoa Parish	LA	100	0.46	100.00	13.00	7	100	0
Terrebonne Parish	LA	100	0.45	100.00	5.00	9	100	0
Vermilion Parish	LA	100	0.29	0.00	9.00	5	0	0
Washington Parish	LA	100	0.21	0.00	7.00	5	0	0
Hancock County	MS	0	0.35	36.31	19.00	5	0	0
Harrison County	MS	0	0.37	100.00	21.00	5	0	0
Jackson County	MS	0	0.34	100.00	18.00	6	0	0
Aransas County	TX	100	0.10	0.00	5.00	6	100	0
Brazoria County	TX	100	0.10	29.79	73.00	6	100	0
Calhoun County	TX	100	0.30	0.00	16.00	7	0	0
Cameron County	TX	0	0.07	0.00	67.00	5	100	1
Chambers County	TX	0	0.09	0.00	12.00	3	0	0
Galveston County	TX	100	0.13	48.76	62.00	5	100	100

(*Continued*)

Table H.1 (Continued)

County/parish	state	plan	serv	crs	pol_frag	declar	citcorp	stready
Harris County	TX	100	0.15	100.00	470.00	5	100	5
Jackson County	TX	0	0.24	0.00	18.00	3	0	0
Jefferson County	TX	100	0.16	68.37	36.00	4	100	54
Kenedy County	TX	0	0.04	0.00	1.00	3	100	0
Kleberg County	TX	0	0.13	0.00	10.00	4	100	82
Liberty County	TX	0	0.06	0.00	31.00	5	0	0
Matagorda County	TX	0	0.19	0.00	26.00	5	0	0
Nueces County	TX	0	0.15	90.52	36.00	8	100	91
Orange County	TX	100	0.08	0.00	23.00	4	0	0
Refugio County	TX	100	0.27	0.00	14.00	5	100	0
San Patricio County	TX	0	0.13	0.00	32.00	9	100	0
Willacy County	TX	0	0.05	0.00	18.00	4	100	0

Infrastructure Resilience

County/parish	state	mobile	vac	bed	roads	house_age	hotels	school
Baldwin County	AL	85.69	25.33	32.06	0.66	0.39	0.02	0.04
Mobile County	AL	90.91	34.07	36.48	0.84	0.42	0.06	0.14
Bay County	FL	86.65	33.28	38.33	1.05	0.50	0.10	0.08
Calhoun County	FL	66.90	14.39	19.15	0.44	0.46	0.00	0.01
Charlotte County	FL	88.22	12.76	46.20	1.02	0.55	0.02	0.05
Citrus County	FL	73.05	14.03	23.14	0.95	0.58	0.02	0.06
Collier County	FL	94.27	11.71	18.55	0.42	0.52	0.03	0.04
Dixie County	FL	48.73	6.96	0.00	0.57	0.53	0.00	0.01

Escambia County	FL	92.32	39.04	42.42	2.04	0.46	0.07	0.17
Franklin County	FL	80.66	9.98	25.05	0.52	0.44	0.02	0.02
Gulf County	FL	78.29	19.26	19.53	0.45	0.43	0.00	0.02
Hernando County	FL	81.81	15.82	25.48	0.93	0.57	0.02	0.06
Hillsborough County	FL	91.99	42.95	29.82	1.36	0.46	0.14	0.37
Jefferson County	FL	64.28	13.49	0.00	1.10	0.45	0.00	0.01
Lee County	FL	89.11	14.23	31.26	1.59	0.48	0.11	0.18
Leon County	FL	90.85	51.08	32.41	1.46	0.50	0.08	0.13
Levy County	FL	54.31	8.34	10.89	0.58	0.50	0.01	0.02
Liberty County	FL	53.90	16.23	0.00	0.30	0.48	0.00	0.01
Manatee County	FL	82.83	19.76	27.47	1.27	0.48	0.06	0.14
Miami-Dade County	FL	98.55	31.00	34.89	0.70	0.41	0.21	0.37
Monroe County	FL	85.02	11.15	27.60	0.67	0.53	0.11	0.03
Okaloosa County	FL	93.18	38.04	23.16	0.93	0.49	0.05	0.07
Pasco County	FL	79.15	19.54	26.02	1.33	0.55	0.03	0.14
Pinellas County	FL	90.55	23.70	37.79	2.48	0.51	0.72	1.01
Santa Rosa County	FL	87.15	29.03	13.88	0.68	0.43	0.00	0.04
Sarasota County	FL	90.82	14.67	30.30	1.08	0.52	0.11	0.16
Taylor County	FL	62.55	12.26	24.52	0.64	0.49	0.01	0.01
Wakulla County	FL	63.61	14.56	0.00	0.51	0.45	0.00	0.01
Walton County	FL	84.60	15.79	20.97	0.89	0.42	0.02	0.02
Washington County	FL	67.08	11.02	27.25	0.81	0.50	0.01	0.02
Acadia Parish	LA	81.90	30.75	40.43	1.81	0.38	0.01	0.05
Ascension Parish	LA	79.88	25.45	16.26	2.32	0.39	0.04	0.10
Assumption Parish	LA	69.72	3.72	2.60	1.66	0.43	0.00	0.03

(*Continued*)

Table H.1 (Continued)

County/parish	state	mobile	vac	bed	roads	house_age	hotels	school
Calcasieu Parish	LA	83.28	37.40	48.67	0.79	0.37	0.04	0.07
Cameron Parish	LA	68.89	6.09	34.25	0.44	0.30	0.00	0.00
Iberia Parish	LA	79.73	31.88	22.62	0.93	0.39	0.01	0.07
Jefferson Parish	LA	98.10	47.51	35.70	2.43	0.47	0.24	0.49
Jefferson Davis Parish	LA	82.78	20.85	19.47	1.19	0.33	0.01	0.02
Lafayette Parish	LA	88.68	42.19	54.65	2.62	0.47	0.17	0.24
Lafourche Parish	LA	82.04	24.81	25.54	0.68	0.41	0.02	0.03
Livingston Parish	LA	71.24	24.26	0.00	1.39	0.43	0.01	0.06
Orleans Parish	LA	97.85	30.78	58.71	3.29	0.22	0.79	0.55
Plaquemines Parish	LA	78.33	21.46	0.00	0.31	0.30	0.01	0.01
St. Bernard Parish	LA	85.95	24.71	29.65	0.66	0.40	0.00	0.02
St. Charles Parish	LA	89.80	30.32	11.31	1.77	0.52	0.03	0.08
St. James Parish	LA	83.47	18.56	7.73	1.94	0.40	0.01	0.05
St. John the Baptist Parish	LA	88.58	28.87	13.32	1.95	0.54	0.06	0.09
St. Martin Parish	LA	74.78	15.27	5.01	0.89	0.46	0.01	0.03
St. Mary Parish	LA	80.11	24.27	14.55	0.93	0.38	0.02	0.06
St. Tammany Parish	LA	91.42	26.71	33.75	1.57	0.47	0.03	0.09
Tangipahoa Parish	LA	78.16	31.00	24.06	1.25	0.46	0.02	0.06
Terrebonne Parish	LA	82.38	24.21	38.31	0.51	0.42	0.02	0.04
Vermilion Parish	LA	77.65	13.78	20.05	0.70	0.35	0.00	0.02
Washington Parish	LA	79.15	15.41	20.80	1.17	0.38	0.01	0.04

Hancock County	MS	82.20	26.75	22.88	0.67	0.34	0.01	0.03
Harrison County	MS	88.22	49.37	47.12	0.89	0.38	0.06	0.13
Jackson County	MS	87.78	42.65	28.91	0.71	0.43	0.05	0.09
Aransas County	TX	79.87	14.87	0.00	0.41	0.51	0.06	0.10
Brazoria County	TX	88.11	36.06	7.95	0.40	0.43	0.03	0.01
Calhoun County	TX	85.09	13.47	12.29	0.39	0.39	0.03	0.20
Cameron County	TX	87.40	20.29	27.50	0.73	0.48	0.08	0.01
Chambers County	TX	82.24	21.88	5.06	0.58	0.37	0.01	0.26
Galveston County	TX	94.62	28.36	37.10	0.93	0.40	0.17	0.03
Harris County	TX	97.27	60.61	30.07	1.44	0.47	0.32	0.07
Jackson County	TX	83.15	20.44	38.23	0.26	0.37	0.00	1.60
Jefferson County	TX	96.79	39.88	57.24	0.67	0.35	0.05	0.01
Kenedy County	TX	91.13	1.16	0.00	0.09	0.54	0.00	0.07
Kleberg County	TX	92.68	29.47	32.37	0.17	0.30	0.01	0.00
Liberty County	TX	68.54	16.71	18.30	0.26	0.47	0.01	0.02
Matagorda County	TX	84.88	17.20	22.36	0.16	0.46	0.01	0.04
Nueces County	TX	96.17	37.18	49.12	0.39	0.41	0.11	0.03
Orange County	TX	82.09	36.60	18.40	0.89	0.41	0.04	0.43
Refugio County	TX	87.26	5.99	26.44	0.20	0.30	0.00	0.04
San Patricio County	TX	90.17	29.74	9.44	0.35	0.37	0.02	0.01
Willacy County	TX	90.05	27.43	0.00	0.25	0.34	0.01	0.06

(Continued)

Table H.1 (Continued)

Ecological Resilience

County/parish	state	imperv	wet	srl
Baldwin County	AL	6.05	-1.54	4
Mobile County	AL	11.20	-1.95	4
Bay County	FL	11.63	-1.16	1
Calhoun County	FL	4.69	-0.15	0
Charlotte County	FL	19.28	-2.39	1
Citrus County	FL	20.95	-2.30	1
Collier County	FL	9.03	-11.54	0
Dixie County	FL	4.66	-0.26	1
Escambia County	FL	17.78	-1.06	4
Franklin County	FL	3.14	-0.81	1
Gulf County	FL	2.47	0.01	1
Hernando County	FL	22.44	-5.05	1
Hillsborough County	FL	31.10	-15.75	4
Jefferson County	FL	3.83	-0.24	0
Lee County	FL	31.03	-24.30	1
Leon County	FL	15.25	0.79	0
Levy County	FL	4.55	-0.40	0
Liberty County	FL	2.56	-0.23	0
Manatee County	FL	15.72	-7.53	3
Miami-Dade County	FL	16.36	-15.14	2

Monroe County	FL	1.04	-0.36	2
Okaloosa County	FL	11.72	-0.62	3
Pasco County	FL	24.18	-5.71	2
Pinellas County	FL	38.14	-2.47	4
Santa Rosa County	FL	10.54	-1.45	4
Sarasota County	FL	30.22	-5.05	3
Taylor County	FL	4.34	-0.31	0
Wakulla County	FL	4.16	-0.43	0
Walton County	FL	6.09	0.11	1
Washington County	FL	6.49	0.24	0
Acadia Parish	LA	9.59	-2.29	0
Ascension Parish	LA	21.51	-2.88	1
Assumption Parish	LA	5.74	-1.21	0
Calcasieu Parish	LA	15.19	-2.43	3
Cameron Parish	LA	1.53	-0.83	0
Iberia Parish	LA	4.82	1.33	0
Jefferson Parish	LA	16.20	-5.49	4
Jefferson Davis Parish	LA	8.02	-0.64	0
Lafayette Parish	LA	33.39	-0.47	0
Lafourche Parish	LA	3.47	-5.37	2
Livingston Parish	LA	8.74	-4.00	4
Orleans Parish	LA	24.80	-2.91	4
Plaquemines Parish	LA	1.44	-24.76	1
St. Bernard Parish	LA	0.82	-6.13	4
St. Charles Parish	LA	12.41	-2.07	4

(Continued)

Table H.1 (Continued)

County/parish	state	imperv	wet	srl
St. James Parish	LA	7.64	-0.74	0
St. John the Baptist Parish	LA	4.65	-6.64	0
St. Martin Parish	LA	3.71	29.93	1
St. Mary Parish	LA	10.36	-3.14	4
St. Tammany Parish	LA	8.99	-1.83	1
Tangipahoa Parish	LA	2.74	-11.24	4
Terrebonne Parish	LA	2.85	-3.95	1
Vermilion Parish	LA	6.58	-0.31	0
Washington Parish	LA	9.51	-1.52	2
Hancock County	MS	10.47	-1.60	4
Harrison County	MS	8.31	-1.40	4
Jackson County	MS	4.20	0.30	0
Aransas County	TX	10.21	0.97	4
Brazoria County	TX	3.43	1.42	0
Calhoun County	TX	12.62	-10.94	1
Cameron County	TX	7.04	-0.25	0
Chambers County	TX	16.15	2.05	4
Galveston County	TX	60.59	-7.83	4
Harris County	TX	4.21	-0.05	0
Jackson County	TX	15.00	-3.28	4

Jefferson County	TX	1.93	0.16	0
Kenedy County	TX	4.17	0.42	0
Kleberg County	TX	6.90	-3.48	0
Liberty County	TX	3.38	0.75	0
Matagorda County	TX	11.43	-0.42	1
Nueces County	TX	20.08	-1.29	0
Orange County	TX	3.69	0.38	0
Refugio County	TX	7.13	-1.14	0
San Patricio County	TX	3.64	0.34	0
Willacy County	TX	3.64	0.34	0

Appendix I
Reliability Analysis of Ecological Resilience

The adaptive capacity index presented in Chapter 5 is the replication of Susan Cutter, et al.'s Disaster Resilience of Place (DROP) index. Therefore, the indicators chosen for social resilience, economic resilience, institutional resilience, infrastructure resilience, and community capital correspond to the measures used in the DROP index. Ecological resilience, however, was not addressed by Cutter et al. because their sample was so large that measures of this component would not have been comparable. The study in this book is restricted to counties within 25 miles of the Gulf of Mexico and, therefore, focuses on a sample where ecological measures should be comparable. Given that the inclusion of ecological resilience is an addition to the DROP model, it is important to examine the reliability of this component.

Reliability refers to the internal consistency of a measure. We are concerned with how consistently the individual indicators chosen for ecological resilience represent this capacity. Cronbach's alpha is often used to measure the reliability of composite indices by assessing inter-correlations. It is calculated by weighing the variance of each individual indicator against the total variance of all indicators in the index. It also incorporates the number of indicators used to create the index; therefore, the alpha coefficient is inflated as indicators are added to the index. Higher alphas, however, do indicate greater internal consistency (or correlation).

Three indicators were chosen to measure ecological resilience, including wetland preservation—the net change in percent wetland area between 1996 and 2006, impervious surfaces—percent in square miles of land area, and floodplain development—index of severe repetitive loss properties (coded as: 0 = 0, 1 = 1 to 20, 2 = 21 to 30, 3 = 31 to 40, and 4 = 41 and over). Wetland preservation should contribute positively to ecological resilience while impervious surfaces and floodplain development should detract from this capacity.

Table G.1 presents the item-test correlations and the Cronbach's alpha for ecological resilience and the three indicators. Item-test correlations show the correlation between each indicator and the overall scale, and the alphas indicate internal consistency. The highest item-test correlation occurred between the ecological resilience index and impervious surfaces ($r = 0.771$). And the

Table I.1 Item-test Correlations and Cronbach's Alpha Coefficients for Indicators of Ecological Resilience

Item	Item-test Correlation	Alpha
Wetland preservation	0.680	0.553
Impervious surfaces	0.771	0.312
Floodplain development	0.722	0.451
Ecological resilience		0.546

highest alpha was obtained by the wetland preservation indicator ($\alpha = 0.553$). While the alphas were below the generally accepted 0.70 level, we must bear in mind that the calculation of the Cronbach's alpha is influenced by the number of items included in the analysis. Given that only three indicators were used in this index and that they are all highly correlated with the index (average item-test correlation of 0.72), we can say that the ecological resilience index is fairly reliable. This points out that constructing this component of resilience is difficult and that future studies should work to identify a set of measures that can be widely used to capture the concept of ecological resilience.

Appendix J
Description of Method to Create Adaptive Capacity Indices

To construct the adaptive capacity measure for each county, the individual indicators were first standardized using min-max rescaling. This procedure subtracts from each case the minimum value of the indicator then divides by the range of values. Observed, not theoretical, values are used. This forces zero to correspond to the lowest observed value of the indicator and one to indicate the highest observed value. For example, consider a hypothetical variable that theoretically ranges from 0 to 100. The observed cases of this indicator, however, range from 25 to 75. To standardize a case with a value of 50, we would calculate the following: [value—minimum]/range = [50 – 25]/50 = 0.5. We can see this without using the formula because we know that 50 is half-way between 25 and 75. This is the method of standardization for all indicators that are believed to have a positive effect on resilience. For those that have a negative effect, the additive inverse is first calculated then the values are standardized.

Once each indicator is standardized, the sub-component scores are calculated by averaging the indicators in the group. This means that each sub-component could range from zero to one. The overall measure of adaptive capacity is calculated by summing all of the sub-component averages. Therefore, has a theoretical range of zero to six. The disaster phase capacity measures are also calculated as the sum of their sub-components. They also were standardized to ensure comparability. Each index was multiplied by a factor so that it could range on the same theoretical scale of zero to six as the overall disaster resilience index. Therefore, the mitigation index was multiplied by 1.2 because it contains five sub-indices; the preparedness index was multiplied by two because it contains three sub-indices. Finally, the response and recovery resilience indices were multiplied by 1.5 because they contain four indicators each.

The raw scores of the resulting indicators were then converted to z-scores to analyze the data. Z-scores were calculated as the mean subtracted from each county's score, divided by the standard deviation. These z-scores were then converted to scale of very low (less than 1.5 standard deviation units below than the mean), low (between 1.5 and 0.5 standard deviation units below than the mean), moderate (between 0.5 standard deviation units lower than the mean and 0.5 standard deviation units above the mean), high (between 0.5 and 1.5 standard deviation units above the mean), or very high (greater than 1.5 standard deviation units above the mean). Finally, these adaptive capacity categories were assigned numerical values: 1= very low; 2 = low; 3 = moderate; 4 = high; and 5 = very high.

Appendix K
Adaptive Capacity for Disaster Resilience Scores

Table K.1   Adaptive Capacity for Disaster Resilience Scores

County/Parish	State	Disaster Resilience
Baldwin County	Alabama	4
Mobile County	Alabama	4
Bay County	Florida	4
Calhoun County	Florida	3
Charlotte County	Florida	3
Citrus County	Florida	2
Collier County	Florida	2
Dixie County	Florida	1
Escambia County	Florida	4
Franklin County	Florida	4
Gulf County	Florida	4
Hernando County	Florida	3
Hillsborough County	Florida	2
Jefferson County	Florida	4
Lee County	Florida	2
Leon County	Florida	5
Levy County	Florida	2
Liberty County	Florida	2
Manatee County	Florida	2
Miami-Dade County	Florida	2
Monroe County	Florida	3
Okaloosa County	Florida	4
Pasco County	Florida	3
Pinellas County	Florida	3
Santa Rosa County	Florida	3
Sarasota County	Florida	3
Taylor County	Florida	4

Wakulla County	Florida	4
Walton County	Florida	3
Washington County	Florida	3
Acadia Parish	Louisiana	4
Ascension Parish	Louisiana	4
Assumption Parish	Louisiana	3
Calcasieu Parish	Louisiana	4
Cameron Parish	Louisiana	4
Iberia Parish	Louisiana	4
Jefferson Parish	Louisiana	5
Jefferson Davis Parish	Louisiana	4
Lafayette Parish	Louisiana	5
Lafourche Parish	Louisiana	3
Livingston Parish	Louisiana	3
Orleans Parish	Louisiana	4
Plaquemines Parish	Louisiana	3
St. Bernard Parish	Louisiana	2
St. Charles Parish	Louisiana	4
St. James Parish	Louisiana	4
St. John the Baptist Parish	Louisiana	4
St. Martin Parish	Louisiana	3
St. Mary Parish	Louisiana	4
St. Tammany Parish	Louisiana	4
Tangipahoa Parish	Louisiana	4
Terrebonne Parish	Louisiana	3
Vermilion Parish	Louisiana	3
Washington Parish	Louisiana	3
Hancock County	Mississippi	1
Harrison County	Mississippi	2
Jackson County	Mississippi	1
Aransas County	Texas	2
Brazoria County	Texas	3
Calhoun County	Texas	3
Cameron County	Texas	1
Chambers County	Texas	2
Galveston County	Texas	4
Harris County	Texas	1
Jackson County	Texas	3
Jefferson County	Texas	3
Kenedy County	Texas	1
Kleberg County	Texas	3

(*Continued*)

Table K.1   (Continued)

County/Parish	State	Disaster Resilience
Liberty County	Texas	1
Matagorda County	Texas	2
Nueces County	Texas	4
Orange County	Texas	3
Refugio County	Texas	3
San Patricio County	Texas	2
Willacy County	Texas	2

Appendix L
Adaptive Capacities for Disaster Resilience Scores across Components

Table L.1 Adaptive Capacities for Disaster Resilience Scores across Components

County/Parish	State	Social Resilience	Community Capital	Economic Resilience	Institutional Resilience	Infrastructure Resilience	Ecological Resilience
Baldwin County	Alabama	5	3	3	4	3	2
Mobile County	Alabama	4	4	3	4	4	2
Bay County	Florida	4	2	4	4	3	3
Calhoun County	Florida	3	2	3	3	2	4
Charlotte County	Florida	2	2	4	4	3	3
Citrus County	Florida	2	2	4	3	2	3
Collier County	Florida	2	1	3	3	2	3
Dixie County	Florida	1	2	3	3	1	4
Escambia County	Florida	3	3	4	4	4	2
Franklin County	Florida	3	5	1	4	2	4
Gulf County	Florida	3	4	3	4	2	4
Hernando County	Florida	3	2	4	4	2	3

(*Continued*)

Table L.1 (Continued)

County/Parish	State	Social Resilience	Community Capital	Economic Resilience	Institutional Resilience	Infrastructure Resilience	Ecological Resilience
Hillsborough County	Florida	4	2	3	4	4	1
Jefferson County	Florida	3	5	3	4	2	4
Lee County	Florida	3	2	3	4	3	2
Leon County	Florida	4	4	3	3	4	4
Levy County	Florida	2	3	2	4	1	4
Liberty County	Florida	3	4	1	2	1	4
Manatee County	Florida	3	2	3	3	3	2
Miami-Dade County	Florida	1	1	3	4	4	2
Monroe County	Florida	3	3	2	4	2	3
Okaloosa County	Florida	4	2	4	4	3	2
Pasco County	Florida	3	1	4	4	3	2
Pinellas County	Florida	4	2	3	4	5	1
Santa Rosa County	Florida	5	2	4	4	3	2
Sarasota County	Florida	3	2	3	5	3	2
Taylor County	Florida	4	4	2	4	2	4
Wakulla County	Florida	3	2	5	4	2	4
Walton County	Florida	3	3	3	3	3	3

Washington County	Florida	3	2	3	3	2	4
Acadia Parish	Louisiana	3	4	2	3	4	4
Ascension Parish	Louisiana	5	3	4	3	3	3
Assumption Parish	Louisiana	3	4	3	2	2	4
Calcasieu Parish	Louisiana	4	4	3	4	4	2
Cameron Parish	Louisiana	3	3	4	3	3	4
Iberia Parish	Louisiana	3	4	3	3	3	4
Jefferson Parish	Louisiana	3	3	4	5	5	2
Jefferson Davis Parish	Louisiana	3	5	3	3	3	4
Lafayette Parish	Louisiana	4	4	3	3	5	3
Lafourche Parish	Louisiana	3	4	2	3	3	3
Livingston Parish	Louisiana	4	3	4	4	2	2
Orleans Parish	Louisiana	1	4	3	4	5	1
Plaquemines Parish	Louisiana	2	3	4	3	2	3
St. Bernard Parish	Louisiana	2	3	3	3	3	2
St. Charles Parish	Louisiana	5	4	5	4	3	2
St. James Parish	Louisiana	3	4	3	3	3	4
St. John the Baptist Parish	Louisiana	3	3	4	3	3	4
St. Martin Parish	Louisiana	3	4	2	3	2	4

(Continued)

Table L.1 (Continued)

County/Parish	State	Social Resilience	Community Capital	Economic Resilience	Institutional Resilience	Infrastructure Resilience	Ecological Resilience
St. Mary Parish	Louisiana	3	3	3	2	3	5
St. Tammany Parish	Louisiana	5	3	4	3	3	2
Tangipahoa Parish	Louisiana	3	3	2	4	3	3
Terrebonne Parish	Louisiana	3	4	3	4	3	2
Vermilion Parish	Louisiana	3	4	2	2	3	3
Washington Parish	Louisiana	3	4	2	2	3	4
Hancock County	Mississippi	4	1	4	2	3	3
Harrison County	Mississippi	4	2	3	2	4	2
Jackson County	Mississippi	4	2	2	2	3	2
Aransas County	Texas	3	2	2	3	2	4
Brazoria County	Texas	4	3	5	3	3	2
Calhoun County	Texas	2	3	4	2	3	4
Cameron County	Texas	1	2	3	1	3	3
Chambers County	Texas	4	2	4	1	3	4
Galveston County	Texas	4	3	4	4	4	2
Harris County	Texas	2	2	3	3	5	1
Jackson County	Texas	3	4	2	1	4	4
Jefferson County	Texas	2	4	3	3	4	2

Kenedy County	Texas	1	3	1	1	2	4
Kleberg County	Texas	2	4	1	2	3	4
Liberty County	Texas	2	2	3	1	2	4
Matagorda County	Texas	2	4	1	1	2	4
Nueces County	Texas	3	3	3	3	4	3
Orange County	Texas	3	3	3	1	3	3
Refugio County	Texas	2	4	2	3	3	4
San Patricio County	Texas	3	3	2	2	3	4
Willacy County	Texas	2	3	3	1	3	4

Appendix M
Adaptive Capacity for Disaster Resilience Scores across Disaster Phases

Table M.1   Adaptive Capacity for Disaster Resilience Scores across Disaster Phases

County/Parish	State	Mitigation	Preparedness	Response	Recovery
Baldwin County	Alabama	4	4	4	3
Mobile County	Alabama	3	4	4	3
Bay County	Florida	4	4	4	3
Calhoun County	Florida	3	2	2	3
Charlotte County	Florida	3	3	3	3
Citrus County	Florida	3	3	3	3
Collier County	Florida	2	2	2	2
Dixie County	Florida	2	3	2	3
Escambia County	Florida	3	4	5	2
Franklin County	Florida	4	4	4	4
Gulf County	Florida	4	4	3	4
Hernando County	Florida	3	3	3	3
Hillsborough County	Florida	2	3	4	1
Jefferson County	Florida	5	4	3	5
Lee County	Florida	2	3	3	1
Leon County	Florida	4	4	4	4
Levy County	Florida	3	3	2	3
Liberty County	Florida	3	2	2	3
Manatee County	Florida	2	3	3	2
Miami-Dade County	Florida	2	3	3	1
Monroe County	Florida	3	3	3	3
Okaloosa County	Florida	4	4	4	3
Pasco County	Florida	3	3	3	2
Pinellas County	Florida	2	3	4	1
Santa Rosa County	Florida	3	3	3	3

Sarasota County	Florida	3	4	4	2
Taylor County	Florida	4	4	3	4
Wakulla County	Florida	4	4	3	4
Walton County	Florida	3	2	2	3
Washington County	Florida	3	2	2	3
Acadia Parish	Louisiana	4	3	3	4
Ascension Parish	Louisiana	4	3	3	4
Assumption Parish	Louisiana	3	2	2	4
Calcasieu Parish	Louisiana	4	4	4	3
Cameron Parish	Louisiana	4	3	3	4
Iberia Parish	Louisiana	4	3	3	4
Jefferson Parish	Louisiana	4	5	5	2
Jefferson Davis Parish	Louisiana	4	3	3	4
Lafayette Parish	Louisiana	4	4	4	4
Lafourche Parish	Louisiana	3	4	3	3
Livingston Parish	Louisiana	3	4	3	3
Orleans Parish	Louisiana	2	4	5	2
Plaquemines Parish	Louisiana	3	3	3	3
St. Bernard Parish	Louisiana	2	3	3	2
St. Charles Parish	Louisiana	4	5	4	3
St. James Parish	Louisiana	4	4	3	4
St. John the Baptist Parish	Louisiana	4	3	3	4
St. Martin Parish	Louisiana	4	3	3	4
St. Mary Parish	Louisiana	4	3	3	4
St. Tammany Parish	Louisiana	3	4	4	3
Tangipahoa Parish	Louisiana	4	4	4	3
Terrebonne Parish	Louisiana	3	4	4	2
Vermilion Parish	Louisiana	3	2	2	3
Washington Parish	Louisiana	3	2	2	4
Hancock County	Mississippi	1	1	1	2
Harrison County	Mississippi	1	2	3	2
Jackson County	Mississippi	1	1	2	2
Aransas County	Texas	3	2	2	3
Brazoria County	Texas	3	3	3	3
Calhoun County	Texas	3	3	3	4
Cameron County	Texas	1	1	1	2
Chambers County	Texas	2	1	2	4
Galveston County	Texas	3	4	4	3

(*Continued*)

Table L.1   (Continued)

County/Parish	State	Mitigation	Preparedness	Response	Recovery
Harris County	Texas	1	2	3	1
Jackson County	Texas	2	1	2	4
Jefferson County	Texas	2	3	4	2
Kenedy County	Texas	1	1	1	2
Kleberg County	Texas	3	2	3	4
Liberty County	Texas	2	1	1	3
Matagorda County	Texas	2	1	1	3
Nueces County	Texas	3	3	4	3
Orange County	Texas	2	2	2	4
Refugio County	Texas	4	3	3	4
San Patricio County	Texas	3	2	2	3
Willacy County	Texas	2	2	2	4

Appendix N
Descriptive Statistics for Chapter 5 Regression

Table N.1   Descriptive Statistics for Chapter 5 Regression

		Mean	Standard Deviation	Minimum Value	Maximum Value
	Factors Associated with Disaster Resilience Scores				
	Dependent Variables				
	Disaster resilience	3.26	0.25	2.54	3.76
Subcomponents	Social	0.70	0.06	0.53	0.86
	Community capital	0.49	0.10	0.24	0.77
	Economic	0.55	0.08	0.25	0.69
	Institutional	0.57	0.17	0.16	0.98
	Infrastructure	0.33	0.13	0.06	0.83
	Ecological	0.62	0.18	0.10	0.90
Disaster Phases	Mitigation	3.52	0.29	2.61	4.05
	Preparedness	3.22	0.43	1.97	4.15
	Response	2.91	0.42	1.69	3.98
	Recovery	3.54	0.34	2.50	4.06
	Independent Variables				
Urban/Rural County	Metro: ≥1 million pop	0.23	0.42	0	1
	Metro: 250,000–1million pop	0.24	0.43	0	1
	Metro: <250,000 pop	0.17	0.38	0	1
	Urban: ≥20,000 pop	0.13	0.34	0	1
	Urban: 2,500–19,999	0.19	0.39	0	1
	Rural: <2,500 pop	0.04	0.20	0	1
Grants	Public assistance grants	492.09	760.90	2	4647
	Hazard mitigation grant	25.05	31.18	1	202
Disaster	Hurricane max intensity	429.53	534.19	0	2500
	Tornado max intensity	1.03	0.84	0	3
State Context	Home rule county	0.39	0.49	0	1
	Alabama	0.03	0.16	0	1
	Louisiana	0.32	0.47	0	1
	Mississippi	0.04	0.20	0	1
	Texas	0.24	0.43	0	1

Appendix O
Descriptive Statistics for Chapter 6 Regression Analyses

Table O.1 Descriptive Statistics for Chapter 6 Regression Analysis

Factors Related to County Emergency Managers Ratings of Coordination				
	Mean	Standard Deviation	Minimum Value	Maximum Value
Dependent Variables				
Citizens	0.87	0.34	0	1
Nonprofits	0.93	0.26	0	1
Private partners	0.87	0.34	0	1
Local government	0.91	0.29	0	1
State EM	0.91	0.29	0	1
Federal EM	0.59	0.50	0	1
Independent Variables				
Urban index	3.98	1.52	1	6
Hurricane max damage	416.58	427.88	0	1333.33
BP oil spill economic loss	1.71	1.30	0	4.75
Coordinator role	0.48	0.50	0	1
Years of experience	19.00	11.28	3	45
EM expenditures	0.20	0.12	0.04	0.46
EM number of staff	1.94	0.71	1	3
Alabama	0.02	0.14	0	1
Louisiana	0.31	0.47	0	1
Mississippi	0.06	0.23	0	1
Texas	0.28	0.45	0	1

Table O.2 Descriptive Statistics for Chapter 6 Regression Analysis

	Factors Related to Municipal Elected Officials Ratings of Coordination								
	Mean	Standard Deviation	Minimum Value	Maximum Value		Mean	Standard Deviation	Minimum Value	Maximum Value
	Citizen ratings (N = 164)					County EM ratings (N = 164)			
Citizens	0.85	0.35	0	1	County EM	0.88	0.32	0	1
Population	65.50	297.09	0.28	2191.40	Population	65.48	297.10	0.28	2191.40
Hurricane	380.33	413.88	0	1333.33	Hurricane	380.62	413.68	0	1333.33
BP oil spill	1.20	1.05	0	4.5	BP oil spill	1.21	1.05	0	4.5
Fiscal resources	0.03	0.17	0	1	Fiscal resources	0.02	0.15	0	1
Human resources	2.09	0.72	1	3	Human resources	2.09	0.73	1	3
Business leader	0.52	0.50	0	1	Business leader	0.51	0.50	0	1
Local govt. leader	0.93	0.26	0	1	Local govt. leader	0.92	0.27	0	1
Faith-based leader	0.70	0.46	0	1	Faith-based leader	0.69	0.46	0	1
Alabama	0.09	0.29	0	1	Alabama	0.09	0.29	0	1
Louisiana	0.09	0.29	0	1	Louisiana	0.09	0.29	0	1
Mississippi	0.12	0.32	0	1	Mississippi	0.12	0.32	0	1
Texas	0.51	0.50	0	1	Texas	0.50	0.50	0	1

(Continued)

Table O.2 (Continued)

	Mean	Standard Deviation	Minimum Value	Maximum Value
	Nonprofit ratings (N=161)			
Nonprofits	0.85	0.36	0	1
Population	65.72	299.73	0.28	2191.40
Hurricane	378.49	413.52	0	1333.33
BP oil spill	1.20	1.06	0	4.5
Fiscal resources	0.02	0.16	0	1
Human resources	2.07	0.73	1	3
Business leader	0.52	0.50	0	1
Local govt. leader	0.91	0.28	0	1
Faith-based leader	0.70	0.46	0	1
Alabama	0.09	0.29	0	1
Louisiana	0.09	0.29	0	1
Mississippi	0.12	0.32	0	1
Texas	0.51	0.50	0	1
	Neighboring municipalities (N = 164)			
Neigh. munis.	0.88	0.33	0	1
Population	65.45	297.10	0.28	2191.40

	Mean	Standard Deviation	Minimum Value	Maximum Value
	State government ratings (N = 159)			
State govt.	0.74	0.44	0	1
Population	67.42	301.55	0.28	2191.40
Hurricane	380.84	411.24	0	1333.33
BP oil spill	1.22	1.06	0	4.5
Fiscal resources	0.03	0.16	0	1
Human resources	2.09	0.74	1	3
Business leader	0.50	0.50	0	1
Local govt. leader	0.92	0.27	0	1
Faith-based leader	0.69	0.47	0	1
Alabama	0.09	0.29	0	1
Louisiana	0.09	0.29	0	1
Mississippi	0.12	0.33	0	1
Texas	0.50	0.50	0	1
	Federal government (N = 154)			
Federal govt.	0.57	0.50	0	1
Population	68.43	306.23	0.28	2191.40

Hurricane	373.94	411.14	0	1333.33
BP oil spill	1.18	1.06	0	4.5
Fiscal resources	0.03	0.17	0	1
Human resources	2.08	0.73	1	3
Business leader	0.51	0.50	0	1
Local govt. leader	0.91	0.28	0	1
Faith-based leader	0.70	0.46	0	1
Alabama	0.09	0.29	0	1
Louisiana	0.09	0.29	0	1
Mississippi	0.12	0.32	0	1
Texas	0.51	0.50	0	1

Hurricane	374.76	405.16	0	1333.33
BP oil spill	1.23	1.06	0	4.5
Fiscal resources	0.02	0.14	0	1
Human resources	2.08	0.73	1	3
Business leader	0.50	0.50	0	1
Local govt. leader	0.92	0.28	0	1
Faith-based leader	0.69	0.46	0	1
Alabama	0.09	0.29	0	1
Louisiana	0.10	0.30	0	1
Mississippi	0.12	0.33	0	1
Texas	0.50	0.50	0	1

Appendix P
Alignment of Resilience Perceptions with County Adaptive Capacity

The scores for alignment of resilience perceptions held by county emergency managers with county adaptive capacities shown in Figure 7.3 are reported in Table P.1. Alignment of resilience perceptions are coded –1 for overestimation of county adaptive capacity, 0 for alignment, and 1 for underestimation.

Table P.1   Alignment of Resilience Perceptions with County Adaptive Capacity

County/Parish	State	Alignment
Baldwin County	Alabama	1
Bay County	Alabama	1
Calhoun County	Florida	1
Charlotte County	Florida	–1
Citrus County	Florida	0
Franklin County	Florida	1
Gulf County	Florida	1
Hernando County	Florida	1
Lee County	Florida	0
Leon County	Florida	1
Liberty County	Florida	–1
Manatee County	Florida	1
Monroe County	Florida	0
Okaloosa County	Florida	1
Pasco County	Florida	1
Santa Rosa County	Florida	0
Sarasota County	Florida	–1
Taylor County	Florida	0
Walton County	Florida	–1
Washington County	Florida	1
Acadia Parish	Louisiana	0

Ascension Parish	Louisiana	1
Assumption Parish	Louisiana	0
Cameron Parish	Louisiana	0
Iberia Parish	Louisiana	1
Jefferson Parish	Louisiana	1
Lafourche Parish	Louisiana	0
Orleans Parish	Louisiana	0
Plaquemines Parish	Louisiana	−1
St. Bernard Parish	Louisiana	−1
St. Charles Parish	Louisiana	0
St. James Parish	Louisiana	1
St. Mary Parish	Louisiana	1
St. Tammany Parish	Louisiana	−1
Tangipahoa Parish	Louisiana	−1
Terrebonne Parish	Louisiana	−1
Washington Parish	Louisiana	1
Hancock County	Mississippi	−1
Harrison County	Mississippi	−1
Jackson County	Mississippi	−1
Aransas County	Texas	0
Brazoria County	Texas	1
Calhoun County	Texas	0
Cameron County	Texas	−1
Chambers County	Texas	−1
Galveston County	Texas	1
Jefferson County	Texas	0
Kleberg County	Texas	1
Matagorda County	Texas	0
Nueces County	Texas	1
Orange County	Texas	1
Refugio County	Texas	−1
San Patricio County	Texas	−1
Kenedy County	Texas	−1

Appendix Q
Alignment of Resilience Perceptions with County Adaptive Capacity across Capacity Components

Chapter 7 considers how hypothetical resilience ratings by county emergency managers overlap with county adaptive capacity. Given that the measure of adaptive capacities is an aggregation of multiple indicators across six components (social, community capital, economic, institutional, infrastructure, and ecological), it is important to examine how perceptions of resilience align with capacity in each area to determine if one component dominates assessments. Figure Q.1 shows the distribution of alignment, underestimation, and overestimation across the components of the adaptive capacity measure. Graph A in the figure reports the percentage of cases with aligned perceptions; Graph B the percentage of cases that underestimated resilience; and Graph C the percentage of cases that overestimated resilience. The horizontal line on each graph marks the percentage of cases that were aligned, underestimated, or overestimated based on comparison of resilience perceptions with the county's *overall* adaptive capacity.

These graphs show that the alignment of resilience perceptions with the components of adaptive capacity does not deviate considerably from the alignment of perceptions with the overall capacity measure. In other words, there is not one component of capacity that dominates resilience assessments. This implies that the assessments of resilience given by county emergency mangers are not driven by one component; rather resilience evaluations seem to capture the range of capacity components. This is supported by correlation analysis.

Pairwise correlations of perceptions of resilience with the components of adaptive capacity indicate that there are no significant associations between the components of resilience and hypothetical resilience ratings. Additionally, the correlation coefficients are not high, ranging from -0.076 to -0.250. The correlation between hypothetical resilience ratings and overall adaptive capacity, however, is statistically significant at the 0.05 level with a correlation coefficient of -0.500.

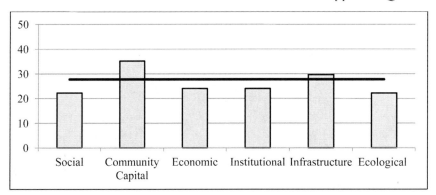

A. Alignment of Resilience

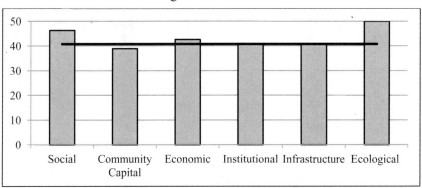

B. Underestimation of Resilience

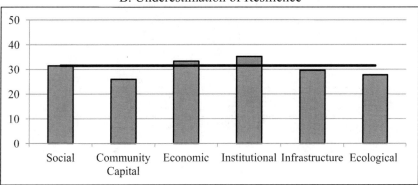

C. Overestimation of Resilience

Figure Q.1 Alignment of Resilience Perceptions with County Adaptive Capacity across Capacity Components

Sources: Data sources for the measures of overall adaptive capacity and its component measures are listed in Appendix G. Data on perceptions of resilience were taken from original surveys of county emergency managers.

Notes: The bars denote the percentage of cases in each category across the components of adaptive capacity. The line marks the percentage for overall adaptive capacities for disaster resilience.

Appendix R
Descriptive Statistics for Chapter 7 Regression Analysis

Table R.1   Descriptive Statistics for Chapter 7 Regression Analysis

	Mean	Standard Deviation	Minimum Value	Maximum Value
Factors Associated with Overestimation of Resilience				
Dependent Variables				
Overestimated resilience	0.33	0.48	0	1
Independent Variables				
Level of disaster resilience	2.20	0.63	1	3
Rural county index	3	1.51	1	6
Hurricane max damage	432.62	434.41	0	1333.33
Tornado max damage	1.02	0.84	0	3
BP oil spill impact	1.72	1.29	0	4.75
Year since severe disaster	6.33	2.75	0	11
PA grants	470.69	585.02	2	3323
HMGP grants	23.10	17.40	1	72
EM office number of staff	1.96	0.69	1	3
EM years of experience	19.90	10.95	3	45
EM college education	1.49	0.51	1	2

References

Adger, W. Neil. "Social and Ecological Resilience: Are They Related?" *Progress in Human Geography* 24 (2000): 347–64.

Alabama Department of Mental Health. "Project Rebound." Accessed June 30, 2013. https://www.mh.alabama.gov/ProjectRebound/.

Alabama Emergency Management Agency. "Emergency Operations Plan." Accessed June 30, 2013. http://www.ema.alabama.gov/filelibrary/Alabama_EOP.pdf.

Alabama Policy Institute. "Home Rule in Alabama." Accessed June 30, 2013. http://www.alabamapolicy.org/research/home-rule-in-alabama/.

Alabama Political Reporter. "Governor announces coastal restoration projects." By Beth Clayton. May 3, 2013. Accessed June 30, 2013. http://www.alreporter.com/al-politics/political-news/state-news/4567-governor-announces-coastal-restoration-projects.html.

Alabama State Legislature. "SB 129." Accessed June 30, 2013. http://www.legislature.state.al.us/SearchableInstruments/2005RS/Bills/SB129.htm.

Alabama Travel Industry. "Economic Impact Report, 2010." Accessed June 30, 2013. http://images.alabama-staging.luckie.com/publications/main-con-tent/2010TourismReport.pdf.

American City and County. *Homeland Security Outlook: Local Governments Reveal Purchasing Plans for 2006.* 2006. Accessed June 30, 2013. http://americancityandcounty.com/site-files/americancityandcounty.com/files/archive/americancityandcounty.com/mag/homelandsecurity06.pdf.

Baltimore Sun. "Letters recall the great Galveston hurricane of 1900." Accessed June 30, 2013. http://articles.baltimoresun.com/2010-09-18/news/bs-md-backstory-galveston-hurricane-20100917_1_galveston-residents-hurricane-leeward-islands/2.

Bea, Keith. "The Formative Years: 1950–1978." In *Emergency Management: The American Experience 1900–2005*, edited by Claire B. Rubin, 81–110. Fairfax, VA, VA: Public Entity Risk Institute, 2007.

Beatley, Timothy. *Planning for Coastal Resilience: Best Practices for Calamitous Times.* Washington, DC: Island Press, 2009.

Berke, Philip R., and Thomas J. Campanella. "Planning for Postdisaster Resiliency." *Annals of the American Academy of Political and Social Science* 604 (2006): 192–207.

Birkland, Thomas A. "Federal Disaster Policy: Learning, Priorities, and Prospects for Resilience." In *Designing Resilience: Preparing for Extreme Events*, edited by Louise K. Comfort, Arjen Boin, and Chris C. Demchak, 106–28. Pittsburgh: University of Pittsburgh Press, 2010.

Birkland, Thomas A. "Focusing Events, Mobilization, and Agenda Setting." *Journal of Public Policy* (1998): 53–74.

Birkland, Thomas A. *After Disaster: Agenda Setting, Public Policy, and Focusing Events.* Washington, DC: Georgetown University Press, 1997.

Bixel, Patricia B. and Elizabeth H. Turner. *Galveston and the 1900 Storm.* Austin: University of Texas Press, 2000.

Bodin, Per and Bo L.B. Wiman. "Resilience and other stability concepts in ecology: Notes on their origin, validity, and usefulness." *ESS Bulletin* 2 (2004): 33–43.

Boin, Arjen, Louise K. Comfort, and Chris C. Demchak. "The Rise of Resilience." In *Designing Resilience: Preparing for Extreme Events,* edited by Louise K. Comfort, Arjen Boin, and Chris C. Demchak, 1–12. Pittsburgh: University of Pittsburgh Press, 2010.

Boin, Arjen. "Designing Resilience: Leadership Challenges in Complex Administrative Systems." In *Designing Resilience: Preparing for Extreme Events,* edited by Louise K. Comfort, Arjen Boin, and Chris C. Demchak, 129–42. Pittsburg: University of Pittsburg Press, 2010.

Bolin, R.C. and L. Stanford. "Constructing Vulnerability in the First World: The Northridge Earthquake in Southern California, 1994." In *The Angry Earth: Disasters in Anthropological Perspective,* edited by A. Oliver-Smith and S. Hoffman, 89–112. New York: Routledge, 1999.

Bonanno, George A. "Loss, trauma, and human resilience: have we underestimated the human capacity to thrive after extremely aversive events?" *American Psychology* 4 (2004): 20–8.

BP Deepwater Horizon Settlements. "Map of Economic Loss Zones." Accessed June 30, 2013. http://www.deepwaterhorizonsettlements.com/Documents/Economic%20SA/Ex1A_Map_of_Economic_Loss_Zones.pdf.

Briguglio, Lino, Gordon Cordina, Nadia Farrugia, and Stephanie Vella. 2008. "Economic Vulnerability and Resilience." Research Paper No. 2008/55. United Nations University. British Monarchy. "Queen's Jubilee Speech Hails U.K.'s 'Resilience'." Accessed June 30, 2013. http://www.cbc.ca/news/world/story/2012/03/20/queen-jubilee-address.html.

Brodie, M., E. Weltzian, D. Altman, R.J. Blendon, and J.M. Benson. "Experiences of Hurricane Katrina Evacuees in Houston shelters: Implications for Future Planning." *American Journal of Public Health* 96 (2006): 1402–8.

Brody, Samuel D. "Are We Learning to Make Better Plans? A Longitudinal Analysis of Plan Quality Associated with Natural Hazards." *Journal of Planning Education and Research* 23 (2003): 191–201.

Brody, Samuel D., Jung Eun Kang, and Sarah Bernhardt. "Identifying factors influencing flood mitigation at the local level in Texas and Florida: the role of organizational capacity." *Natural Hazards* 52 (2010): 167–84.

Buckle, Philip. "Assessing Social Resilience." In *Disaster Resilience: An Integrated Approach,* edited by Douglas Paton and David Johnston, 88–103. Springfield, IL: Charles C Thomas Publisher Ltd., 2006.

Butler, David. "Focusing Events in the Early Twentieth Century: A Hurricane, Two Earthquakes, and a Pandemic." In *Emergency Management: The American Experience 1900–2005,* edited by Claire B. Rubin, 11–48. Fairfax, VA, VA: Public Entity Risk Institute, 2007.

Butler, David. "The Expanding Role of the Federal Government: 1927–1950." In *Emergency Management: The American Experience 1900–2005,* edited by Claire B. Rubin, 49–80. Fairfax, VA, VA: Public Entity Risk Institute, 2007.

Campanella, Thomas J. "Urban Resilience and the Recovery of New Orleans." *Journal of the American Planning Association* 72 (2006): 141–6.

Chamlee-Wright, Emily and Virgil H. Storr. "Community Resilience in New Orleans East: Deploying the Cultural Toolkit within a Vietnamese American Community." In *Community Disaster Recovery and Resiliency: Exploring Global Opportunities and Challenges,* edited by DeMond S. Miller and Jason D. Rivera, 102–24. Boca Raton, FL: Auerback Publications, 2011.

Cigler, Beverly A. "The Big Question of Katrina and the 2005 Great Flood of New Orleans." *Public Administration Review* 67 (2007): 64–76.

Citizen Corps. Accessed September 5, 2012. https://www.citizencorps.gov/cc/Council MapIndex.do.

Clary, Bruce B. "The Evolution and Structure of Natural Hazard Policies." *Public Administration Review* 45 (1985) 20–8.

CNN. "Empty Nets in Louisiana Three Years After the Spill." Accessed June 30, 2013. http://www.cnn.com/2013/04/27/us/gulf-disaster-fishing-industry.

CNN. "Family: Oil disaster devastated captain who committed suicide." By Rich Phillips. June 25, 2010. Accessed June 30, 2013. http://www.cnn.com/2010/US/06/25/gulf.oil.disaster.suicide/index.html.

Coastal Recovery Commission of Alabama. *Roadmap for Resilience: Toward a Healthier Environment, Society and Economy for Coastal Alabama.*2011. Accessed June 30, 2013. http://crcalabama.org/wp-content/uploads/2011/02/CRC-Report-02-2011.pdf.

Coastal Recovery Commission of Alabama. "Beyond the Oil Spill." Accessed June 30, 2013. http://crcalabama.org/.

Col, Jeanne-Marie. "Managing Disasters: The Role of Local Government." *Public Administration Review* 67 (2007): 114–24.

Comfort, Louise K. "Crisis Management in Hindsight: Cognition, Communication, Coordination, and Control." *Public Administration Review* 67 (2007): 189–97.

Comfort, Louise K., Namkyung Oh, Gunes Ertan, and Steve Scheinert. "Designing Adaptive Systems for Disaster Mitigation." In *Designing Resilience: Preparing for Extreme Events,* edited by Louise K. Comfort, Arjen Boin, and Chris C. Demchak, 33–61. Pittsburgh: University of Pittsburgh Press, 2010.

Common Ground Relief. "Wetlands Restoration." Accessed June 30, 2013. http://www.commongroundrelief.org/wetlands.

Community and Regional Resilience Initiative. *Community and Regional Resilience: Perspectives from Hazards, Disasters, and Emergency Management.* By Susan L. Cutter, Lindsey Barnes, Melissa Berry, Christopher Burton, Elijah Evans, Eric Tate, and Jennifer Webb. CARRI Research Report 1. Columbia: Hazards and Vulnerability Research Institute, University of South Carolina, 2008. Accessed June 5, 2011. http://www.resilientus.org/library/FINAL_CUTTER_9-25-08_1223482309.pdf.

Congressional Research Service. *Federal Emergency Management Policy Changes After Hurricane Katrina: A Summary of Statutory Provisions.* By Keith Bea, Elaine Halchin, Henry Hogue, Frederick Kaiser, Natalie Love, Francis X. McCarthy, Shawn Reese, and Barbara Schwemle. RL33729. Washington, DC: CRS, 2006. Accessed June 30, 2013. http://www.tisp.org/index.cfm?cdid=10986&pid=10261.

Cottrell, Alison. "Weathering the Storm: Women's Preparedness as a Form of Resilience to Weather-Related Hazards in Northern Australia." In *Disaster Resilience: An Integrated Approach,* edited by Douglas Paton and David Johnston, 128–41. Springfield, IL: Charles C Thomas Publisher Ltd., 2006.

Cutter, Susan L., Bryan J. Boruff, and W. Lynn Shirley. "Social Vulnerability to Environmental Hazards." *Social Science Quarterly* 84 (2003): 242–61.

Cutter, Susan L., Christopher G. Burton, and Christopher T. Emrich. "Disaster Resilience Indicators for Benchmarking Baseline Conditions." *Journal of Homeland Security and Emergency Management* 7 (2010): 1–22.

Cutter, Susan L., Lindsey Barnes, Melissa Berry, Christopher Burton, Elijah Evans, Eric Tate, and Jennifer Webb. "A Place-Based Model for Understanding Community Resilience to Natural Disasters." *Global Environmental Change* 18 (2008): 598–606.

de Bruijne, Mark, Arjen Boin, and Michel van Eeten. "Resilience: Exploring the Concept and Its Meanings." In *Designing Resilience: Preparing for Extreme Events,* edited by Louise K. Comfort, Arjen Boin, and Chris C. Demchak, 13–32. Pittsburgh: University of Pittsburgh Press, 2010.

DeSalvo, Karen. "Delivering High-Quality, Accessible Health Care: The Rise of Community Centers." In *Resilience and Opportunity: Lessons from the U.S. Gulf Coast after Katrina and Rita,* edited by Amy Liu, Roland V. Anglin, Richard M. Mizelle Jr., and Allison Plyer, 45–63. Washington, DC: The Brookings Institution, 2011.

Drabek, Thomas E. "The Evolution of Emergency Management." In *Emergency Management: Principles and Practice for Local Government,* edited by Thomas E. Drabek and Gerard J. Hoetmer, 3–29. Washington, DC: International City Management Association, 1991.

Drabek, Thomas E. *Strategies for Coordinating Disaster Responses.* Boulder: University of Colorado, Natural Research and Applications Information Center, 2003.

Dyer, Christopher L. and James R. McGoodwin. "Tell Them We're Hurting: Hurricane Andrew, the Culture of Response, and the Fishing Peoples of South Florida and Louisiana." In *The Angry Earth: Disasters in an Anthropological Perspective,* edited by Anthony Oliver-Smith and Susanna M. Hoffmann, 213–31. New York: Routledge, 1999.

Edwards, Francis L. "All Hazards, Whole Community: Creating Resiliency." In *Disaster Resilience: Interdisciplinary Perspectives,* edited by Naim Kapucu, Christopher V. Hawkins, and Fernando I. Rivera, 21–48. New York: Routledge, 2013.

Edwards, Francis L. and Daniel C. Goodrich. "Organizing for Emergency Management." In *Emergency Management: Principles and Practices for Local Government, Second Edition,* edited by William L. Waugh Jr. and Kathleen Tierney, 39–53. Washington, DC: International City/County Management Association, 2007.

Enarson, Elaine and Betty Hearn Morrow. "Women Will Rebuild Miami: A Case Study of Feminist Response to Disaster." In *The Gendered Terrain of Disaster: Through Women's Eyes,* edited by Elaine Enarson and Betty H. Morrow, 185–98. Westport, CT: Praeger Publishers, 1998.

Encyclopedia of Alabama. "Home Rule." Accessed June 30, 2013. http://www.encyclopediaofalabama.org/face/Article.jsp?id=h-1153.

Erikson, Bonnie. "Social Networks: The Value of Variety." *Contexts* 2 (2003): 25–31.

Federal Civil Defense Administration. "Annual Statistical Report." Accessed June 30, 2013. http://training.fema.gov/EMIWeb/edu/docs/HistoricalInterest/FCDA%20-%201955%20-%20%20Annual%20Statistical%20Report.pdf.

Federal Emergency Management Agency. Citizen Corps. *A Guide for Local Officials.* Washington, DC: FEMA, 2011. Accessed June 30, 2013. http://www.ready.gov/guides.

Federal Emergency Management Agency. "Categories of Work." Accessed June 30, 2013. http://www.fema.gov/public-assistance-local-state-tribal-and-non-profit/categories-work#catC.

Federal Emergency Management Agency. "Community Rating Fact Sheet." Accessed June 30, 2013. http://www.fema.gov/library/viewRecord.do?id=2635.

FEMA. "CRS Eligible Communities." Accessed April 2, 2012. http://www.fema.gov/library/viewRecord.do?id=3629.

Federal Emergency Management Agency. "Disaster Mitigation Act 2000." Accessed June 30, 2013. http://www.fema.gov/library/viewRecord.do?id=1935.

Federal Emergency Management Agency. HAZUS [Online database]. Accessed April 2, 2012. http://www.fema.gov/hazus-software.

Federal Emergency Management Agency. "Historical Disaster Declarations." Accessed April 2, 2012. http://gis.fema.gov/DataFeeds.html.

Federal Emergency Management Agency. "Improving Preparedness and Resilience through Public-Private Partnerships." Accessed June 30, 2013. http://training.fema.gov/EMIWeb/IS/courseOverview.aspx?code=is-662.

Federal Emergency Management Agency. "Learn about Presidential Policy Directive—8." Accessed June 30, 2013. http://www.fema.gov/learn-about-presidential-policy-directive-8.

Federal Emergency Management Agency. "Mitigation Plan Status." Accessed April 2, 2012. http://www.fema.gov/multi-hazard-mitigation-plan-status.

Federal Emergency Management Agency. "National Planning Frameworks." Accessed June 30, 2013. http://www.fema.gov/national-planning-frameworks.

Federal Emergency Management Agency. Number of Severe Repetitive Loss Properties per County 2007. Accessed April 2, 2012. http://www.fema.gov/library/viewRecord.do?id=2711.

Federal Emergency Management Agency. "Severe Repetitive Loss Program." Accessed June 30, 2013. http://www.fema.gov/severe-repetitive-loss-program.

Federal Emergency Management Agency. "Whole Community." Accessed June 30, 2013. http://www.fema.gov/national-preparedness/whole-community.

Federal Emergency Management Agency. FEMA Library. *FEMA Public Assistance Funded Projects Summary* [Downloadable Data File]. Washington, DC: FEMA, 2012. Accessed June 30, 2013. http://www.fema.gov/library/viewRecord.do?id=6299.

Federal Emergency Management Agency. FEMA Library. *FEMA Hazard Mitigation Program Summary* [Downloadable Data File]. Washington, DC: FEMA, 2012. Accessed June 30, 2013. http://www.fema.gov/library/viewRecord.do?id=6293.

Flanagan, Barry, Edward W. Gregory, Elaine J. Hallisey, Janet L. Heitgerd, and Brian Lewis. "A Social Vulnerability Index for Disaster Management." *Journal of Homeland Security and Emergency Management* 8 (2011): 1–22.

Flores, Christopher III, Michael Kelly, Roberta A. Ritvo, and Natasha Borges Sugiyama. "Local Government Structure and Function in Texas and the United States," Paper Prepared for the Policy Research Project: Fiscal Capacity of Texas Cities, September 15, 1997. Accessed June 30, 2013. http://uts.cc.utexas.edu/˜rhwilson/fiscalprp/structure.html.

Florida Association of Counties. "Charter County Information." Accessed June 30, 2013. http://www.fl-counties.com/about-floridas-counties/charter-county-information.

Florida Division of Emergency Management Office of Private Sector Coordination. "Public Sector-Private Sector Disaster Preparedness Summit." Accessed June 30, 2013. http://www.floridadisaster.org/publicprivatesector/documents/2013%20PPP%20Disaster%20Preparedness%20AAR_FINAL%202-27–13.pdf.

Florida Emergency Preparedness Association. "Our History." Accessed June 30, 2013. http://www.fepa.org/index.php/about-fepa.

Florida League of Cities. "Understanding Florida's Home Rule Power." Accessed June 30, 2013. http://www.floridaleagueofcities.com/Resources.aspx?CNID=645.

Florida, the State of. *Comprehensive Emergency Plan.* 2012. Accessed June 30, 2013. http://floridadisaster.org/documents/CEMP/Final%20Draft_2012%20Basic%20CEMP%20and%20Annexes.pdf.

Florida, Richard. *The Rise of the Creative Class: And How It's Transforming Work, Leisure, and Everyday Life.* New York: Basic Books, 2002.

Fox 10. "2012 Baldwin CO. tourism numbers released." By Hal Scheurich. November 2, 2012. Accessed June 30, 2013. http://www.fox10tv.com/dpp/news/local_news/baldwin_county/2012-baldwin-county-tourism-numbers-released.

Gall, Melanie and Susan L. Cutter. "2005 Events and Outcomes: Hurricane Katrina and Beyond." In *Emergency Management: The American Experience 1900–2005*, edited by Claire B. Rubin, 185–206. Fairfax, VA, VA: Public Entity Risk Institute, 2007.

Garnett, James L. and Alexander Kouzmin. "Communicating Throughout Katrina: Competing and Complementary Conceptual Lenses on Crisis Communication." *Public Administration Review* 67 (2007): 171–88.

Gerber, Brian J., David B. Cohen, and Kendra B. Stewart. "U.S. Cities and Homeland Security: Examining the Role of Financial Conditions and Administrative Capacity in Municipal Preparedness Efforts." *Public Finance and Management* 7 (2007): 152–88.

Glavovic, Bruce and Gavin Smith. *Adapting to Climate Change: Lessons from Natural Hazards.* London: Springer, forthcoming.

Godschalk, David R., Timothy Beatley, Philip Berke, David J. Brower, and Edward J. Kaiser. *Natural Hazard Mitigation: Recasting Disaster Policy and Planning.* Washington, DC: Island Press, 1999.

Gregg, C.E. and B.F. Houghton. "Natural Hazards." In *Disaster Resilience: An Integrated Approach,* edited by Douglas Paton and David Johnston, 19–37. Springfield, IL: Charles C Thomas Publisher Ltd., 2006.

Gulf of Mexico Alliance. "Coastal Community Resiliency." Accessed June 30, 2013. http://www.gulfofmexicoalliance.org.

Gulf Restoration Network. "Natural Lines of Defense." Accessed June 30, 2013. https://healthygulf.org/our-work/natural-defenses/natural-defenses-overview.

Handbook of Texas. "Home Rule Charters." Accessed June 30, 2013. http://www.tshaonline.org/handbook/online/articles/mvhek.

Harrald, John R. "Emergency Management Restructured: Intended and Unintended Outcomes of Actions Taken Since 9/11." In *Emergency Management: The American Experience 1900–2005,* edited by Claire B. Rubin, 161–184. Fairfax, VA, VA: Public Entity Risk Institute, 2007.

Harrald, John R. "The System Is Tested: Response to the BP Deepwater Horizon Oil Spill." In *Emergency Management: The American Experience 1900–2010 2nd Edition,* edited by Claire B. Rubin, 213–36. Fairfax, VA, VA: Public Entity Risk Institute, 2012.

Hazard Reduction and Recovery Center. *Advancing the Resilience of Coastal Localities: Developing, Implementing and Sustaining the Use of Coastal Resilience Indicators: A Final Report.* By Walter G. Peacock, Samuel D. Brody, William A. Seitz, William J. Merrll, Arnold Vedlietz, Sammy Zahran, Robert C. Harriss, and Robert R. Stickney. College Station: Texas A&M University, 2010.

Hazards & Vulnerability Research Institute. *The Spatial Hazard Events and Losses Database for the United States, Version 10.0* [Online Database]. Columbia, SC: University of South Carolina, 2013.Accessed September 5, 2012. http://www.sheldus.org.

Henstra, Daniel. "Evaluating Local Government Emergency Management Programs: What Framework Should Public Managers Adopt?" *Public Administration Review* 70 (2010): 236–46.

Holling, C.S. "Resilience and Stability of Ecological Systems." *Annual Review of Ecology and Systematics* 4 (1973): 1–23.

Hoyman, Michele and Christopher Faricy. "It Takes a Village: A Test of the Creative Class, Social Capital, and Human Capital Theories." *Urban Affairs Review* 44 (2009): 311–33.

Hurricanes: Science and Society. "1965—Hurricane Betsy." Accessed June 30, 2013. http://www.hurricanescience.org/history/storms/1960s/betsy/.

Hurricanes: Science and Society. "1969—Hurricane Camille." Accessed June 30, 2013. http://www.hurricanescience.org/history/storms/1960s/camille/.

Hurricanes: Science and Society. "1972—Hurricane Agnes." Accessed June 30, 2013. http://www.hurricanescience.org/history/storms/1970s/agnes/.

Insurance Institute for Business and Home Safety. *Survey of State Land-Use and Natural Hazards Planning Laws,* 2009. Accessed June 30, 2013. http://ofb.ibhs.org/page;jsessionid= 549644DA1BD1147F56D5BD822A8AE566?execution=e1 s1&pageId=state_land_use.

Insurance Institute for Business and Home Safety. "General State Planning Legislation." Accessed June 30, 2013. http://ofb.ibhs.org/content/data/file/statutes2009.pdf.

Johnston, David, Julia Becker, and Jim Cousins. "Lifestyles and Urban Resilience." In *Disaster Resilience: An Integrated Approach,* edited by Douglas Paton and David Johnston, 40–64. Springfield, IL: Charles C Thomas Publisher Ltd., 2006.

Kahan, Jerome H., Andrew C. Allen, and Justin K. George. "An Operational Framework for Resilience." *Journal of Homeland Security and Emergency Management* 6 (2009): 1–48.

Kendra, James M. and Tricia Wachtendork. "Community Innovation and Disasters." In *Handbook of Disaster Research,* edited by Havidan Rodriguez, Enrico Quarantelli and Russell R. Dynes, 320–34. New York: Springer, 2007.

King, David. "Planning for Hazard Resilient Communities." In *Disaster Resilience: An Integrated Approach,* edited by Douglas Paton and David Johnston, 288–304. Springfield, IL: Charles C Thomas Publisher Ltd., 2006.

Klein, Richard J.T., Robert J. Nicholls, and Frank Thomalla. "Resilience to Natural Hazards: How Useful is this Concept?" *Environmental Hazards* 5 (2003): 35–45.

Labao, Linda and David S. Kraybill. "The Emerging Roles of County Governments in Metropolitan and Nonmetropolitan Areas: Findings from a National Survey." *Economic Development Quarterly,* 19 (2005): 245–59.

Leong, Karen, Christopher A. Airriess, Wei Li, Angela Chia-Chen Chen, and Verna M. Keith. "Resilient History and the Rebuilding of a Community: The Vietnamese American Community of New Orleans East." *The Journal of American History* 94 (2007): 770–79.

Lester, William and Daniel Krejci. "Business 'Not' as Usual: The National Incident Management System, Federalism, and Leadership." *Public Administration Review* 67 (2007): 84–93.

Louden, Robert J. "Who's in Charge Here? Some Observations on the Relationship Between Disasters and the American Criminal Justice System." In *Disciplines, Disasters, and Emergency Management,* edited by David A. McEntire, 223–33. Springfield, IL: Charles C Thomas, Ltd., 2007.

Louisiana Coastal Area. "Louisiana's Coastal Area—Ecosystem Restoration." Accessed June 30, 2013. http://www.lca.gov/learn.aspx#.

Louisiana Resiliency Assistance Program. "Home." Accessed June 30, 2013. http://www.resiliency.lsu.edu/.

Louisiana Resiliency Assistance Program. "Resiliency." Accessed June 30, 2013. http://www.resiliency.lsu.edu/resiliency.

Louisiana Seafood Promotion and Marketing Board. "Economic Impact." Accessed June 30, 2013. http://louisianaseafood.com/why-buy-louisiana/economic-impact.

May, Peter J. *Recovering From Catastrophes: Federal Disaster Relief Policy and Politics.* Westport, CT: Greenwood Press, 1985.

McEntire, David and Gregg Dawson. "The Intergovernmental Context." In *Emergency Management: Principles and Practices for Local Government, Second Edition,* edited by William L. Waugh Jr. and Kathleen Tierney, 57–70. Washington, DC: International City/County Management Association, 2007.

McGuire, Michael and Chris Silva. "The Effect of Problem Severity, Managerial and Organizational Capacity, and Agency Structure on Intergovernmental Collaboration: Evidence from Local Emergency Management." *Public Administration Review* 70 (2010) 279–88.

Meeting of the Coastal Resiliency Coalition. Personal observation by Ashley D. Ross. Gulf Shores, Alabama. April 3, 2011

Meeting of the St. Bernard Parish Department of Homeland Security and Emergency Preparedness. Personal observation by Ashley D. Ross. Chalmette, Louisiana. June 7, 2012.

Merriam-Webster Online. "Resilience." Accessed August 1, 2012. http://www.merriam-webster.com/dictionary/RESILIENCE.

Mileti, Dennis S. *Disasters by Design: A Reassessment of Natural Hazards in the United States.* Washington, DC: Joseph Henry Press, 1999.

Militello, Laura G., Emily S. Patterson, Lynn Bowman, and Robert Wears. "Information Flow During Crisis Management: Challenges to Coordination in the Emergency Operations Center." *Cognition, Technology & Work* 9 (2007): 25–31.

Mississippi-Alabama Sea Grant Consortium. "Resilience: A Community Self-Assessment." Accessed June 30, 2013. http://www.masgc.org/page.asp?id=591.

Mississippi Association of County Board Attorneys. "Home Rule." Accessed June 30, 2013. http://www.macbanetwork.org/book/2004/home_rule.pdf.

Mississippi, the State of. *Mississippi Comprehensive Emergency Management Plan, Section I: Basic Plan.* 2012. Accessed June 30, 2013. http://www.msema.org/wp-content/uploads/2012/07/BasicPlan.pdf.

Morrow, Betty. "Disasters in the First Person." In *Hurricane Andrew: Ethnicity, Gender, and the Sociology of* Disasters, edited by Walter G. Peacock, Betty Hearn Morrow, and Hugh Gladwin. 1–17. College Station: Hazard Reduction and Recovery Center Texas A&M University, 2000.

Morrow, Betty and Walter G. Peacock. "Disasters and Social Change: Hurricane Andrew and the Reshaping of Miami?" In *Hurricane Andrew: Ethnicity, Gender, and the Sociology of* Disasters, edited by Walter G. Peacock, Betty Hearn Morrow, and Hugh Gladwin. 226–42. College Station: Hazard Reduction and Recovery Center Texas A&M University, 2000.

Moss, David. "Courting Disaster? The Transformation of Federal Disaster Policy since 1803." In *The Financing of Catastrophe Risk,* edited by Kenneth A. Froot. 307–62. Chicago: University of Chicago Press, 1999.

Moss, Mitchell, Charles Schelhamer, David A. Berman. "The Stafford Act and Priorities for Reform." *Journal of Homeland Security and Emergency Management* 6 (2009): 1–21.

National Association of Counties. *County Authority: A State by State Report.* By Matthew Sellers. Washington, DC: NACO, 2010.

National Association of Counties. *Dillion's Rule or Not?* By Adam Coester. Washington, DC: NACO, 2004.

National Center for the Study of Counties. *Emergency Management in County Government.* By Wes Clark. Athens: Carl Vinson Institute of Government University of Georgia, 2006.

National Science and Technology Council. Subcommittee on Disaster Reduction. *Grand Challenges for Disaster Reduction.* Washington, DC: National Science and Technology Council, 2005. Accessed June 30, 2013. http://www.sdr.gov/docs/SDRGrandChallengesforDisasterReduction.pdf.

New Orleans Historical. "Civil Defense Control Center." Accessed June 30, 2013. http://neworleanshistorical.org/items/show/274#.Udi_Dazlf2x.

New York Times. "Protecting the City, Before Next Time." Accessed June 30, 2013. http://www.nytimes.com/2012/11/04/nyregion/protecting-new-york-city-before-next-time.html?pagewanted=all&_r=0.

New York Times. "Text of Obama's Speech in Afghanistan." Accessed June 30, 2013. http://www.nytimes.com/2012/05/02/world/asia/text-obamas-speech-in-afgha-nistan.html?_r =1&pagewanted=all.

National Oceanic and Atmospheric Administration. CSC Coastal Change Analysis Program (C-CAP) Land Cover Atlas. Accessed September 5, 2012. http://stateofthecoast.noaa.gov/wetlands/welcome.html.

National Oceanic and Atmospheric Administration. "Coastal Services Center." Accessed June 30, 2013. http://csc.noaa.gov/regions/gulfcoast/.

National Oceanic and Atmospheric Administration. "Hurricane Andrew's Legacy: 'Like a Bomb' in Florida." Accessed June 30, 2013. http://www.npr.org/2012/08/23/159613339/hurricane-andrews-legacy-like-a-bomb-in-florida.

National Oceanic and Atmospheric Administration. "Hurricane Ike." Accessed June 30, 2013. http://www.nhc.noaa.gov/pdf/TCR-AL092008_Ike_3May10.pdf.

National Oceanic and Atmospheric Administration. "Hurricanes in History." Accessed June 30, 2013. http://www.nhc.noaa.gov/outreach/history/.

National Oceanic and Atmospheric Administration. "Fujita Tornado Damage Scale." Accessed June 30, 2013. http://www.spc.noaa.gov/faq/tornado/f-scale.html.

National Oceanic and Atmospheric Administration. "NOAA and FDA Announce Chemical Test for Dispersant in Gulf Seafood; All Samples Test Within Safety Threshold." Accessed June 30, 2013. http://www.noaanews.noaa.gov/stories2010/20101029_seafood.html.

National Oceanic and Atmospheric Administration. *Storm Prediction Center Severe Weather GIS (SVRGIS)* [Online Database]. Norman, OK: Storm Prediction Center, 2012. Accessed October 5, 2012. http://www.spc.noaa.gov/gis/svrgis/.

National Oceanic and Atmospheric Administration. StormReady!. "StormReady Guidelines." Accessed June 30, 2013. http://www.stormready.noaa.gov/guideline_chart.htm.

National Oceanic and Atmospheric Administration. "Storm Ready Communities." Accessed September 5, 2012. http://www.stormready.noaa.gov/communities.htm.

National Oceanic and Atmospheric Administration. "Storm Surge and Coastal Inundation." Accessed June 30, 2013. http://www.stormsurge.noaa.gov/event_history_1940s.html.

National Oceanic and Atmospheric Administration. "The Great Galveston Hurricane of 1900." Accessed June 30, 2013. http://celebrating200years.noaa.gov/magazine/galv_hurricane/welcome.html#intro.

National Oceanic and Atmospheric Administration. "Thirty Years After Hurricane Agnes-The Forgotten Florida Tornado Disaster." Accessed June 30, 2013. http://www.srh.noaa.gov/media/mlb/pdfs/Agnes30.pdf.

National Oceanic and Atmospheric Administration. "What is resilience?" Accessed June 30, 2013. http://oceanservice.noaa.gov/facts/resilience.html.

Norris, Fran H., Susan P. Stevens, Betty Pffefferbaum, Karen F. Wyche, and Rose L. Pfefferbaum. "Community Resilience as a Metaphor, Theory, Set of Capacities, and Strategy for Disaster Readiness." *American Journal of Community Psychology* 41 (2008): 127–50.

Oliver-Smith, Anthony and Susanna M. Hoffmann, editors. *The Angry Earth: Disasters in an Anthropological Perspective.* New York: Routledge, 1999.

Paton, Ann. "Collaborative Public Management." In *Emergency Management: Principles and Practices for Local Government, Second Edition,* edited by William L. Waugh Jr. and Kathleen Tierney, 71–84. Washington, DC: International City/County Management Association, 2007.

Paton, Douglas and David Johnston. "Disasters and Communities: Vulnerability, Resilience and Preparedness." *Disaster Prevention and Management* 10 (2001): 270–77.

Paton, Douglas and David Johnston. "Identifying the Characteristics of a Disaster Resilient Society." In *Disaster Resilience: An Integrated Approach,* edited by Douglas Paton and David Johnston, 11–18. Springfield, IL: Charles C Thomas Publisher Ltd., 2006.

Paton, Douglas and Kathryn Gow. "Rising from the Ashes: Empowering the Phoenix." In *Phoenix of Natural Disasters: Community Resilience,* edited by Kathryn Gow and Douglas Paton, 1–9. New York: Nova Science Publishers, Inc., 2008.

Paton, Douglas and Li-ju Jang. "Disaster Resilience: Exploring All Hazards and Cross-Cultural Perspectives." *Community Disaster Recovery and Resiliency: Exploring Global Opportunities and Challenges,* edited by DeMond S. Miller and Jason D. Rivera, 81–99. Boca Raton, FL: Auerback Publications, 2011.

Paton, Douglas. "Community Resilience: Integrating Individual, Community and Societal Perspectives." In *Phoenix of Natural Disasters: Community Resilience,* edited by Kathryn Gow and Douglas Paton, 13–31. New York: Nova Science Publishers, Inc., 2008.

Paton, Douglas. "Disaster Preparedness: A Social-Cognitive Perspective." *Disaster Prevention and Management* 12(2003): 210–16.

Paton, Douglas. "Disaster Resilience: Building Capacity to Co-Exist with Natural Hazards and Their Consequences." In *Disaster Resilience: An Integrated Approach,* edited by Douglas Paton and David Johnston, 3–10. Springfield, IL: Charles C Thomas Publisher Ltd., 2006.

Paton, Douglas. "Disaster Resilience: Integrating Individual, Community, Institutional and Environmental Perspectives." In *Disaster Resilience: An Integrated Approach,* edited by Douglas Paton and David Johnston, 305–319. Springfield, IL: Charles C Thomas Publisher Ltd., 2006.

Peacock, Walter G., Betty H. Morrow, and Hugh Gladwin. *Hurricane Andrew: Ethnicity, Gender, and the Sociology of Disasters.* College Station: Hazard Reduction and Recovery Center, Texas A&M University, 1997.

Peguero, Anthony A. "Latino Disaster Vulnerability: The Dissemination of Hurricane Mitigation Information Among Florida's Homeowners." *Hispanic Journal of Behavioral Sciences* 28 (2006): 5–22.

Perilla, Julia, Fran H. Norris, and Evelyn A. Lavizzo. "Ethnicity, Culture, and Disaster Response: Identifying and Explaining Ethnic Differences in PTSD Six Months After Hurricane Andrew." *Journal of Social and Clinical Psychology* 21 (2002): 20–45.

Platt, Rutherford H. *Disasters and Democracy: The Politics of Extreme Natural Events.* Washington, DC: Island Press, 1999.

Police Jury Association of the State of Louisiana. "Parish Government Structure." Accessed June 30, 2013. http://www.lpgov.org/PageDisplay.asp?p1=3010.

Pooley, Julie Ann, Lynne Cohen, and Moira O'Connor. "Links between Community and Individual Resilience: Evidence from Cyclone Affected Communities in North West Australia." In *Disaster Resilience: An Integrated Approach,* edited by Douglas Paton and David Johnston, 161–70. Springfield, IL: Charles C Thomas Publisher Ltd., 2006.

Pratt, Andy C. "Creative Cities: The Cultural Industries and the Creative Class." *Geografiska Annaler* 90 (2008): 107–17.

Press-Register. "Baldwin Business Support Center gets $50,000 boost from BP grant." By Staff. September 28, 2011. Accessed June 30, 2013. http://blog.al.com/live/2011/09/baldwin_business_support_cente.html.

Press-Register. "2012 Census data shows Baldwin County continues its growth; international migration into Mobile and Jefferson counties." By John Sharp. March 20, 2013. Accessed June 30, 2013. http://blog.al.com/live/2013/03/2012_census_data_shows_baldwin.html.

Press-Register. "Baldwin Business Support Center gets $50,000 boost from BP grant." By Staff. September 28, 2011. Accessed June 30, 2013. http://blog.al.com/live/2011/09/baldwin_business_support_cente.html.

Press-Register. "Coastal Resiliency Coalition continues mission two years after spill." By Guy Busby. May 7, 2012. Accessed June 30, 2013. http://blog.al.com/press-register-business/2012/05/coastal_resiliency_coalition_c.html.

Press-Register. "Coastal Resiliency Coalition looks for new ways to shape south Baldwin County." By David Ferrara. April 25, 2011. Accessed June 30, 2013. http://blog.al.com/live/2011/04/coastal_resiliency_coalition_l.html.

Press-Register. "Marine scientist: Gulf fish 'absolutely safe' to eat now." By Casandra Andrews. August 20, 2010.Accessed June 30, 2013. http://blog.al.com/live/2010/08/marine_scientist_gulf_fish_abs.html.

Press-Register. "Supper on the Sand: Guy Fieri hosts as hundreds celebrate oil spill recovery." By David Ferrara. April 18, 2011. Accessed June 30, 2013. http://blog.al.com/entertainment-press-register/2011/04/supper_on_the_sand_guy_fieri_h.html.

PSFK Labs. "Digital Persuasion: How Social Media Motivates Action and Drives Support for Causes." Accessed June 30, 2013. http://www.psfk.com/2013/04/melissa-waggener-zorkin-psfk-2013.html.

Putnam, Robert. "Bowling Alone: America's Declining Social Capital." *Journal of Democracy* 6 (1995): 65–78.

Rausch, Stephen and Cynthia Negrey. "Does the Creative Engine Run? A Consideration of the Effect of Creative Class on Economic Strength and Growth." *Journal of Urban Affairs* 28 (2006): 473–89.

Riveria, Fernando I. and Marc R. Settembrino. "Sociological Insights on the Role of Social Capital in Disaster Resilience." In *Disaster Resiliency: Interdisciplinary Perspectives,* edited by Naim Kapucu, Christopher V. Hawkins, and Fernando I. Rivera, 48–60. New York: Routledge, 2013.

Rose, Adam. "Defining and Measuring Economic Resilience to Disasters." *Disaster Prevention and Management* 13(2004): 307–14.

Rose, Adam. "Economic Resilience to Disasters: Towards a Consistent and Comprehensive Formulation." In *Disaster Resilience: An Integrated Approach,* edited by Douglas Paton and David Johnston, 226–45. Springfield, IL: Charles C Thomas Publisher Ltd., 2006.

Schneider, Robert O. "Hazard Mitigation: A Priority for Sustainable Communities." In *Disaster Resilience: An Integrated Approach,* edited by Douglas Paton and David Johnston, 66–86. Springfield, IL: Charles C Thomas Publisher Ltd., 2006.

Schneider, Saundra K. *Dealing with Disaster: Public Management in Crisis Situations.* New York: M.E. Sharpe Inc, 2011.

Schoch-Spana, Monica, Crystal Franco, Jennifer B. Nuzzo, and Christiana Usenza. "Community Engagement: Leadership Tool for Catastrophic Health Events." *Biosecurity and Bioterrism: Biodefense Strategy, Practice, and Science* 5 (2007):8–24.

Sherwood, Frank P. *County Governments in Florida.* New York: iUniverse, 2008.

Smith, Gavin. *Planning for Post-Disaster Recovery: A Review of the United States Disaster Assistance Framework.* Fairfax, VA, VA: The Public Entity Risk Institute, 2011.

Somers, Scott and James H. Svara. "Assessing and Managing Environmental Risk: Connecting Local Government Management with Emergency Management." *Public Administration Review* 69 (2009): 181–93.

South Baldwin Chamber of Commerce. "Baldwin Business Center Relocates." Accessed June 30, 2013. http://www.southbaldwinchamber.com/chamber-news-item/1496733-chamber-news-baldwin-business-support-center.

Sports Illustrated, "New York Giants prove resilient again in Super Bowl XLVI." February 5, 2012, Accessed August 2, 2012. http://sportsillustrated.cnn.com/2012/writers/don_banks/02/05/super.bowl.xlvi.snaps/index.html

The St. Augustine Record. "1944: A Dangerous Year." Accessed June 30, 2013. http://staugustine.com/news/local-news/2010-11-01/1944-dangerous-year.

StormSmart Coasts. "National StormSmart Coasts Network." Accessed June 30, 2013. http://stormsmartcoasts.org/.

Subject #8. Personal interview by Ashley D. Ross. Gulfport, Mississippi, February 20, 2011.

Subject #10. Personal interview by Ashley D. Ross. Biloxi, Mississippi, February 20, 2011.

Subject #13. Personal interview by Ashley D. Ross. Gulfport, Mississippi, February 21, 2011.

Subject #25. Personal interview by Ashley D. Ross. Gulf Shores, Alabama, March 16, 2011

Subject #30. Personal interview by Ashley D. Ross. Gulf Shores, Alabama, March 18, 2011.

Subject #41. Personal interview by Ashley D. Ross. Chalmette, Louisiana, June 7, 2012.

Subject #42. Personal interview by Ashley D. Ross. New Orleans, Louisiana, June 7, 2012.

Subject #43. Personal interview by Ashley D. Ross. Niceville, Florida, June 12, 2012.

Subject #47. Personal interview by Ashley D. Ross. Tallahassee, Florida, June 13, 2012.

Subject #49. Personal interview by Ashley D. Ross. Port St. Jo, Florida, June 14, 2012.

Subject #52. Personal interview by Ashley D. Ross. Port Richey, Florida, June 20, 2012.

Subject #54. Personal interview by Ashley D. Ross. Robertsdale, Alabama, June 21, 2012.

Sutphen, Sandra and Virginia Boot. "Issue Salience and Preparedness as Perceived by City Managers." In *Cities and Disasters: North American Studies in Emergency Management,* edited by Richard T. Sylves and William L. Waugh Jr., 133–53. Springfield, IL: Charles C Thomas, Ltd., 1990.

Sylves, Richard T. "Federal Emergency Management Comes of Age: 1979–2001." In *Emergency Management: The American Experience 1900–2005,* edited by Claire B. Rubin, 111–60. Fairfax, VA: Public Entity Risk Institute, 2007.

Sylves, Richard T. *Disaster Policy & Politics: Emergency Management and Homeland Security.* Washington, DC: CQ Press, 2008.

Telegraph. "Texas Rebuilds After Hurricane Ike with Resilience and Resolve." Accessed June 30, 2013. http://www.telegraph.co.uk/expat/5201437/Texas-rebuilds-after-Hurricane-Ike-with-resilience-and-resolve.html.

Texas, the State of. Department of Emergency Management. *Hurricane Ike Impact Report.* Austin: Office of the Governor, 2008. Accessed June 30, 2013. http://www.fema.gov/pdf/hazard/hurricane/2008/ike/impact_report.pdf.

Texas A&M University. "Commencement Speech Transcript: Martha L. Loudder, TAMU Faculty Senate Speaker. May 14, 2004, 7pm." Accessed June 30, 2013. http://graduation.tamu.edu/04A_MarthaLoudder.html.

Texas Department of State Health Services. "Disaster Behavioral Health Services: Resilience—Empowerment—Recovery." Accessed June 30, 2013. http://www.dshs.state.tx.us/mhsa-disaster/.

Texas State Historical Association. "Emergency Management: Handbook of Texas Online." Accessed June 30, 2013. *http://www.tshaonline.org/handbook/online/articles/mze01.*

Texas State Historical Society Texas Almanac. "Galveston's Response to the Hurricane of 1900." Accessed June 30, 2013. http://www.texasalmanac.com/topics/history/galvestons-response-hurricane-1900.

Texas Sustainable Coast Initiative. "Sustainable Texas Coast." Accessed June 30, 2013. http://coastalatlas.tamug.edu.

Tierney, Kathleen J., Michael K. Lindell, and Ronald W. Perry. *Facing the Unexpected: Disaster Preparedness and Response in the United States.* Washington, DC: Joseph Henry Press, 2001.

Tierney, Kathleen J. "Emergency Medical Preparedness and Response in Disasters: The Need for Interorganizational Coordination." *Public Administration Review,* 45 (1985): 77–84.

Tierney, Kathleen J. "Conceptualizing and Measuring Organizational and Community Resilience: Lessons from the Emergency Response Following the September 11, 2001 Attack on the World Trade Center." Accessed June 30, 2013. http://udspace.udel.edu/bitstream/handle/19716/735/PP329.pdf?sequence=1.

Tierney, Kathleen J. "Recent Developments in U.S. Homeland Security Policies and Their Implications for the Management of Extreme Events." Paper presented at First International Conference on Urban Disaster Reduction, Kobe, Japan, January 18–20, 2005.

Tierney, Kathleen J. "Social Inequality: Humans and Disasters." In *On Risk and Disaster: Lessons from Hurricane Katrina*, edited by Ronald J. Daniels, Donald F. Keitl, and Howard Kunreuther, 109–29. Philadelphia: University of Pennsylvania Press, 2006.

Times-Picayune. "Congress passes Restore Act, flood insurance extension in massive transportation bill." By Bruce Alpert. June 29, 2012. Accessed June 30, 2013. http://www.nola.com/politics/index.ssf/2012/06/congress_passes_restore_act_fl.html.

U.S. Census. USA Counties Database. Accessed June 30, 2013. http://censtats.census.gov/usa/usa.shtml.

U.S. Census. American Communities Survey 5 Year. 2010.Accessed September 5, 2012. http://factfinder2.census.gov/.

U.S. Department of Agriculture. Economic Research Service. *2003 Rural-Urban Continuum Codes* [Downloadable Data File]. Washington, DC: USDA, 2004. Accessed April 5, 2012. http://www.ers.usda.gov/data-products/rural-urban-continuum-codes.aspx#.Udj8CKzlf2w.

U.S. Department of Homeland Security. "Written Statement of Craig Fugate, Administrator, Federal Emergency Management Agency, before the House Committee on Homeland Security, Subcommittee on Emergency Preparedness, Response, and Communications, Five Years Later: An Assessment of the Post Katrina Emergency Management Reform Act." Accessed June 30, 2013. http://www.dhs.gov/news/2011/10/25/written-testimony-fema-house-homeland-security-subcommittee-emergency-preparedness.

U.S. Department of Homeland Security. Federal Emergency Management Agency. *National Disaster Recovery Framework: Strengthening Disaster Recovery for the Nation*. Washington, DC: DHS, 2011.Accessed June 30, 2013. http://www.fema.gov/national-disaster-recovery-framework.

U.S. Department of Homeland Security. Homeland Security Advisory Council. *Community Resilience Task Force Recommendations*. Washington, DC: DHS, 2011. Accessed June 30, 2013 http://www.dhs.gov/xlibrary/assets/hsac-community-resilience-task-force-recommendations-072011.pdf.

U.S. Department of Homeland Security. Homeland Security Advisory Council. *Report of the Critical Infrastructure Task Force*. Washington, DC: DHS, 2006. Accessed June 30, 2013. http://www.dhs.gov/xlibrary/assets/HSAC_CITF_Report_v2.pdf.

U.S. Department of Homeland Security. *National Mitigation Framework*. Washington, DC: DHS, 2013. Accessed June 30, 2013. http://www.fema.gov/library/viewRecord.do?id=7363.

U.S. Department of Homeland Security. *National Preparedness Goal*. Washington, DC: DHS, 2011.Accessed June 30, 2013. http://www.fema.gov/pdf/prepared/npg.pdf.

U.S. Department of Homeland Security. *Quadrennial Homeland Security Review*. Washington, DC: DHS, 2010. Accessed June 30, 2013. http://www.dhs.gov/quadrennial-homeland-security-review-qhsr.

U.S. Senate. Committee on Homeland Security and Government Affairs. *Hurricane Katrina: A Nation Still Unprepared*. Washington, DC: U.S. Government Printing Office, 2006. Accessed June 30, 2013. http://www.gpo.gov/fdsys/pkg/CRPT-109srpt322/pdf/CRPT-109srpt322.pdf.

University of Oklahoma Health Science Terrorism and Disaster Center. "Communities Advancing Resilience Toolkits (CART)." Accessed June 30, 2013. http://tdc.missouri.edu/doc/cart_description_021510.pdf.

van Eeten, Michel, Arjen Boin, and Mark de Bruijne. "The Price of Resilience: Contrasting the Theoretical Ideal-Type with Organizational Reality." In *Designing Resilience: Preparing for Extreme Events,* edited by Louise K. Comfort, Arjen Boin, and Chris C. Demchak, 158–79. Pittsburgh: University of Pittsburgh Press, 2010.

van Heerden, Ivor Ll. "The Failure of the New Orleans Levee System Following Hurricane Katrina and the Pathway Forward." *Public Administration Review* 67 (2007): 24–35.

van Zandt, Shannon, Walter G. Peacock, Dustin W. Henry, Himanshu Grover, Wesley E. Highfield, and Samuel D. Brody. "Mapping Social Vulnerability to Enhance Housing and Neighborhood Resilience." *Housing Policy Debate* 22 (2012): 29–55.

Waggener Edstrom Worldwide. "Disaster Relief is the Tip of the Iceberg for Social Media." Accessed June 30, 2013. http://www.psfk.com/2013/04/melissa-waggener-zorkin-psfk-2013.html.

Wall Street Journal. "Euro Resilience Hints at Shift in Currency's Role." Accessed June 30, 2013. http://online.wsj.com/article/SB1000142405270230334340457751636052 9967418.html.

Washington Post. "Haiti's Earthquake Tests Resilience of Capital's Hair Stylists, Now Working in Streets." Accessed August 1, 2012. http://rapadoo.com/2012/07/10/haitis-earthquake-tests-resilience-of-capitals-hair-stylists-now-working-in-streets-the-washington-post/.

Waugh, William L. Jr. "EMAC, Katrina, and the Governors of Louisiana and Mississippi." *Public Administration Review* 67 (2007): 107–13.

Waugh, William L. Jr. "Emergency Management and State and Local Government Capacity." In *Cities and Disasters: North American Studies in Emergency Management,* edited by Richard T. Sylves and William L. Waugh Jr., 221–37. Springfield, IL: Charles C Thomas, Ltd., 1990.

Waugh, William L. Jr. "Management Capacity and Rural Community Resilience." In *Disaster Resiliency: Interdisciplinary Perspectives,* edited by Naim Kapucu, Christopher V. Hawkins, and Fernando I. Rivera. 291–308. New York: Routledge, 2013.

Waugh, William L. Jr. and Gregory Streib. "Collaboration and Leadership for Effective Emergency Management." *Public Administration Review* 66 (2006): 131–40.

The White House. *National Security Strategy.* Washington, DC: The White House, 2010. Accessed June 30, 2013. http://www.whitehouse.gov/sites/default/files/rss_viewer/national_security_strategy.pdf.

The White House. *Presidential Policy Directive/PPD—8.* Washington, DC: The White House, 2010. Accessed June 30, 2013. http://www.dhs.gov/xlibrary/assets/presidential-policy-directive-8-national-preparedness.pdf.

Wildavsky, Aaron. *Search for safety.* New Brunswick: Transaction, 1988.

Wolensky, Robert P. and Kenneth C. Wolensky. "Local Government's Problem with Disaster Management: A Literature Review and Structural Analysis." *Review of Public Research* 9 (1990): 703–25.

Zahran, Sammy, Samuel D. Brody, Walter G. Peacock, Arnold Vedlitz, and Himanshu Grover. "Social Vulnerability and the Natural and Built Environment: A Model of Flood Casualties in Texas." *Disasters* (2008): 537–60.

Index